Days & Nights
by
The Red Sea

David Dundas

'And almost thence my nature is subdued
To what it works in like the dyer's hand'
Sonnet iii
William Shakespeare

Table of Contents

1 Down and out

I crawled across the floor onto the bed and asked for milk and a boiled egg.

When the waiter arrived, I couldn't sit up to take the glass. "I think you better call a doctor." I said.

When the doctor came, he pummelled my stomach and his face grew serious, as if searching for something which wasn't there. A sheet was draped over me and I was moved out of the room. The last thing I remember, was determining to save my scream until the first spadesful of earth fell on me. When they told me it was polio, I felt relieved that it was something important, but I guess morphine may have had something to do with it.

After several weeks in the wind tunnel of an ancient iron lung, dreaming I was swimming in the Red Sea, I graduated to the ward status of flopper.

In the complex hierarchy of the ward, this was below the play putty men, who could just hold position when sitting up, and the wobblers who couldn't. But both of us were below the TB patients, who whizzed up and down the ward in wheelchairs, flicking the weights of patients-in-traction for being late in paying their betting slips.

One of these wheelchair cowboys later told me, on one of his night time forays, he'd come across a nurse crying in the corridor who'd just held in her arms the thalidomide child, nick-named Flipper, whom the Sisters called 'our little cherub from heaven.'

One day, out of the blue, the Doc told me, he could let me have my little outing, adding, "But you'll have to get used to one of these first," and slid from a plastic wrapper, the sort of thing I imagined popular around the time of Queen Victoria – a whalebone corset. My ego was badly ruffled, for I saw no reason why I should have to go into the world trussed up like Oscar Wilde. But the contents of the second package were as disturbing as the first: the frame of an aluminium backpack, of which my back was to be the pack. Several days of staggering about in that Meccano set, had me trussed up like Oscar, and ready for launch.

Two weeks later, my brother arrived, dangling his car keys, very much the man about town. He manoeuvred me in my wheelchair into the car park and assisted me onto an orange crate, hidden behind a van. "I'm very sorry," he said, "but the car's crook. I can return the wheelchair and handle the crate, if you can manage the bus, ok?"

Twenty minutes later, the two of us and the crate were aboard a double-decker. When we came to a stop, he got into an altercation with a lady who wanted to put her baby carriage under the stairs. "This isn't Covent Garden," she said.

Up to that moment it had been as thrilling as a ride on the Hindenburg, but like our own R101 airship, also ended badly. I don't know if you saw the newsreel of men swinging on the tethering ropes, trying to decide when to jump. My brother handled the crate and I jumped. There was a blinding flash and I woke up with blue dots running round the edges of my vision, and an excruciating headache. My brother told the doctor, I'd fallen off a moving staircase.

Several months passed, exercising with beanbags and the play putty men. Then one day, the sexy physio let me feel her surprisingly buoyant breasts beneath her modest chemise, but only underwater, and I became charged with a new restlessness. On my next meeting with the Doc, he remarked as if fearing I was getting too used to things, "Ever thought about long-distance swimming, job in a warm climate, that sort of thing?"

After a few weeks thinking of that sort of thing, falling off buses, crawling in and out of taxis, lying flat on my back, shouting at the advertisements in empty tube stations, I eventually found myself standing in a swaying group in the local employment office, from which various odours emanated, none of which could be described as after-shave lotion.

If the man in the front, turning the pages of *The Daily Telegraph*, paused too long before villas-for-rent in sunny Greece, or the obits, a Greek chorus would rumble forth from the rear and direct him to the bottle-washers, cloakroom attendants and watchmen of the night.

Then one morning, I saw it: AIRWICK, a popular English air-freshener. Call enough for it surely, then looked again. AIRWORK. Saudi Arabia. Instructors of English required immediately. *Shouldn't strain the back muscles too much, plus it's by The Red Sea, a 365 days-a-year swimming pool!*

Two days of Montezuma's revenge then laid me low. And when I phoned about the job there were only two vacancies left. Next day I was up early and waiting on Marble Arch station, when it struck again. I made my way to the mop room under the iron stairs. In one corner was a steel bucket half-full of Pine disinfectant, the colour of grey milk, and a heap of newspapers with a model Spitfire on top, the plane my aunt had flown from factory to the squadron in our finest hour.

While furiously planning what to do, a black woman station-attendant looked in. She never said a word, but the back of her head said, 'This is one for the Super.'

Sometimes a bad situation made suddenly worse, can galvanize one into action. Newspapers, dipped in disinfectant were crumpled up and flew about in all directions. Finally, dumping a wad of them down the seat of my pants, I walked like a clockwork man towards my train.

"Mind the gap!" said a friendly voice as I sat back on a cushion of newsprint, my scrotum singing.

≈

An old geezer in a plush office had me signed up in all of twenty minutes. Told me work started at seven a.m. and all sorts of interesting things.

"Are we near a beach?" I asked.

"The coast's one long beach," he said, "There's a weekday afternoon bus run to beach and souk (the local market) and on Friday mornings, which is their weekend, they being of the Muslim faith."

While I signed this and that, I could feel his eyes on me as if I were a dodgy consignment that might combust at a later date, and cost him commission.

When I'd finished, he relaxed. Told me how he'd made his bit in Bahrain and I could too, if sensible. I nodded and coughed politely, "How come you're doing this then?"

"Ha, hah! Not really my line at all. Just helping out". He leaned forward and I got a whiff of alcohol above the loamy pines and hint of ferret. "Money for old rope," he said. "There's a rush on. Never seen anything like it."

3

2 Up and away

"And why have you come to Casablanca?"
"I've come to Casablanca to take the waters."
"But there are no waters in Casablanca."
"Then I was misinformed."

And so it proved. The man sitting next to me on the plane, gold-capped teeth flashing like Aladdin's cave, informed me, we weren't going to Jeddah at all, but Khamis-Mushayt, 6000 feet above sea level and 50 miles inland. Seeing despondency settle on my face, he told me about this own arrival in Libya and how at first he'd been unable to sell a single cassette tape. "What did I do?" he asked.

"Beats me," I replied, "Sold some gold fillings?" This set him off again. "Wiped the lot. Recorded prayer calls and sold them to the local mosques. Now I'm into *Desert Footprints*" (the most successful pirated tapes in the Kingdom, though he didn't put it like that). Then he fished out a sample cassette for me. And though it had this dodgy-looking belly-dancer *Umm Kalthoum* on the label I gratefully accepted as a good omen.

After landing at Fort Lamy in Chad and Entebbe in Uganda because of some trouble in Suez, the plane then crossed the Red Sea and made a stop in a place called Gizan. As large bales of densely packed green leaves went bouncing over the hard-packed runway, the stink of dead fish filled the plane. Distant moving shapes, deliquesced into a line of women on donkeys, modulating as if in Madame Tussaud's funny mirrors.

Black-tented mamas climbed aboard and eased past me on the daintiest of feet, leaving behind a heady exhaust of perfume and incense. Then we were off.

Stepping onto the tarmac at Khamis-Mushayt was as if a sheet of cling-wrap had been peeled from my face. The air was spicy; mountains showed far-off and there rode upon the breeze, the odour of wood-smoke, goats and hint of urine.

4

"Low precipitation", said a percipient gent, the medic, come to greet us and wearing a pistachio-and-nougat patterned shirt for the occasion. Then another man, with long hair, looking like a superannuated hippie, gave us a cheery wave and swung himself into our minibus as if practicing for *Swan Lake*.

"Devrill-Smith," said the medic, in muted tones, "Plays the violin beautifully."

This was another thing my brother had warned me about, Florence of Arabias, and if not mistaken, they were popping up all over the place — like the desert in bloom.

At the first opportunity, I asked the medic about roads to the Red Sea and swimming pools.

"Good lord man!" He said. "There're no swimming pools here and no roads to the Red Sea, either."

3 On probation

For reasons I needn't go into here, I was put on probation. When I innocently asked a beady-eyed instructor with specs, named Barnes, who worked for another Company, what the Present Perfect Tense was, he looked at me in amazement. He could help me, but as quid-pro-quo (typical Barnsey lingo for a hefty bribe) I'd have to get him a pass to our film nights.

Easy enough. A week earlier, he'd re-spliced an unscheduled break in the movie *Gordon of Khartoum,* and prevented a right old rumpus between Ali's kitchen staff and the Brits. And the man in charge, whom everyone called the Major, was more than happy to issue him one.

Ali, the long time head of kitchen staff, was a *Fuzzy Wuzzy,* and sported the original Afro. His idea of fair play was to show you wallet photos of his two marriageable daughters (of remarkably tender years) next to a mercifully ancient newspaper clipping depicting two decapitated Italians, caught prospecting for oil in his tribal domains without permission.

Somehow he'd already picked up on my problem. Told me his brother was big in goat-smuggling for the Hadj. If push came to shove, I could simply disappear, and he'd set me up, teaching English at an esteemed ladies' establishment in Port Sudan, next to Tin Town (for light entertainment) and the Dhalak islands (for swimming).

I considered this a very generous offer from a man whose hero was the Mahdi (whose skull, Lord Kitchener had intended to use as an inkpot), and informed him, I'd be honoured if he'd keep a place for me, preferably above the goat deck.

But Barnes warned me, Port Sudan was no great shakes. Told me how a French Cavalry officer at the local Sports Club, on handing over several landing craft had, in the interests of fraternité and egalité, taken a dip in the moribund pool. Then exhibited liberté, by abruptly leaping out on finding himself doing laps with a rather energetic rat.

In the meanwhile, we were sent into the field under Devrill-Smith to train the Bedhu as airport managers. Windsock managers, we called them. For although their airfields amounted to little more than patches of level grazing, radio comms and a water tower, these wizened patriarchs of the desert always seemed to know well which way the wind was blowing and the best moment to soften us up with a goat grab, just before the graduation exam.

Then, one bright morning, Barnes presented me with a special trainee and two English grammars.

"Thought you'd arranged things?" I said.

"This is the arrangement. One lesson a day. The new Boss arrives in two weeks. There isn't much time. So suggest you get on with it."

My trainee, chosen for some esteemed reason of compassion, was of indeterminate years, had been burned in a petroleum fire, and only spoke two inappropriate words of English. Nevertheless, he passed the course with flying colours (his mum weeping copiously like a sack of chickens outside the perimeter fence). He being the only one able to clear the airfield in ten minutes flat, which he did by cranking himself up vocally like one of the local donkeys. Then, instead of letting all the air out at once, went careening down the runway with his arms out and a noise like an F-5.

4 Fuddy Duddy

Because Devrill-Smith was thought too much a fuddy duddy (worrying about whose goats or donkeys were being deprived of grazing etc.) we were moved back to base to instruct young farmers. One old fellow thought Saudia's jet engines were air-conditioners, which Leo (my villa mate) and the Major, confirmed by jerry-building a mobile fan, which wretched contraption careened round the classroom like a demented alien, desperate to go to the bathroom.

When Devrill-Smith's students got tenses wrong, he made them stand up and apologize for their stupid mistakes. But when one was able to correct another's spelling, he himself stood up and apologized for English's stupid spelling.

His class was so popular that the Base Training Officer, Captain Turkestani, attended and even Lieutenant Mufti, (when he could drag himself away from weightier matters, such as which ancient bedhu should be given the position of tea-wallah and which to carry the biscuits).

One trainee, who found all this unspeakably wearisome, was our lesser princeling, Abdul Aziz, hauled in from the flesh-pots of the West as part of King Faisal's retrenchment program; Faisal's predecessor King Saud, having almost bankrupted the Kingdom.

I'd already learned from Devrill-Smith that one of the many Abdul Azizes, after a legendary raid on Riyadh, had tupped the daughters of the most important Sheikhs, produced a hundred sons and founded a Kingdom, (whereas his pal Philby, produced but one son, who betrayed his). He also freed the slaves, and as there are few people more wearisome than a freed slave (what's for dinner?), Abdul Aziz bestowed on the best of them, top commissions in the National Guard. With the result, most were more loyal to him (he may have been daddy) than to any tribal Sheikh. Lesser commissions were bestowed on the second sons of the aforementioned Sheikhs; offers, they too, were unable to refuse.

The National Guard protected the ammunition of both the North and South armies (who never met) and their artillery ranges ran alongside the airforce's airfields. And some people still say there are no checks and balances.

By absorbing some of the above, I was better able to tell why our own lounge-lizard princeling, now a lowly Warrant Officer, was congenitally unable to obey Capt. Turkestani.

Explaining military rank to W.O. Abdul Aziz was as painful as having our Pakistani Officers (cleverly insinuated into the system to check on us), explain to us Brits, why we were being thrashed in the first Test, despite our persistent ball-tampering. To bolster his own argument, Abdul Aziz let slip details of a coup attempt by Pilot-officers returning from Egypt and subsequently invited to take a hike in the Empty Quarter, albeit it from 20,000 ft.

And one day, watching sand blowing-off the tops of the dunes, I felt I understood a little better something of his complaint: *Officers? What officers? Here today, gone tomorrow.* Thinking of which reminded me of my own ephemeral prospects, not helped by Barnes reminding me, I might have to pay back the return airfare, and other items in the small print.

≈

Our new boss was a Lebanese-American ex-bible salesman nicknamed Bible John. His brief was to promulgate the Defence Language Institute's Training Course.

When ushered into his office, well briefed by Barnes as to the Present Perfect 'being a very human tense, expressing a living past, as opposed to the Past Simple', my mouth was half open --to be greeted with an incisive gesture, more a karate chop, to be honest. "*Faswat Dab*," sibilated Bible John, which I took to be the Arabic equivalent of 'Stow it!' (Later more fully translated by Devrill-Smith as 'the soundless flatulence issuing from the rear end of a hyena'). "We don't educate," he went on, "We train, for jobs. And you Sir, if you achieve the objectives in the timeframe given to the standard set, will hold down yours. If not …" and here delivered a more elevated karate chop, the high-jump clearly indicated.

"Will do," I said, and was dismissed with another kinder, gentler chop.

When I informed Barnes that everything he'd told me had simply flown right out the window, he said. "You mean you caved in?"

"Basically, yes."

And he's despised me ever since, but I'm hoping to set things right, when we reach the Red Sea.

5 Bible John

Bible John proved more a mix of hokum and horse-sense than a bad bloke. Apparently he'd joined the Company as a *bona fidé* member of catering staff, but had found academe more congenial to his prospects. He was really keen on speeding up 'throughput' in the new canteen. "We don't want trainees late back to the Training Centre because they didn't know what to order, do we?" And had us spending hours chanting The Defence Language Institute's dialogue, under creaking fans:

Instructor: 'What would you like today?'

Trainee: 'I won't have the peach melba today, I'll have the apple pie, a-la-mode.'

If we flagged there was gnashing and grinding of teeth behind us. "Why are you Brits such hypocrites?" they gnashed. "When the time comes, you'll gobble it down like all the rest, and not a squeak will I hear about your spotted-dick and custard." He was right, of course.

Side-burns came next, no longer permitted to extend below the earlobes. Devrill-Smith's did, but he'd wisely switched contract to The Presidency of Civil Aviation. "Look what's happening to the Shah," he warned us.

"Won't happen here," retorted Bible John, "Royal family's too big. Wahabis will be placated, Shias (or was it the Shiites?) restrained."

This was way above my head, and it was actually our own new uniforms (canary-yellow polyester shirts and brown trousers) which did Barnes in. He called us *Bible John's Pizza Service,* but being on a separate contract didn't help him. He was exiled to the radar-site, a Westinghouse white-elephant, which turned and turned surveying all things from the highest point of the escarp.

One day, he heard that two willowy maidens, entirely encased in black-chiffon, accompanied by a bulkier version, had stepped out of a dark-windowed, chauffeured limousine parked outside his compound, and asked about English teachers. But the gormless gate-guard became so tongue-tied, they left crestfallen and frustrated.

We scarcely saw him after that, and I had to spend quality time in Marsden's bar after the movie, with my new pal Cowboy. His girlfriend was a vet at Military City, and often called him out to help exercise the horses. When he came in for a drink, I'd wind him up, by coming on like Lawrence of Arabia, or quoting bits of Devrill-Smith's and Bible John's repartee as if my own. "What about Kermit Roosevelt and Moussadeq?' I'd say.

"Kermit who? Get Real! What about Suez?"

I'd mention the Sykes-Picot Agreement, which Devrill-Smith said no one could understand, including Sykes and Picot.

To be honest, I had absolutely no interest in this stuff and certainly didn't worry about as Devrill-Smith did, but it got us off to a good start. "Bullshit!" was his favoured rejoinder. If I then spelled the matter out, he'd say "Old hat," and if I persisted, "So what?" So effective was this technique, I thought he might be working for State or whoever, undercover, deep cover. After all, he was often out at Military City, so what better way to pick up tips: a small bloke, hidden under a jockey cap, among military types, horsing around? One evening, who should come in, but Bible John and Barnes, who'd long ago made up. Neither drank alcohol, but needed to slake their thirsts after a vigorous squash game.

Barnes said he liked it up at the Radar; no lounge-lizard princes, and ok, no princesses. And had Bible John ever thought about that market? He had. "Remote TV in a booth? You'd go bonkers." And did we know that even King Faisal's wife was unable to start a girls' school. Had to be an orphanage? "All your Shakespeare's fault."

"Old Will's?"

"Not old Will, new Will, the firebrand officer, Lt. Shakespeare, who fought alongside Abdul Aziz, against the Turks."

"Abdul Aziz never fought against the Turks." said Barnes. "You're muddling up your Abdul Azizes."

Bible John ignored this. "Lt. Shakespeare insisted on wearing a pith helmet and died standing beside his Gatling gun. The Turks paraded his head around on a pike, so all could see that Abdul Aziz had been in the pay of the Infidels. Nine years in the snake-pit of the Nedj, he had to spend, under the fanatical Ikhwan. Earned their respect, but had to promise Saudi Arabia would become an Islamic State. The House of Saud is still shackled to that promise. But as in your Shakespeare's *Merchant of Venice,* there's many ways to keep a promise."

≈

We now had to work 8.4 hours a day, but got Thursdays and Fridays off. Getting to the Red Sea became a possibility time-wise, and even Barnes began to express interest.

Then Bible John departed. We missed him immediately. He'd gotten things up-and-running ahead of schedule, and never bore a grudge. But what we didn't know was that on one of his early morning fitness runs, he'd sensed he was being followed and run faster. A vehicle had drawn up beside him; some choice epithets been exchanged, and he'd ended up in the clink. They said it took a phone call from big George of Betchel Corporation to get him transferred to Okinawa.

Other things began to speed up. No longer was it only F-5s on the runway. On the apron, 200 yards from the old Training Centre, Agusta Bell helicopters and British Lightnings revved up, their blasts rocking the wooden walls.

Once I thought I saw my Lebanese friend from the plane, under an orange hard-hat, tagging along with some brown-cloaked, gold-trimmed VIPs. Could have been. Because a week later, the muezzins' impassioned calls to prayer, once floating from minaret to minaret like morning doves over the sleeping earth, were now replaced by ominous cracklings high in the air from loudspeakers slung between the enormous hangers of Raytheon and Bin Laden.

6 Leo and Rix

Leo, my American villa mate, I only ever saw reading but two books, *Catholics and Divorce* and *The Willy's Jeep Manual.*

Rix, my fellow Brit villa mate, had been in the Merchant Marine (Leo initially thought he'd been in the Marines) looked like The Players Cigarette man, and like Marlboro man had a health problem: one rheumy eye which fixed on you while the other did a survey of your upper portions. He was sometimes known as the Ancient Mariner.

Leo believed in seeing things through, whereas with Rix, no sooner was one job half-done than the next begun. 'Make a table' you'd say, and it was finished, one leg maybe a bit short because he was building a greenhouse or starting a vegetable garden.

One day they claimed to have found the oldest jeep in the kingdom half-buried in the sand. Rix stripped it, and Leo began assembling it inside the villa. 'Be out in a jiffy,' he said, but it stayed on. Then they acquired a wrecked Land Cruiser, and asked me if I thought we could get to the Red Sea in it. When I said we had to, or I'd resign, they were impressed. And off we went to see an American named Pitsos. On the way we picked up a new Welsh lad, Steve, who seemed dead keen on everything and Rix deemed advisable to bring on board right away.

Pitsos offered us Ethiopian coffee and went to get a map, 'a matter best kept to ourselves', he said. And I was immediately impressed by his air of authority and forthright manner, with one reservation. *Could a person wearing Rupert Bear trousers, really be our leader?*

Not long ago, I'd completed my National Service as a scatter-brained subaltern on the borders of the Yemen, and made some map-reading errors of my own. And if I wasn't mistaken, here was another man so fed up with having everything organized from above, wanted to make some of his own, too.

After a suitable pause and in a voice a shade louder than strictly necessary (considering there were only four of us and the smallness of the room) he informed us, we were in the highest part of Saudi, the Province of Asir (meaning rough) next to the Red Sea. And below us was a long low-lying coastal plain, the Tihama (meaning hot earth). "You get the picture?"

"Hot and rough" said Steve.

"Hah!" said he. "I see you pick up things quickly. So maybe you've noticed, the escarpment is split in several places by some big wadis, Al Lith, Beesha and Nazran," pointing to them and naming each respectfully, as if he'd spent many sleepless nights exploring their winding ways – at least on his map. "Unfortunately, they're too far away for a weekend trip, "he went on, "so our best bet is probably this one", and pointed to a much closer, forbidding cluster of contour lines, "The Wadi Ghawan. Let's go and look at it."

Half an hour later, we were clunking over an ironstone high plateau, when we suddenly came to a drop-off with several valleys floating away into a haze, 6,000 feet below.

Fantail ravens performed acrobatics along the edge, and high above us, vultures wheeled expectantly. On our left was the zigzag cicatrice of the old camel trail to lowland Yemen, and immediately beneath us, a newly built wall, blocking all access.

I was frankly shocked to meet the proverbial brick-wall so early in our enterprise, but Pitsos didn't seem too upset. "So that's where they're going to build the new road," he mused. "Looks like we may have to find our own way down. Might even be better in the long run. Less crowds."

Less crowds? I had no idea what he meant. As none of us at the time had any notion about the oil boom to come, I simply asked to look at his map again.

"Too dangerous," he said, "like jogging."

I could understand that being caught reading a map might get one arrested for spying, but knowing nothing about Bible John's encounter with the authorities, simply asked what was wrong with jogging.

"A Bedhu will run after a camel if he has to. But what sort of man chases nothing?"

"One running *away* from something." said Steve.

"And what sort of man is that?"

Sensing this might be some kind of admittance test, I piped up quickly, "A coward."

"A thief." says Steve.

"Their way of thinking, exactly." says Pitsos. But Steve's no mere pushover or side-kick. "What about the Hash House Harriers? They allow them, don't they?"

"Only in the bondu. Half-naked men and women, running together, doing ziggy-ziggy in the streets. No way."

"Men *and* women?" asks Steve.

"They don't know they're women. All ladies are welcome, but must tie up their hair, hide their boobs and not to worry if they have to pee. The locals squat too."

Then Steve asks, when and how he can join, and I hope loses some Brownie points – for dilettantism.

≈

For many weeks now, we've been practicing getting stuck in sand, backing out of gullies and digging ourselves out of the miasmal muck beneath saltpans. But alas, been unable to acquire the sense of humour Rix considers *de-rigueur* for descending the escarpment.

That's not to say funny things haven't been happening. They have. In some of the narrower steep-sided wadis, without escarp top or skyline visible, it's sometimes difficult to know if you're going up or down. Steve says Cezanne would have loved it. Apparently, in his oeuvres, Cezanne liked to flatten the occasional chimney, bank-up the sea, and get under the skin of apples and mountains, alike. But Steve's meant to be navigating, not carrying on as if in one of those Californian art museums, where he tells me you can sit down at *The Last Supper* in one gallery, then enjoy the company of *The Venus de Milo* with her arms back on, in the next.

Of course the inevitable happens. One bright morning, we come full tilt round a bend in a gully, onto the lip of a high dry waterfall, and would have taken off into the bosom of Abraham, had not Rix the presence of mind, to spin the steering wheel this way-and-that and zigzag down an endless scree, ending up beneath the original overhang.

The engine block ticked away. The cicadas started up a welcoming chorus. Only Steve was out of it – shot through one of Cezanne's oeuvres. Then Rix fixed each of us in turn with a single eye, and said the last thing I expected. "Not a word to anyone you guys, or everyone will be wanting to come down it."

7 Recruitment party

Tomorrow's the big day. The Red Sea excursion will be on its way.

Since we're still a bit short of volunteers, Rix decides to bring a big bottle of uncut sid to Marsden's bar for a recruitment party. Sid is the name given to expats' locally distilled moonshine. (Sidiki, the diminutive, meaning little friend, more commonly used by people already half-pissed.) You can buy an authorized cut version in Marsden's bar. But if you bring your own, it must pass the blue-flame test, given in a side room, appropriately equipped with bucket and fire-extinguisher.

When I arrive, Steve is putting up photographs in the main room to make it more homely. As I'm not sure if he's still on for the trip, I wander around, peering at them in respectful silence. They're of people with their dogs, dogs with their people, and a Saudi Prince with his Saluki (which isn't a dog). A Toyota pick-up with a camel in the back, entitled *Ship of the Desert* (scatological joke omitted), a gasoline station, a museum and art gallery – but only of the attendants. *Weird.*

A new skinhead, name of Warner, decides he wants to buy one of a petrol station, blown-up to poster size. It's been taken with a telephoto lens, and looking closer see why, the attendant is leaning on the pump, having a quiet smoke.

I also gather that Steve's Hash House Harrriers hadn't gone entirely to plan. His idea had been to hang about in the rear, in the hope of chatting up a few birds. After a while a gent in a pick-up turned up, told him to hop in as he was becoming dehydrated. Then wrote 'disoriented' on a clipboard against his name and put a consoling hand on his knee.

"You're the one who disoriented." said Steve, but before I hear the end of it, two new lads come charging up. "We hear you're the navigator," they say breathlessly.

"First I've heard of it." But on they go. "Can you tell us how we're going to get down the escarpment? Not by camel, is it? Because I got very sick in Lanzarote once."

"Not the first part. But that's as much as I can tell you, the rest's a surprise. However, if you go over there, the gentlemen with the big bottle of sid, will fill you in on the details and maybe offer you a drink. Come to think of it, could do with one myself!" On the way, I notice a strange Italian-American, called Lambourski, eyeing me suspiciously. "Don't take any notice of him", Marsden said earlier. "He's just back from a six-month stint at Sharorah, in the middle of the Empty Quarter. Has enormous debts, and Rix already has him down to go. Told him it was "a great place for swimming and nowt to spend money on."

Not much later, I overhear the two lads saying to the Italian, "That navigator chap hasn't a clue either."

Obviously, things aren't going too well, but I'm happy to see that the skinhead and Steve are getting along like a house on fire. "You're a bit of a stalker then," says a clearly inebriated Warner. A startled Steve grins. "Well, not exactly. It's just that art galleries and museums are the best places to pick up girls, good-lookers with specs, more interested in how the exhibits look, than how they do. For example, you'd be surprised at how many twig that *Dejeuner sur l'Herbe* is making fun of corpulent nudes posing as goddesses."

"Um." Says Warner. "So what you doing out here then?"

As if suddenly remembering where he is, the light bulb in Steve's face dims. "Didn't last, and I developed a bit of a drinking problem. The Recruitment Officer recommended here as the best place, no alcohol, no ifs and or buts about it, period."

"Well, you've certainly landed in the lion's den. But cheer up! I've got a request. Could be right up your street. Can you get a shot of me floating in the sea, beer in one hand, *The Sun* in the other, for my mates and my mum back home?"

At this, the efficient looking older man, called the Major, stands up as if for God Save the Queen, mutters "Muddling up the Red Sea with the Dead", and is about to give the young man a geography lesson, when Rix puts a friendly arm round his shoulder and wheels him away. "We need the bods, Major," he says quietly, pouring him a sid with his other hand, and adding, "The good news is we have two vehicles!"

"Now you tell me. Since when?"

"For some time." Actually it's since Pitsos and he went 'cray-fishing' while TDY (Temporary Duty) at Wedj. But after following too many mirages, ended up at midnight in the middle of nowhere, wearing nothing but swimming trunks, with Rix drawing a large crayfish in the sand for two distinctly perturbed policemen.

"Easy on old man," Pitsos had said, "They might think you're on some kind of high." Later confiding to us that although Rix was the best man to get us out of the shit, he was also the most likely to put us in it in the first place, "I actually think, he likes getting lost."

"Who's driving?" the Major now asks.

"Pitsos, Barnes, and myself".

"Makes more sense. Let's go see what Gaspar thinks." Rix follows, bottle firmly in hand. Gaspar, full name Gaspareti, is a cantankerous old sod, who seems to have had a pretty chequered career in various fields. He's established himself as the grey-eminence of the local bird-watching community and is always on the lookout for acolytes wanting to score Brownie points over one another.

Casting my eye over the room, I'm shocked to see several new lads are already seriously adrift, and it's only 8 o'clock. "It's going to be chaos," I warn Pitsos.

"So what's new?" he says. This is his standard response to rumours and scaremongers, but here the evidence is plain to see. It's not just that the lads are whooping it up like feeding-time at the zoo, it's what they're jabbering about.

"See that one, jerking about like Joe Cocker?" I say. "Honestly thinks we're going to some glorified beach resort," Then Pitsos interrupts, "With Galla girls dancing like entwined cobras in a place called the Snake-Pit," and adds, "as it used to be in Port Sudan's Tin Town, in the good old days."

"How do you know?"

"The thing about Rix, despite his odd way of doing things, is that he's not a complete turnip-head. He's already factored-in getting stuck and, don't take offence, the getting out's been delegated to you."

"Me?"

"Not your fault, your responsibility."

"Flipping hell! Could at least have warned me. It'll be my fault tomorrow – for sure."

"Relax. Think of it as a promotion. You're not a pusher-out or a digger, are you? And just look around you. There's enough new blood here to excavate the Terra Cotta Army."

"Hardly. They're all half-pissed."

"A passing phase. As your Churchill said, 'Tomorrow they'll be sober.'"

"So, what's Rix up to now with Gaspar and the Major?"

"Attempting to promote or encourage a bit of community spirit or whatever you want to call it, from our two senior citizens."

But when we go over, it seems a non-starter. The Major appears to be still prodding Gaspar awake. "How about it?" *Prod.* "What am I saying? *Prod.* What do you think?"

Gaspar, then noticing Rix, sits up, "A small one will do nicely," and adds. "You've extra water, spare tyres, that sort of thing?" This humourless focusing on the downside, isn't what Rix wants to hear. "Basics Gaspar. Basics." This doesn't sit too well with Gaspar, either. He takes off his glasses and stares at Rix as if it will make his next point clearer. "What about emergency tucker?"

"Swiss cheese and energy drinks. What more do you want?"

For some reason, this causes a shadow to cross Gaspar's brow and his jaw to drop, as if the prospect of ending up in some nameless wadi, gouging Velveeta cheese from a tin, and rinsing out with warm Vimto, held a special menace. It did. But only Steve knew what it was. On one of Gaspar's bird-watching picnics, when everyone else's eyes were focused on a pair of hoopoes, Steve noticed him tucking into the Velveeta.

Now the Velveeta experience, like the cuckoo clock, can mean different things to different persons. To babes-in-arms is often greeted with delight, dribbles and giggles. To pubescent girls, it can have the impact of a first kiss or imploding bubble gum. To older persons, one experience is enough, usually more than enough. And so it was with Gaspar. As he bit down, it stuck to his palate then to his lower teeth, as if he was being fitted for dentures by Lawrence Olivier in *The Boys from Brazil*. In an instant, he was fighting for life-giving oxygen and scared of losing his teeth. Steve leapt forward, thumped him on the back, or so he said, and all was well.

So what does Gaspar do here and now? What anyone would, turned on his erstwhile mentor and bit back, "Don't get yourself sucked-in Major. It will be hotter than the devil's own asshole down there."

"Stuff and nonsense," he replied. "Bringing those Italian POW's from Kassala to Tobruk, the heat never bothered us, did it?"

"Apart from killing a quarter of us. No".

All I remember of the end of the discussion is Rix's pouring the last of the sid, the Major urging everyone to walk in front of the convoy when approaching a new wadi, and himself departing in the wrong direction with a hearty wave and a sanguine, "Count on me, lads. Crack of dawn. I'll be there."

8 To the Red Sea

Six a.m. Most of the lads, halfway across the Empty Quarter the evening before, don't even make it to the gate. "I'll be there. Count on me," that Major chappie had said. But no Major.

Rix decides to drive and the skinhead Warner elects to sit up front in Rix's vehicle, a decision he may come to regret. Steve is here, and surprisingly, the sombre Italian-American, Lambourski and the two new lads.

Rix has the numbers, so there's no hanging about, and by 6:30, we're off.

It's quiet and peaceful as we skim over the soft sand in a grey dawn. A thin mist weaves here and there and hangs softly among the modest ruins of ancient Juraish, one of the too many places where Solomon met Sheba.

We turn left by a single rock rising out of the mist, with a Toyota perched on top. Whenever we passed it, someone always said "How the fuck did they manage that" as if the bedhu had done it, they alone being able to go up-and-down impassable wadis, no one having told them, they couldn't. In fact, the catering manager had parked it there, moments before the big flood. And when he came to retrieve it, everything else had been swept away.

When we pass it, Warner leans out the window and hollers, "How the fuck did they manage that?"

Beady-eyed Barnes is our driver, and excellent he is. His problem is bird-watching while doing it. He tells us that before he came here, he had no interest in our feathered friends, but in this land of desert and rock, it slowly crept up on him. Now, it's impossible to shake off.

As we head up to the escarp top, Pitsos does his best to keep him entertained by describing the other occupants, but he's unimpressed. "No great train robbers, unfrocked priests? And are you positive, that pseudo-hippie Devrill-Smith, isn't Lord Lucan?" Pitsos hasn't a clue whom he's talking about, but continues trying to be helpful. "Leo here was once thinking of taking the cloth, weren't you Leo?"

Leo smiles amiably. "Bonnie Raitt," he says, giving a thumbs-up sign and closes his eyes.

"Better let sleeping dogs lie," murmurs Pitsos. That's fine by me, for with the mist now closing in, I've quite enough on my plate.

For some reason Leo starts moaning, as if communing with departed spirits. Once or twice I hear them, but no louder than mice scratching. All of a sudden he says, "Listen to this Dave, quick now!" and thrusts these itsy-bitsy earplug things into my ears. I am immediately transported into an utterly captivating world of wrap-around sound, my first Walkman experience, have one moment of breathless vision – as of a far country – then we dip over the escarp.

It grows darker as we sink into shadow. All I can see are Rix's rear lights going this way-and-that, below us. It turns cold. I take the earphones out and it's totally silent. Even the vehicle makes no sound. Finally Barnes draws up beside us, "Piece of cake," he says. And one of the new lads throws up onto the sand.

"Cheer up." Says Barnes encouragingly, "You've made it! Pretty much plain sailing from here on."

"So far so good." says Rix to our lot, "Now comes the difficult part." On we go. House-high rocks loom out of the mist. We slow to a crawl, stop, and probe forward once more. It's difficult to tell what's moving, us or the fog.

7:30 a.m. We're driving through an abandoned village of fallen towers, with flowers painted on ancient whitewashed walls, still deep in the escarpment's shadow. Then to a place of enchantment, by a tiny stream, where Nile Sunbirds cavort in the first rays of the sun and camels amble contentedly on steep hillsides, munching exotic herbs.

By 8 o'clock we're in a different climate, gliding along on soft sand by groves of teberinth, tamarisk and acacias; cicadas blasting from every tree. We spy a couple of black-winged tents tucked-up a side wadi, silver bangles gleam – but no faces show.

Soon the wadi – fed by others – widens, and small bushes grazed down to mere bristle, give way to hard-baked earth, which breaks off in chunks. "Keep your eye on the road," says Leo.

"What road?" retorts Barnes, as he makes his way towards an impressive stand of acacias on the far side.

"Stop!" I shout, suddenly remembering what the Major said. Leo and I get out, check the ground, and feeling slightly foolish, plod on ahead.

When I next look up, the massive flank of the Jebel Adam is in full sunlight and the crushed mica on its face hurts the eyes. The acacias are dusty and loud with cicadas. As I usher Barnes forward, have to shout, "By the shade of that big one, looks good!" And he promptly gets stuck. "There's no shade here" he says. Everyone disembarks, and with a lot of huffing and puffing, we manage to push him out, then collapse round the vehicles and go to sleep.

I must have been considerably chastened by this turn of events, because I notice later two severe quotes in my diary. The first from Bruce Chatwin:

'The secret is to know when to get out and inspect the route, and having inspected it, to interpret the consequences of proceeding further.' And the second from Winston Churchill:

'It's not sufficient for you to be right, you must also implement your plan in a practical way and see it through, such that it is brought to a successful conclusion.' And it didn't occur to me, both were probably the result of screw-ups and rebukes received and endured, long before producing these pithy aphorisms.

As I doze beneath the tarry underbelly of the Toyota, fresh doubts begin to crowd in.

Beyond this point, crossed somewhere by the Tihama road, Pitsos's map had said only 'dunes.' And in the sea, where cartographers once put sea-monsters and mermaids to fill the empty spaces in men's minds, they'd simply inscribed crenellations like those of the Great Wall of China, signifying reefs.

I wake from a musty dream, which has no reef or beach, only mangroves and mud, and miles of gently lapping waves, like milky tea.

10:00 a.m. The wadi opens into a parched and sun-baked plain. "Look out for bustards," says Barnes enthusiastically. But with the rising heat, a torpor has settled on the troops, and if anyone sees so much as the shadow of a bird, simply hopes it will go away.

Feeling let off lightly for my navigational blunder, I dutifully scan the landscape for the lesser bustard and the more elusive, greater houbara bustard. (In Gaspar's sketch he's done little to differentiate them, except give the former less feathers than the latter, as if to save ink). Neither puts in an appearance. We have entered the bad lands, where wanted men go underground, and few birds dally.

Rix, tired of eating our dust, comes barrelling alongside. A clownish Steve, powdery and rubbery-lipped, leans out the window and points toward the horizon. "Huts, just like in Africa!" he shouts, and there looms up, no secret Tin Town with dancing girls and beer, but a miserable cluster of half-sunken beehive dwellings. The desiccated body of a hyena hangs from a nearby pole, but no humans appear. We top a rise and there's the reason: dunes, in endless waves like the sea.

The heat rises up like a wall and we blast through it. After half an hour, we've almost given up trying to find a way through the cursed sands. *Should we go on or turn back?* Pitsos points to a thick black line on his map. "This is the Tihama Road lads. We should be on it."

Half-formed thoughts careen round in my head. Perhaps the real road hasn't been started yet and like the one in the Wadi Ghawan, is only on a map. Confusion abounds. I remember reading that in BC 24, Aelius Gallus, a Roman General, had made a famous journey along this very coast, all the way to Umm Ladj. "His road lay by a desert country," wrote his chronicler Strabo, "which had only a few watering places." *But had it in fact, been a road?*

I also recalled that in the 6th century, wheeled vehicles had virtually disappeared from Morocco to Afghanistan because people had no need of them, camels doing the job better. In that case, we could be on the Tihama Road, without knowing it.

A rubicund Rix comes over. "Map letting you down?"

Pistos has to make a decision. "The Red Sea is dead ahead, or I'm a Dutchman." Fair enough. Compass out, we take another back-bearing, put down our second last bamboo pole, let more air out of the tires, and plunge on.

After a time I notice Rix appears to be going down the dunes sideways. *They've been at the wine for sure.* "What a bunch of shitheads!" I hiss.

26

"Don't worry about them," says Pitsos, "Worry about us. How about letting me know how steep the next dune is, before I'm down this one."

Suddenly, quicker than you'd imagine possible, we are surrounded by lakes of shimmering light. Beside us, the dunes levitate. The mirage in front, dispenses with desert completely, and gives us the illusion of infinite ocean. "Holy Jesus…a whiteout," whispers Pitsos. Compass out, we ride over a sea of crackling glass, hoping for the best.

Then it is there – a gentle curved beach and the bluest of blues imaginable. We climb out and plunge into the sea, like shipwrecked sailors seeking land.

As we dash through the shallows, a little cinnamon-red octopus comes gliding over the seabed. Pitsos stands there grinning. "A long way to come for a swim, lads. Bring on the wine!" He bellows and carries an empty crate into the sea. "Stevie, your camera, Warner! Over here! Sit down. Keep your legs straight; easy does it. Here's the newspaper – don't get it wet. This will really confuse the Major." He chuckles.

We don goggles, and in we go. How serenely and unhurriedly the fish move! This is the way we should live. Far away to the left, some silvery fish are feeding, a haze of glittering sand and shell grit drifting off them, as they rise and fall.

Chugging along in the calm lagoon, we're soon beset by beginner's ills: misty masks, mis-angled snorkels, and much too much enthusiasm. Down we go, up we come. Peter Pans in a bright airy room, bouncing round like balloons, bumping our heads against a silken roof. A dark form galumphs away beneath me. Just as I'm about to make out what it is, something swoops down to distract me. It's only a sand cloud billowing up from the seabed reflected in the surface. But it works. Scaramanga's trick on James Bond Island, done with mirrors. A deep excitement pervades my being. This isn't a morphine dream in an iron lung, this is under the Red Sea.

On a smooth dome of coral, as brightly lit as an expensive aquarium, small feathered creatures peer at us. Some open like miniature shuttlecocks, some wave daintily, others like miniature blue Christmas trees in souvenir snow globes, don't move, and still others, like red and yellow tufted BB gun pellets, shrink back as if fired at all at once, into a dart board. A striped butterfly fish with raccoon eyes comes by. A small school of silver jacks edges past us, turns about in a delicate shivering pirouette and not touching each other, thread back the way they came. All are bright silver except one, which is half smoky lamp-black, as if someone had started to clean it, and stopped. A small mystery.

We part the last strands of kelp. And one, two, three, four, large sharks cruise by. I see a black-tipped fin and a white-tipped one. In the shark book, the names had been boring, but we aren't bored. *What had Dr. Randall's shark book said?* Count the gills. I try to, like I did the slats in the Venetian blinds when the dentist's drill approached, but am hopelessly confused. *What else had he said?* "Don't urinate." Too late. When one turns round in front of a long ribbon of glittering fish, it passes so close, I could touch its sand-papery side. We withdraw in good order but kind of sideways.

Back on shore, a shadow falls over our little company, similar no doubt to that which darkened Crusoe's mind, when he spied that footprint in the sand.

7:00 p.m. The troops are still confused. "You say you saw a black tip on top of the white bit? What fin are you talking about?" asks Steve, "The one on the top of the back or the tail?"

"Dorsal, caudal or tail fin?" says Barnes. "Better start using the correct terms."

"Simpler to start with what we know," says Steve. *Natter, natter, natter.* However, as it's not the niggardly barman Marsden pouring the shots, the siddiki soon gets to work. "It wasn't a Great White for God's sake. It was only a reef shark."

"What do you mean *only*? Was big enough to swallow Warner here."

Into the second bottle, attitudes begin to lighten up. "They may have turned up because they were curious," says Steve. "A special occasion, perhaps?"

"A sharks' convention, you mean?"

"Why not? Something we've been privileged to witness, a one-off event, we can tell our grandchildren about – should we live that long. Ha, ha!"

I lie back, half listening to the conversation, and stare at the night canopy stretching from horizon to horizon every way you look. It's as if an artist, stunned by being given so grand a canvas, has filled it with stars all the same size, making none smaller towards the edges, so all are pressing their faces against the window of the world.

"Beats the planetarium, eh Stevie?" says the skinhead, Warner.

"Beats sleeping under Charing Cross Bridge," says Steve.

"You never slept under Charing Cross Bridge."

"I did that. Two weeks before I came here. Had my suit nicely pressed under a newspaper, and the old gaffer signed me up in a jiffy."

"Taking all comers, aren't they?" says one of the new lads.

"Beggars can't be choosers." Says Steve modestly.

"Speak for yourself. How much you putting away then?" Says the other lad.

"Before tax of after? Come on," mutters Steve sarcastically.

"You an accountant, tax-informer or what?"

"Stow the shop." growls Leo beside me. And my eavesdropping is also brought to an abrupt end, for the skinhead is staring straight at me through the fire. Class warfare about to begin.

"What about you? What's wrong with you then?" he says.

"Fucked up too. Had a fall."

"Mountain climbing were we? The Matterhorn?"

"Number 29 bus."

He laughs. "Let you out here though, didn't they? We may be the walking wounded, but I've a feeling we may have walked in the right direction. Cheers, mate!"

"Cheers."

A shooting star burns across the heavens.

"Magic," he says. "Fucking magic."

≈

Slept well, towel for a pillow, breeze for a blanket, no sand flies or mosquitoes. One odd incident. Lambourski, suddenly sat up in the middle of the night and hollered, "Louisa! Louisa! I've found the answer. It's all sorted out!" Then, demanded a pencil. By the time we'd found the flashlight, got him his pencil and a piece of paper, he'd forgotten what it was, and we all went back to sleep.

7:00 a.m. Just time for a quick dip and, under the principle the hair of the dog, a swim out to the kelp. As we push the inflated inner tube ahead of us, the privileged aspect of our previous meeting with the sharks begins to fade. As our dark dirigible perambulates over the lagoon attended by a coterie of sky-divers, peering down, even small fish flee in surprise. We gingerly part the kelp and peek through. Nothing.

Back on shore we slosh fresh water over ourselves and into salt-rashed groins, gulp down warm Vimto, and are on our way.

Near the escarp top, we tug on warm clothes again.

Later, Lambourski thinks he's contracted malaria. The medic gives him a couple of aspirins. "What are these for?" he demands disgustedly.

"Bit of sunburn and the sniffles."

9 North. We're as clueless as pigeons at Wimbledon

Today we walk north, hugging the coast and taking a dip whenever we feel like it. Most of the glades are full of small fish, layered in clouds, among which Forster's barracuda hang motionless, awaiting their chances.

Only in one place does the coral come close to shore. Almost immediately, we see a large trout-like fish hanging off an overhang. It idles down beneath a coral table. And a second one, pale as speckled-sand, dashes out and waves its pectoral fins at us from open water. Leo dives down to check-out the one hiding under the coral, but sees nothing. We then realize that it and the second fish are the same one. When we approach it, yet another slides off the top of the very coral table under which Leo had just been looking. And if you can unravel that, you're on your way to understanding something of their antics. We follow them, or rather, they lure us on, and in the end, simply fade away.

Looking back, further on, I see the first one has returned to its original location, like an old river trout, which has found the best place below the bank, and intends to keep it.

By the first reed bed, we come across a school of plump, iron-grey fish with big mouths, out on an early morning stroll. When almost opposite us, they become possessed with the manic friskiness of a sidewalk peddler's wind-up toys.

We don't know it yet but these are the young of some very large fish, later called the Korean fish. To see these bigger ones, we should stop and wait in the reeds for anything up to half-a-day, but we don't know that, either. To be frank, we are as clueless as pigeons at Wimbledon.

Chugging along as we do, at the pace of a gentle walk, is the perfect warning for any respectably-sized fish to ease back into the reeds till we're gone. But we don't know that either. After an hour or so, the only one who's got close enough for a shot, is

Warner, and though his spear tip couldn't have been more than a foot from a fish, it bounces off.

We plod across the shallows of large bays, where baby shark make bee-lines for our ankles, veering off like bats out of hell the instant they see the giants attached. Soon the glassy surface is etched with large V's, criss-crossing among the floating clouds.

Beach leads to beach. Behind us, rise table-high macaroon-coloured, windswept plateaus of iron-hard dead coral. On the seaside, they drop abruptly, as if bitten-off, giving the impression that the Red Sea is narrowing, which it is in the short term, but in deep time (the sort that tells fossil hunters, the peak of Everest was once under water) it's widening.

Old lava fields come right down into the sea, and the heat right up through the soles of our sandals. Swimming among gleaming boulders, we see next to nothing, though home to some very big snapper, but of course we don't know that, either. After a while, by a bleak amphitheatre of rock, a pod of mullet come in from deep water, dither-about, then head out. The sea gets deeper. Only when we begin to wonder where they'd been going, do we backtrack along the amphitheatre wall. But no entrances or exits do we find.

Beginning to get fed up, we climb out onto a basalt area with several large pools. Skittish terns swoop down on us. I slip on the hot basalt, slosh sea water over it, sit down and ponder what to do.

A single rock monolith about a quarter of a mile out, appears and disappears in the blinding glare. Naturally no one wants to swim to it. Lambourski, who before we set out, had stood rooted to the spot as if trying to decide if more insulted by the tepid sea or burning sand, has hardly uttered two words all day and stares at his feet.

A bad feeling comes over me. In the silence broken only by the scuttling of crabs and the petulant screeching of terns, I wonder. *Is this Red Sea caper really going to warrant multiple visits? Maybe that's not the way it's going to work out, at all.*

After a long wait, Lambourski says out of the blue, "The pool's moving and there's no wind". And he's right. We jump up and start searching for where the water must be coming in. Under a large overhang we eventually find the entrance to a tunnel and ease down cautiously, one by one. Small schools of coppery fish, scatter like windblown leaves.

In the soft-blue light at its end, mullet come by. The water fizzes like champagne and we lose them. They appear again, moving more like new recruits than the cool customers who usually jumped over our spears like children skipping rope. Their outriders bunch up, wheel, and the whole pod retreats down the tunnel, where they end up going round in circles. We stay quite still.

After a while, as if pretending we don't exist, they advance again. *Thwack! Thwack!* Warner pins one to a rock where it vibrates like a tuning fork. Another twirls on Lambourski's spear, shedding scales like a one-armed bandit, loose change.

In ten minutes, we have three good fish, heads blunt as turtles, silver-bright bodies, tinged with violet where the fins and tails attach. Within minutes it's all faded. They've become fishmonger's grey mullet, much as one might say Red Indian or white man.

Back at camp, Pitsos and Rix can't imagine how we got close enough.

"Gloomy grumps here, kept his eyes open and asked the right question." Warner explains.

"Not your usual method, then." Says Pitsos. "Any shark?"

"No shark."

"What about the reef?"

"Never went to the reef. Chicken."

10 South. We're lost

The coast is more open south, with many low-lying sandy islets. We see black and white dolphins leaping high, hundreds of oyster catchers – dressy little waders who don't like swimming, so flit back and forth along the shore as we pass. We see two antelopes.

"Not antelopes," says Barnes. "Gazelle." Leo thinks they're trail bikes. Soon we're lost.

In the evening, the light of our fire is joined by another far over a large lagoon. A line of almost naked figures appears, the man in the middle, holding aloft a flaring torch. We can just make out a pale ribbon of surf, lapping at his feet.

Once they formed an excited circle, as a great flapping ray was lifted up on the spears, before being laid on the exposed coral and bludgeoned to death. They are the Koreans, whom we've been half-expecting. Soon they are back on the beach and we go over to join them.

A man with hooded-eyes and larger than the rest, comes forward, peering into the night. When he sees us, his face breaks into a big smile. "Welcome. Welcome! Ha, ha! You bring number one wine! Thank you Mr. Lixie. With or without, always welcome. I'm Captain Kim, and these are my men."

They half rise, not out of discourtesy or lethargy, but because their lower extremities are tucked under a huge slab of polished steel, under which there appears to be a fire. At first glance, you might imagine them to be a band of pirates or murderers, undergoing some gentle persuasion, courtesy of the captain. "Sit down please. Make yourselves at home." He beams.

We crumple down, close to the ironwork as best we can. He tells us it comes from a wreck on the reef, and makes a cracking sound with his knuckles, possibly to indicate popping rivets. "We bring back on a raft. Big work."

Wine is poured. The wings of the ray are already filleted and bubbling away in the soup. Other small slices are now dipped in a mustard-like condiment and offered to us. Each man lays out what he wants: squid, octopus, garfish, on the steel plate, slaps on a brick-red sauce, plies his chopsticks to skate it round, flips it over and conducts it to a grinning face. To them, taste seems to be a matter of fire-on-fire, and nothing matters about the wine, either – save it have the kick of a rutting camel.

Another man, Kim number two, looms up out of the night, thrusts a bucket of creepy-crawlies into our faces and grabs a handful of raw sausages. "So sorry," he says, "Must go beat more fish," and he's off.

"You want to go too?" inquires Captain Kim, catching my eye. "Yes? Good idea! When you come back, soup will be ready."

Under a raggedly flaring torch, which has to be dipped in kerosene every so often, bright green garfish pirouette away like the spokes of a big wheel.

Not far off, a humped wave makes seawards. *What is it?* But they gabble away in their own tongue, adding to the confusion. Meeting a submerged sandbank, the creature turns about and comes directly towards us. Spears fly in all directions. *Eeeh… Aaaargh!"* Comic strip expletives burst out, as a big ray passes through our line, its tail, taut as steel wire.

Next we surround some squid, the colour of rabbits, which stream away into the deeps.

Eventually the torch dies out, we hit the beach and walk back. But it's not a beach. There are rushing sounds all around us and big waves come looming out of the night. It's some kind of sand bank. Phosphorescence streams past us, and underwater, clusters of dark ovoid, vertical shells, spew forth plumes of sand as if from an encampment of extra-terrestrials. We pick our way carefully through patches of dark sea, towards the small light of our fire.

Back at camp, we quaff down the fiery soup and wine, while Kim number one tells us about a great fish, with a large mouth and big rubbery lips, they caught a month ago. Part of its meat was white, for long-distance swimming, and part red, for shorter bursts. The red part, they prefer for raw fish, sliced very thin and eaten just after the fish is caught. The white, with head and lips, is favoured for soup, which is their custom to eat last.

By the time we stagger away, Orion the hunter, is well over the horizon. "Must be something to do with the sea air," muses Pitsos, sliding down a dune. "I don't feel a bit tired."

Soon we're lost, something Rix seems happy to have achieved twice in one day (which is, why we are camped where we are, wherever that is). But he's now going to guide us back by the Big Dipper. In a while, voices singing in a savage oriental harmony, reach us over the dunes. We're approaching the Koreans again. Rix seems bewitched. "They're like the three musketeers, only more of them, popping up all over the place. All for one and one for all."

"You're right," say I. "Explains why they need such a big fish, doesn't it?"

"Yes. But not why you promised to get them one, tomorrow."

"Did I?"

"Yes. Several times."

11 Pursuit of Korean fish

Over the next weeks, I took several swims to the reef where the Koreans said they'd seen the big fish. One time I saw a dim shape in the distance then fade away, too still to be a shark, too high in the water, a grouper. "We'll have to find out where it lives" I report to the lads.

"Whose this 'we', you're talking about?" says Warner. "You're the one going to bell this cat."

One day, after a long swim, I catch a glimpse of an enormous head with big white lips, peeping out of a cave. The entrance is encrusted with sea urchins. I settle down to wait, well back from the rim, the water barely covering my head.

After a goodish time, a pod of mullet stream by on their own concerns, then a nurse shark – thuggish but harmless – circles, causing my testicles to squirm when it dallies overlong behind me. Reminds me to send the hospital wheelchair cowboys a postcard with a shark on it, to keep their spirits up. I also recall our Olympic Gold medallist, Gordon Pirie's ward visit to encourage us to persevere. (If your memory needs a jolt, think Charlie Chaplin in short pants). But he kept me going, furiously exercising with play putty and trying to nudge a matchbox across my blanket by splaying my fingers.

Then the Books on Wheel's lady set me up with *Gun Runners of the Caribbean,* whom I happily envisaged bobbing away on the Gulf Stream with half fish-eaten faces, while their protagonists frolicked with beautiful Asst. District Attorneys, after a rigorous weekly regime of long-distance swimming and Jamaican rum punches.

However, it soon dawned on me, the author spent far less ink on the long-distance swimming than on the fisticuffs and powerboat crashes, which had put his combatants in need of the long distance-swimming in the first place. And in between these incendiary episodes, were never allowed to clutter the deck, wearing prosthetic devices, or God forbid, ramble on like The English Patient.

I must have dozed off under the sheer drama of these reminiscences, for the next thing I remember is the gentle lapping of the waves and being surrounded like Gulliver, by scores of sea urchins come out on the falling tide. One lot was already snuffling round my extremities like hedgehogs looking for nuts while my own, true to the code of the genes (each to his own) having shrunk to walnut size without telling me.

I poked two away with my snorkel and spear gun, but they continued to advance — not exactly at a brisk trot, true enough — but a perseverance and pace that old Gordon himself would not have disparaged. I soon got a better understanding of how the lesser creatures of the sea could be mesmerized by the sparkling sapphires and pearl necklaces laid out on black velvet, beneath the come-hither twinkle of ebony spines, then stabbed! Their way of protecting smaller residents who kept the surface free of detritus. (The palpitating cocktail centrepiece, Barnes later informs me, being the anus.)

When another sea urchin got entangled in my T-shirt, I tried to stand up, but found I'd lost the knack. And things grew more serious.

To cut a long and pathetic story short; when the lads found me drifting in after merciful lift-off and mumbling on about an attack by man-eating hors d'oeuvres, in a Japanese horror movie, they generously promised to help me next time, provided I could show them the place and had a plan.

≈

It's now the next time and here's the plan, into the spirit of which, the Korean fish also seem to have entered. There are three of them, one of which is a monster, and they've elected to make their stand by a rocky outcrop near the cave. Pitsos and I will drive them towards it, where Warner, Lambourski and Leo are waiting.

It goes fine until the last moment, when they explode in all directions, each to watch us from a different point of the compass, as if daring us to have another go, which we do, with exactly the same result. Barnes is delighted, as he always roots for the fish. The others conclude they've helped enough.

The Koreans remain optimistic.

≈

Early morning, a few weeks later. The gentle swell of the lagoon is punctured by three or four large drops of rain. Of course, it's not rain but the dorsal fins of big fish, turning over.

In five minutes, gear half-on, we're all wading out. About fifty yards in, we feel a jolt in our stomachs, as if a shockwave was passing through the sea.

At first, we thought someone must be dynamiting in the old Greek quarry. Then it happens again. A solid long wall of small fish rises from the surface of the sea in a single curved wave, and falls back. In a few seconds, we are in the middle of huge school. It is scary and dark, like having a ton of confetti dumped on one and nothing to celebrate. At intervals, the entire mass jerks first to the left, then to the right, drawing us with it. I try to resist moving, but can't. It has the impact of the demon-drum at Rio Carnival. You have to move, and having moved, can't stop.

I later learned, each of us imagined, the school was being impacted by big fish first from one side, then the other, and was as if our nervous systems and bodies had decided they were better off trusting to instinct, than to the indecisiveness of our brains.

After being bumped by a particularly vicious blow from the right, the whole mass jumps two or so yards to the left and we find ourselves expelled into clear water, with only a pair of small jacks skittering away – and us feeling very foolish. So we swim back in, to see who can stay longest.

After no more than a minute of excruciating jolting, the school opens, and two huge Korean fish, mouths agape, come powering through the middle, carving out a tunnel of clear water like air at the centre of a water-spout. We shrink back into the panicky mass, which streams around us in a river of fright, but the big fish have gone before we've gathered our wits together.

They return again and Pitsos hits one hard. My gun jams, but I thrust my arm deep into the fish's gill-case to get a better grip. This is a mistake.

Though the front of the mouth is entirely devoid of teeth, the back isn't, having several rows of spectacular molars, not unlike small versions of those domed-studs used as speed bumps, which it now grinds like a cow chewing the cud, only in this case an arm which, until this moment had entirely belonged to me.

While its ownership was being contested, I was being drawn down into the deep, and truly fancied my foolish existence was about to end. It would have, had not Lambourski, put another spear in the fish, and with Leo's help begun to raise the great beast upwards.

As we drifted inshore, I saw myself pass over a squadron of Forester's barracuda, aloof, almost still, but no doubt inching upwards. Head-on for a moment, their bodies offering no reflecting surfaces to the sun, they looked like pleasant spheroid creatures with big innocent eyes and no evil intentions.

That afternoon the Koreans arrived by bush telegraph, with meat cleavers, mallets, long blood-thirsty looking knives and small plastic bags full of brick-red powders. They went over to Rix's grill, from where we heard nothing but heavy blows, scuffling – like several beasts trying to strangle each other – and more blows. Twenty-five minutes later, they emerged laden with platters of razor-thin red meat and a bowl piled high with fish fillets.

The latter are slapped on a domed grill (made from the top of a petrol drum) and doused with a blood-red sauce. A tureen of soup, in which a calf's head appears to be bobbing about, is then brought forward. "Number one soup," says Captain Kim enthusiastically.

After we've devoured most of the fish steaks and partaken modestly of the soup; the remains of the fillets and soup are born away under bamboo poles, for a whole family of more Paks, Kims, and Chungs, shortly coming off shift.

Next time we eat, the newest arrivals become the cooks and hewers of meat, and the old team gives the orders. The next time again, the old team sat with us, quaffing wine and ale, and the erstwhile hewers of flesh gave orders to a new collection of Paks, Kims, and Chungs. And woe betide you if you got muddled up and offered the new Kim a drink before the old.

12 Our place

I wake at six. Over earth and sky, an immense silence reigns. Far-off, small waves rise up and march in long parallel lines towards the reef. Each one tautens, winks, and falls. 'Slow kisses on the eyelids of the sea' wrote Rimbaud, and he was right.

I listen for the hoopoe lark, but I hear no sound. Closer to, the sand is criss-crossed by the tracks of the night-revellers. We hear them almost every night, scuffling in the tinfoil and dancing in the kettle. We call them the hermit-crab band. When their high jinks are finished, they roll over and go to sleep, wherever they are.

The lagoon's shallows, like the beach, are criss-crossed by early morning hunters, baby reef-shark. One or two, look as if they are going backwards. These are not shark at all, but blue crabs moving fast this way-and-that, fending for themselves.

Most early mornings, we can see in the lagoon the almost static duets between solitary barracuda and schools of fish. We wondered why the latter put up with it, but have not pursued the issue.

The first hoopoe lark now calls: three plaintive notes, followed by another three, slightly higher, repeated at intervals, endlessly. It is muted yet insistent, like the advancing heat.

Further out, mysterious upwellings, taut and sinuous, gently rock the pale face of the sea and tilt the sky this way-and-that. Beyond them, there's nothing to tell one where sea ends and sky begins, and what is beyond doesn't matter.

Behind us, the two bamboo poles used to mark the way in and out, have disappeared (camels had knocked them down and eaten the pennants). Several times since, we've entered through different configurations of dunes, and realize this is how it is going to be. We're a bit like the lads from *Lord of the Flies* 'come to a new imagined, but no means realized coast', grown older, as Jimmy Buffet sings, 'but not necessarily up'.

We camped by sleepy backwaters, week after week, often not ten yards from the waters edge, chased fish and sometimes got chased in return. Used no boats or scuba-gear and carried our spiny loads in a sack, slung from spear guns on our shoulders. All in all, we spent more time in the sea and caught less fish than any fishermen I know.

For this, we pretty much blamed Pitsos. Many persons said we should have bought a boat, proper spear guns and gone to remoter reefs. And we'd have gotten more and bigger fish, in half the time. He maintained that without a boat, we could spend more time in the water, horizontally, have longer to fish, and less of them to carry. And rather than concentrating on upgrading our technology, be better served, directing half our minds to studying how the fish conducted themselves, and half to out-thinking them. Warner, on the other hand, maintained fish couldn't think, dispensed with all philosophizing and caught more than any of us.

In the beginning, we towed what we caught in a sack and inner tube behind us as the Shark Book said, but under the pitiless tutelage of the sun, soon abandoned sack and tire, buried our catch on the reef-top, and caught only what we could carry.

On our stretch of coast, there was neither surface water nor permanent wells. The few wandering bedhu of the area were not fishermen. Though the Prophet had stated, 'it was lawful to fish in the sea, as a provision for those who travel', the Wahabis of the area had their own notions: 'A man of his hands is disgraced by eating the three mean foods: chicken, eggs and fish,' as Lawrence had noted in *The Seven Pillars of Wisdom. P*ilgrims didn't tarry on the Tihama road either, and visitors from the sea were a rarity. Too many reefs, too many days of drifting sand and enough malaria to go round for all.

The few expeditions of past times are now generally prefaced 'ill-fated.' If they mastered the environment, they upset the locals, and vice versa. In the Forskall-Neibuhr expedition of 1761-67, the low-key Neibuhr survived; the brilliant Forskall, not so. He wowed the natives by predicting an eclipse, but provoked jealousy in high places. Dispensing medicine one time, an old man complained to him of being unable to see in the dark. Forskall suggested he try lighting a candle. This went down exceptionally well. Then Forskall blew the situation, calling for volunteers to catch snakes then openly bottling them in alcohol.

Of the riff-raff who drifted onto these shores, one AWOL chancer named Thomas Keith, formerly of the Cameron Highlanders, stood out in my mind. He was offered the usual hospitality; head-off or foreskin? Probably made the right decision because in 1815, he was appointed Governor of Medina.

The acacias that we stopped by on our first trip have now become a half-way house to the coast. Because they are the last trees worthy of the name between here and Africa, all sorts come to them, for shelter, shade, food or firewood. So one can hardly blame them for presenting a prickly face to the world. Let in a single goat, and it would strip the bark and scuff-up the humus in next to no time.

But I've also learned the acacias have a few tricks up their sleeves. Over-browsers are encouraged to move on by the tree's ability to produce a bitter-tasting tannin in a matter of moments, as well as airborne pheromones to warn the neighbours.

On peering in that the first time, I fancied only a fakir seeking his bed of nails would feel welcome. The lugubrious explorer Charles Doughty, a bit that way inclined, also spoke only of the acacia's 'shimmering dimness'. For its leaves, well-protected by inch-long crossed thorns, also like to curl up between them during their own midday siestas.

Adept as the acacias are at keeping at bay most creatures larger than a bird, they remain extremely hospitable to the smaller citizenry of the world. That first peek revealed a bustling metropolis, full of scurrying pedestrians bearing trophies, backed-up traffic, removal services and funeral processions. All using the over-and-underpasses, and no doubt crammed into the enclosed, elevated subways, running like exposed veins over the tree's sinewy arms.

Imagine my surprise when on gently nudging away one harmless dead-looking branch, it snapped, spraying me with a host of ants. Not your common-a-garden variety either, but aggressive members of a rapid-deployment force, similar to our Parachute Regiment, without the sissy parachutes.

Barnes tells me, they are kept up-to-the-mark on a supplementary diet of protein-rich albumen, with aromatic gum-arabic as the come-on. But not that another line of defence, also waits for me. For when I stepped back for a good scratch, I was stung on the back of the neck by a thorn as tenaciously barbed as a well-cast trout fly.

The Major had warned us about these first cousins of 'the come-back-don't-go-away thorn of the Matabele', but not that they liked to dance a meter or more from the thorn wall on the end of long springy out-riders, sprouting from the very crown of the tree.

And after observing them from a distance, I understood a bit better why the bushman out hunting, on coming to such a grove squats down for a careful look-see and friendly chat, before pushing on.

I mention this stuff here because, though we came to love this place, it certainly didn't start out so.

13 Everything's going wrong

While crossing the coastal saltpan this morning, instead of going round it, I'm reminded of Rix's burned fish: break the crust and God knows what's underneath! And chooses this same moment to tell me, Warner's been posted to Sharorah.

This is serious bad news. Not only is he the sort of cold-blooded killer we need to get the show on the road, but he's the only one capable of doing it on a regular basis.

Suddenly, everything is going wrong. The local fish no longer want to know us. We scare away a few, and naturally, they keep away. This affects others. Big groupers (we called them the snarlers), which used to go to their holes and look out, don't look out anymore.

Then there's the matter of the great Bayad. This is a fish of dignified and solitary mien, which often comes over the turtle grass on his way out after an early morning breakfast. Though he doesn't carry himself with the lightness and grace of the smaller jacks, nevertheless looks splendid in his all-silver skin.

Young Ben, our villa neighbour, who claimed to come from the Seychelles, but lives in Wimbledon, told us it was the very best for making his mum's fish curry, (the flesh of other jacks breaking-up too soon). This was a bit like pointing at the moon, and expounding on its mineral resources. And that's pretty much how it remained to us, so much so that after a few weeks, we hardly noticed it, a bit like a silver Bentley, which regularly passes you on your way to work.

Then one morning, a wave, not a white-cap, but more a powerful heave of water, caught me just right and I knew I could get it. I kicked and fired in one go. At first, the fish didn't seem to connect me with what hit it. And though blood was pumping from it like red smoke, I almost managed to climb on its back. But the instant I laid my hand on the spear shaft, it had the leverage it needed, and with two mighty whacks of its tail, sailed away. 'The whole world is a fish and the fish is gone.' says the author of *A River Runs Through It*. And so it is.

I swam round in circles, replaying over and over again what I should have done, determined to do it properly at the very next opportunity. At the same time, seized with remorse, I determined not to commit such folly again. These two states of mind existed, side-by-side, for quite a while. And when Lambourski told me one time, never to try and shoot a big fish with a small gun, I replied. "How do I know it's too big unless I try it first", and maybe added "asshole", *sotto voce*.

Next morning I was back in exactly the same place.

The sea was grey and still.

The small pan-sized jack I'd just shot, was vibrating like a tuning-fork on the end of my spear. I reached forward to break its back and a huge shark, fatter than a full-grown porker, came in like an express train. Even as I was knocked-off balance like a child playing too near the tracks, I saw clearly its snaggled teeth and enormous belly.

It raced round in a big circle. Everyone yelled. Barnes rushed to the water's edge, the rest walked backwards out of the shallows. Then it was gone, the jack untouched. '*If they want you they've got you,*' I kept mumbling to myself. Fear came later, in dribs and drabs, usually when a fish vibrated on the end of the spear.

In later discussions, the size of the shark grew with each telling, as if repetition itself diminished the effect and needed compensating for. We did however, settle on Pigeye Shark, after careful scrutiny of details and pictures in the Shark Book. I was disappointed by the name, but at least the caption had this to say: Although not implicated in any shark attacks on man, it seems likely that it has been implicated and misidentified as some other species such as *Leucas* (the bull shark).

That night I dreamed, not of shark but that I'd been abandoned on a lonely beach, Pitsos and Lambourski had joined the Bridge Club (though neither plays) and Rix had had his beer contract with Marsden's Club, renewed. Whereupon I woke, because I knew this last item couldn't be for real.

Then over-stretched catapults began to snap. More powerful ones to bend the spear shafts or explode, their piano wire V's ripping open our hands. We called them the finger-stingers, in distinction to Rix's fearsome ring-stinging curries.

Next I was banned from making the soup, too many fish scales.

And one day on reading about the Burke and Wills expedition across Australia south to north, I came across the following sentence. *Burke had left them provisions for six months and they had plenty of duck to eat until the constant shooting scared them off.* And despite the incredible hoop-la and fanfare of that expedition's send-off, realized we were them and they were us. It was time for radical action.

We agreed not to move from our beach, as this would only export the problem, which was after all, us.

This was probably the least stupid thing we ever did.

The second least stupid thing we did (despite trying otherwise) was to forgo more powerful guns. Here we were a bit like that Spartan lad who whinged to his mom that he needed a longer sword and was told "Try taking a step closer, son".

And here Lambourski went over the top in the opposite direction! Said we should try and enter the sea, like a mother peering at her sleeping baby!

But it only took one plate of calamari from a large squid, shot not three yards from the water's edge, to have us paying attention.

My guess is, not to lose face, we practised his technique in secret. My way was to affect to notice a rare shell by the water's edge, kneel down, pick it up, rinse it (man see monkey do) then kind of rolling sideways (like those fish which imitate a piece of wood) float gently forward.

On the reef top, where as carefree youths we'd bantered about which way to go, then simply jumped in, we now pedantically scrutinized the surface for the slightest ripple and something Barnes called the *Coriolis Effect* (apparently due to the spin of the earth). Pitsos said we should drift with the current, but here was in error. For the moment we entered the water, sweat, suntan lotion, mineral oil, breakfast crumbs etc., were telegraphed way ahead. Also, to avoid being swept past any target fish, no last second paddle-steamer adjustment could be made because it invariably put the frighteners on the fish, never mind which way they were facing.

But the hardest thing to do, was to show respect to those small fish, we'd previously not given the time of day. Three examples should suffice.

Silver Wrasse. These little beauties usually hang about where seabed meets vertical rock-face and sand swirls about. All we are likely to see are a few beady eyes and flickers of silver. *So what's the problem?* Most of the time, nothing. But every so often, when we peer over the reef's edge, they get it into their tiny brains, it's them we're after. They dash back-and-forth just above the seabed in a state of high dudgeon. If they could speak, they'd be screaming "Flee for your lives. Help! Help! The reef-rapers are here!" There's nothing to be done, but back-off, and take ourselves elsewhere.

Rabbit fish. These scruffy little specimens, of no fixed of abode, drift all over the sand flats like wind-blown leaves.

One morning, Pitsos, on his best behaviour, came across a large school, some of whom were wearing rather fetching green eye-shadow, dainty smudges of trypsin granules, to cut-down the glare from the sand flats.

He courteously bade them pass and they immediately went into a tizzy, rabbit fish for shock-and-awe. 'Don't tell a soul,' one bubbled, 'but did you hear the naughty word the traffic warden just used?' I don't know what it was, but must have been good because several did doo-doos right there in the water before streaming away to tell their mums, who informed the P.T.A, who told Dame Parrott-Fish herself. And was subsequently quoted in *The Reef Gazette,* under the headline 'School Girls in Street-Crossing Shocker', saying 'I won't comment, but can assure you, it wasn't a local fish.'

And we'd learned our lesson: Don't play the goat with rabbit fish.

Finally, the soldier fish. This little fellow, we've built up a certain respect for. Always smartly turned-out in bright orange, he resolutely mans his little sentry box, any suitable porthole in the reef's hulk. Whenever we come by, he presents arms, clicking his gill-cases open-and-shut, like a flick-knife.

Pretty impressive stuff, you might think and you're right, but perhaps not quite as you imagine. His gill-cases also connect to his swim-bladder and cause it to send out low staccato reverberations into the warrens and caves behind him, warning the occupants to stay put. And this mix of ceremonial ostentation, obsequious display and street smarts, has earned him extra employment as the doorman to certain dubious local establishments.

"This little critter has us by the balls", as Warner put it before his untimely departure to Sharorah. "To take him out now would only involve us in some sort of mafia trouble."

So whenever we meet now, we cross to the other side of the street, leaving him to beat his little drum and help his own. Some of whom are no doubt, those big snarlers we no longer see and others, yet unseen: big snappers with no intention of meeting us socially, inside or outside their premises.

14 Burying the beer

Our troubles are not yet over. This morning Rix wakes us, He's been digging and looks it. "Sorry, no rations," he says. "*Huff.* The shit's hit the fan. *Puff.* They're going to raid the compound."

"So what's new?" says Pitsos.

"Barnes and I need a bit of help. I've buried half the beer in the greenhouse and the rest's here."

"Great," says Pitsos, "Where?"

"Down the beach."

"Right, let's get on with it."

I'm detailed to keep watch from a dune while they proceed to dig a pit on Beer Bottle Beach, destined no doubt to become a passing-out parade ground for future recruits, and begin to wonder if it's such a good idea.

The thing about Rix's beer is, most customers (here I include myself) needed it more than liked it, and he was quick to exploit this. 'Cheers!' He'd say to any new face about to sample a glass, 'Down the hatch!' They'd immediately grimace, but before they'd time to say a word, he'd be beaming "Noticed the nutty piquance have you? Mark of real ale. Thought a bright lad (or old timer) like you would." By the time the bright lad (or old timer) was ready to contest the issue, they often found they'd lost the capacity for speech and he'd moved onto the next victim.

That the same 'nutty piquance' turned up in his wine, didn't faze him either. And I once heard him apprising the Major in all earnestness. "This bin (a pink plastic dustbin) has a nutty piquance which might find favour with your palate." The Major, who rather fancied himself in this regard, raised his glass to appreciate its nose, and sipped cautiously. "Mm…don't put yourself down my boy. First grade horse-piss. Make no mistake about it."

After several in-house promotions, we sometimes found the less squeamish customers, having parted with the needy and partaken too liberally of the needful, wandering round the villa in various states of difficulty. One woke up under Leo's jeep, hollering for an ambulance in the middle of the night.

I am jolted out of these pitiful reminiscences by Barnes bringing me a bottle of water. "Risky business", he says, "And I don't even drink the stuff. The old bastard let me assume we were carrying ordinary rations, till we reached Juraish, then it was too late. I'd really hate to see us all being arrested because of a bunch of drunks on a beach."

"You think it could come to that?"

"From Pitcairn to the wreck of the SS Batavia, there comes a point in groups such as ours when the booze takes over. Then the murders start."

"Who'll be first, d'you think?"

"Rix, or Jack – he wants to set up a rival taxi-service to the coast."

"That's no joke," I blurt out. "We could all end up for the chop."

I watch a couple of dust devils sweeping towards us across the badlands. Could be the coast guard, but they veer off in the direction of Shekeik. "You'll have to take care of it," I say, "I had enough trouble with the Korean fish."

The sand over the last crate is finally tamped down. Then Rix produces another bottle from the shallows. Pitsos, who up to now has been clueless as to the fearsome nature of Rix's black beer, takes a generous swig. His face tightens like a fist. I thought the beer was going to come spraying out all over the place, but only his eyebrows went up, and stayed there for the remains of the day, which he later told us, he spent planning where to bring down and bury his own sid.

When I asked Rix what had happened to the brew room, he told me it had been taken care of.

"What's that's supposed to mean? Hasn't just disappeared, has it?"

"As a matter of fact, it has. It's now officially a dark room."

"What about the stink?" He'd lost the last club beer contract because, when the mash was tipped over the compound wall, the local donkeys began braying like it was happy hour at the Hilton.

"Not to worry. It's all hypo now." He chunters gaily on. "And at this very moment, Steve is probably retouching the Site Manager's silver-wedding photos."

"What if he pays us a visit?"

"She's getting the next best thing to plastic surgery, fraction the cost, and I'm sure he understands a creative artist like Steve needs to work undisturbed. Relax Dave! Have another swig! Look on the bright side! We've enough booze here, to last a year."

Next week, there's a hardboard partition up in the living room with a red light and a sign saying, Dark Room.

'Sorry, can't go in there just at the moment," Rix says to nosey-parkers, "something's being developed.' And Leo mumbles "Trouble brewing, more like." But they're just having a bit of fun, there's not a drop of booze in the place. It's all being managed by Grattan-Bellew and Bradley, behind Marsden's bar.

15 A shark tugs Leo's shirt

Our luck begins to change. Word's out that Warner's back, but avoiding us.

Rix asks him what's up. Apparently, some paper-pusher told him we were now a club and had no more vacancies. "Fucking clubs," says Rix. "We're open to everyone – like Van's parties." Van was an American Indian who invited everyone to his. But then not wishing to denigrate Warner's special status, Rix adds, "You're a founding member, in fact, you can't leave."

"Easy on," says Pitsos, "he might start to consider his options." The thing is, Pitsos *has* made us into a club, *The Red Sea Snorkelling Club* no less, to by-pass the rigmarole in extracting individual passes from Lt. Mufti, a shadowy figure at the best of times, on whose office doorstep, supplicants not only camped, but visibly aged.

Warner's sojourn in Sharorah had been unsettling too. He'd been fired for head-butting the Yemeni cook, who'd tried to remove his watch while he dozed in the Recce hall. Later the cook was apprehended exchanging various missing items for the demon drink, and Warner found himself back in Khamis.

≈

Our first spear-fishing outing, started well enough, but soon deteriorated.

Bright fusilier fish were sparkling between the reefs, and olive-green saddleback groupers could be seen socializing below, over a place called the plains.

I decided to concentrate on a group of three. The best method was to choose one and stick with it, so I chose the biggest and dived.

The biggest looking, I soon saw was only so because it was the nearest, and the biggest was the deepest – but by how much I had no idea. Down I went. The water grew colder and the surroundings, if you could call them surroundings, began to drain of colour. The plains became rubble, then rocks, then large boulders. For a moment, I had a clear portrait of a great fish with a predatory drooping mouth then it went all wobbly in updrafts of cold water.

I looked up to find myself staring at the side of a great slag-heap, with Lambourski and Warner suspended happily above it, under two parachutes of pale-blue light.

When I reached the surface, I coughed up gobs of brown phlegm and swore to myself, *never again*. But in a few minutes was down once more – with exactly the same result. After spending the rest of the morning trying to outdive each other, we ended up with nothing but headaches.

Back on shore Pitsos gave us a couple of sids to clear them, lent a sympathetic ear, and even blamed the fish. "The green groupers usually prefer the reef-top," he said. "So what were they doing on the plains?"

"Beats me" I said, letting the description 'plains' pass.

"Probably some pressing social engagement, like sex," he went on, "and chose the area because they could see predators far off. That being the case, they should be returning home to the second reef, about now."

After a couple more sids, it began to make more sense. The net result being, after one more for the road, Warner and I find ourselves back on the reef top, full of optimism.

The fusiliers, earlier in the day, as bright and cheery as summer leaves in a breeze, have now descended to reef level, and a soft haze settled over the erstwhile plains.

A stingray glides by far below, but still nothing comes up.

A school of gape-mouthed plankton-eating mackerel come by, like disembodied heads.

"There," says Warner. "There!"

"Where?" I cover every nook and cranny.

"A big one. Right in front of you!"

Then I see it, right before my eyes. Olive-green, the colour of the water, no spots at all, and have the feeling it's been watching me for quite some time. Then it's gone, and Warner too.

I hear a shot. In a moment, it's back in front of me, bio-luminescent spots shining. This is something entirely new, but before I can decide which end is which, the fish switches its lights off, and vanishes. A grey blur looms up. It's Warner. Instead of wasting time criticizing my ineptitude, he asks for my gun. "Quick!" he says, "A big one." I hand the gun over, and seeing nothing, begin trying to reload his confounded contraption.

As the sun sets, I lose sight of him in the intense glitter of sun-sculpted waves. After a time, I hear another shot and spy his periscope as he returns trailing a dark shape behind him. It's a saddleback, almost the size of the one I dived for earlier. Its handsome olive-green body turning to bronze, and a faint apricot flush already come to its belly.

≈

Most weekends now, Warner sets to with the nonchalant insouciance of those dapper bow-tied young men, you increasingly see on TV in hushed competition round the green baize. Sometimes you'd think he was treating the reef as a mere extension of the pool table. He was, but he kept to the rules, never shot a parrotfish, and no puffer fish (mistaken for a grouper in some gloomy cave) ever ballooned on the end of his spear.

But it was with the trevally, pelagic (open water) hunters that he came into his own. Steve and I first saw the big ones, when Warner was at Sharorah. They were in a compact pod, so far off that we thought they were blue-fin jacks, which generally follow their leader and become confused, when asked to do anything requiring personal initiative. But these were golden trevally, upon us and gone before we'd gathered our wits. Steve at least, tried to hide, ending up waving his speargun around like a lead tennis racket, whereas I remained suspended in open water, as if I was nothing more than a disembodied pair of eyes.

The next time we saw such trevally, Warner was with us, but the gold had gone from their bodies, leaving just barely perceptible grey stripes on pale oyster-grey backgrounds.

They came in like a barrage of tennis serves, but tennis serves with a difference – able to change speed and direction in mid-flight – becoming torpedoes, whacked soundlessly about in the corner of a vast glassed-in squash court and ricocheting silently all over the place. I fired at one and missed. When it returned to look where the spear had gone, Warner hit it mid-riff, and it took off again.

We eventually found it upside down in a cave. When we pulled it out, it grotesquely extended its mouth, vibrated like a tuning fork, its whole body suffusing with gold, slashed with coal-black stripes. We were stunned by so much beauty, not to say sexual exuberance, in its moment of death.

Later I learned, it was probably an instance of evolutionary altruism, a hormonal burst, of no advantage to the individual fish (which was doomed), but by distracting its predators, happened to give its dowdier companions a better chance of escape.

Over many months, Warner seemed at times able to read a pattern in the trevallys' frenzied movements, and hit his target. At others, he withdrew as coolly as a snooker player, to contemplate the configuration on the green baize anew. Natural History was to him pretty much studying the competition, and the fishes' skill the measure of his respect for them.

That's not to say, in the early days, he wasn't a pain and a pillock, he was. Due to some murky childhood trauma, he was incapable of handling live fish, and was forever coming over, tapping us on the shoulder and asking us to unfish his spear.

"I'm not your caddy" Leo would grumble, and I'd follow suit, "Not your gun boy, either. Sorry." If we relented, he'd as often as not the nerve to pick up your gun and dispatch another fish, come by to see what all the commotion was about. Any reluctance to hand over the said weaponry was met with utter incomprehension. "You're not going to let it escape are you?" He'd say. "Won't see another like it for months, I can tell you." On such occasions, as likely as not, you'd end up with two fish to unspear, and none for yourself.

One day, Leo was outside a cave, occupants long gone, when he felt a familiar tap on his shoulder. "Go away," he hissed, "there's a big one in here, and it's mine." It happened again. "Can't you see I'm busy, dickhead?" He turned around and found himself talking to a ruddy-great nurse shark, tugging his shirt.

The shark pissed off and the shirt ended up behind the bar, until Rix removed it as being detrimental to recruitment.

16 Visitors

Today, when we pick up two barred-bream in the big lagoon, three plump but graceful sandy reef shark, with much the same colouring as Thompson's Gazelle, sweep in and circle us. They're clever and fast, and it's obvious they want the fish. Two nip round behind us. When I turn back, the big one comes straight at me. Perhaps I should have waited, but I don't, I fire and hit it in the side.

It races round, body going up and down as well as sideways. Each time it circles, Warner has to duck under the line. I doubt it was more than twice, but it seemed to go on forever. Eventually the spear tip snaps at the thread, and the shark flashes away. I ask Warner if it was the right thing to do. "As they pissed off, probably was," he says. "Anyway, what else could you do? We can't let them make a habit of it." *My sentiments exactly.*

Back at camp, Rix complains something has absconded with the baked potatoes. This isn't exactly a new event. One time, they'd simply carbonized, and slipped through the grill. Another time, he thought the culprit was a fox, but no footprints were in evidence. This time it's probably a black kite.

We often see them circling above the camp, when we are away, but when Rix stayed, hid behind the gulls. If he went to the ice box, they remained at their stations. If he took out the cooler tray and rummaged in the ice, they'd often dive down and skim an item off the grill.

Today's intrusions aren't over yet. At 7:45 p.m., there were two barred-bream on the tailgate. At 7:55 p.m., only one. "Wild cat!" we shouted, grabbed flashlights and ran along the top of the dune. Rix's beam caught the light in its eyes, but it didn't give up till several well-aimed rocks put paid to its resolution. We dine on one and a half bream.

In the cool morning sun, six or seven heads peep over the dunes like animated bean sprouts. Twenty or so flamingos are stepping about on the saltpan, fastidious as debutants avoiding puddles. By eight o'clock, their deportment is shot to hell. Heads upside down, they are slurping shrimp cocktails at teeth-chattering speed. After a brief beauty sleep, preening-and-gossip session, it's show-time. They fly round and round us, head-to-tail, as if threaded on a single wire: graceful marathon flyers, at the very extreme of elegance, which is saying something, considering all our beach has come up with so far on the fashion front, are Pitsos' floppy hat and hermit crabs in hand-me-downs.

Another morning, we find ourselves facing a row of turbaned warriors, impressively draped in bandoliers and wearing the burning colours of the high Yemen. They are totally unimpressed by the modest catch, Rix has laid out for them to admire. In fact they seem embarrassed that grown men should think it fit to spend time in such a footling occupation, and go away smiling and shaking their heads.

"At least they didn't think we were *Israe-elis*." Says Rix sheepishly, a bit like a sidewalk vendor, the police have let-off with a warning.

≈

Today we swim out to the third reef for the first time. Hardly have we gone twenty yards along it, before the largest barracuda we've ever seen, glides in and parks itself broadside on, right in front of us.

Most big barracuda so far, have been extremely cautious, taking up position, where they were least likely to be observed. We imagined they possessed the patience of police dogs, but once prey fled, a trigger was pulled and the silver missile on its way. We thought we'd come to an understanding about this trigger-pulling business, but were apparently about to witness a new development.

The great fish turned very slowly towards us, opened its lower jaw about thirty-five degrees and snapped it shut, four or five times in rapid succession.

Then something beyond it caught my eye. The dim outline of the reef was expanding and contracting in a strange way. On closer scrutiny we saw it was a densely packed school of silversides, held together as if by a magnet. We'd heard of balling the bait, but so far around here, the rule seemed to be, when in trouble, scatter! But I now sensed this jaw-boning could be exerting influence in the opposite direction, freeze, don't flee, backed-up by the barracuda's baleful stare.

"Fair's fair," said Lambouski (the most indulgent assessment of reef life I'd yet heard), "it's preparing to dine, and we're not invited." And to save face, we hovered over a large specimen of brain coral like a bunch of clueless interns mulling over a preliminary prognosis, before moving on.

When we return at the end of the day, we're amazed to see neither the barracuda nor the silversides have moved. We observed the situation for a while and when the barracuda began to exercise the cutlery again, we turned inshore.

Next morning, a dense school of silversides hangs over the turtle grass like a brooding storm cloud. A fair-sized barracuda peeps round one edge as if wondering if we can be depended upon to provide a reliable backstop.

I ask Lambourski if it's too big to shoot. "Well, it's not half as big as the one behind you, if that's any help."

I turn round. No slim silver birch this time, but a sawn-off tree trunk with teeth at one end, fins bristling down its back like broken-off branches. Not wishing to make eye contact, I stare into the turtle grass. *Don't panic. Use your imagination.* Bubbles stream up from every blade as if from a lemonade factory. It must be the Plutonium facility, M briefed us about. At the same moment, a voice booms over the intercom:

"So sorry Mr. Bond. If I'd known you were dropping by, I'd have called off the welcoming committee. But they're not like guard dogs, you know. Je suis désolé, and now it's too late. All I can recommend is my dear grandmother's advice: a strong belief in reincarnation."

But what the triple-nippled schizoid psychopath doesn't realize is at this very moment, the delectable Elke Sommer, in lustrous lycra, is poised above the command module. "Come in 007" she says brightly.

"Bond here. Over."

"James, I'm here, but it's terribly confusing."

"Calm yourself Miss Sommer. I'm not going to ask you to do long division or anything. Just tell me where here is. Splendid! Now read-off what's on the TV thing in front of you."

"Malidol 3 grams. Nandrolone 5 grams. Once a day."

"That's his breakfast regime. Explains why he has three nipples, but otherwise is not germane to our concern."

"Oh, what a silly billy I am," she interrupts gaily. "This is more like it. Arm perimeter fence. Activate nuclear response. Now I'm told to press this lovely red light which has just popped on." Whoomph!

An orange light lifts from the seabed, ionizing the turtle grass and microwaving two large barracuda, which glow like the bars of a large electric fire, before turning belly up.

When I open my eyes, the biggest fish has gone, but the medium-sized one is still there. The kidney-shaped cloud of silversides in front of it,   has begun to curl round at the edges like the buffalo-horn manoeuvre used against Michael Caine by the Zulus at *The Battle of Rorke's Drift,* we saw the other night. The crescent moon shape ends up a large double circle, inside which some silversides are going clockwise, some anti. I won't say the barracuda actually became cross-eyed, but it began to weathervane as if dizzy then faded away.

For a long time after this, our attitude to barracuda remained confused.

Ben and I still ate small ones. He always had, and I did because I'd once eaten them in Barbados, washed down with avocado milk-shakes in a spotlessly clean hole-in-the wall eatery, called *The Flying Fish Club.*

Lambourski never ate them because of a type of fish-poisoning (ciguatera) in his part of Florida. Barnes backed him up, I suspect, because he liked to prognosticate about ciguatera's interesting symptoms: Fish sometimes tasted peppery, hot drinks cold and cold, hot. And silver cutlery turned black should you happen to be dining 'in the mansion on the hill.'

But Pitsos felt that such observations, because they took no account of our own environment, were no more relevant to us than those of the famous dancers of Yap, who never ate barracuda 'lest they acquired the dumb stare of the fish'. "But at least, their rule stood the test of time." He concluded.

"Except, there's been no test," retorted Barnes.

"No scientific test, it's true. "But they'd passed the loyalty test. No individual dancer ever being egotistical enough to put the reputation of the troupe in jeopardy, merely for the sake of a meal."

And to date, that's pretty much where our attitude to large barracuda has remained.

17 Months of burnt fish explained

In winter, if you could call it winter, the kelp grew up over the reef. No matter how slowly we moved through it, smaller fish bolted. To them, we were as combine-harvesters to rabbits. At the same time, unknown to us, big snapper retreated into their strongholds in the heart of the kelp.

One day, Steve and I were watching a squadron of liver-spotted squid approach the kelp beds in a big V. They broke formation and changed colour to speckled-brown. At the same time they curled-up their tentacles, making themselves into small kelp-like clumps. Then one, manoeuvring like the moon module, upended itself and dove down towards the sand, where it landed delicately on tiptoe, making an inviting grotto for a school of guppies hanging about, a bit farther off.

I decided to watch events. But neither the little guppies nor the squid were to be hurried. To keep my mind focused, I tried to think up an intelligent question, such as, was it possible for a deaf-and-dumb squid to consciously use its own shadow as a lure? And if it stayed put only until the sun was directly above it, then moved on, did this mean it knew its shadow would also move out from the grotto?

While thus engrossed, I sensed a presence behind me, as if a curious promenader had paused, and was craning forward to watch proceedings. I turned round cautiously.

A large dog-toothed snapper was observing the set-up, before moving away. And when I looked down again, the squid had gone too. Did I feel disappointed? Yes. But I also felt privileged. It was the first time I'd been still, 'not locked-and-tense still, but loose-and-relaxed still', as a lady muskrat stalker so succinctly put it. And maybe that was why the snapper had come so close.

And why are they called snapper? One day Warner casually happened to wave a hand in front of one, laid on the cutting board and it bit him.

≈

Back up in the Marsden's bar that evening, he was having a whip around for Lambourksi. "Whatever for?" We asked.

"So he can have a decent length natter with his family. His kid's going into hospital for a big operation."

"First we've heard of it. Never said a word to us."

"Heard it all on the phone. He had to shout, then was cut off."

As I reached into my pockets, Marsden adds unnecessarily loudly "A big hand for the man from Aberdeen!"

≈

The morning is still. Water laps idly along the reef. Lambourski and I have walked too far collecting wood, and the prospect of lying in the kelp appeals to us. We dump our loads and hit the water.

Lambourski, his son out of hospital, the operation a success, is a new man, and I have difficulty keeping up with him. Three-quarters of the way to the kelp, he stops to wait for me. As it happens to be one of those rare, completely calm days, perfect for drifting, we decide to float on till we come to a glade.

On arrival, we gently pick the last strands of kelp away, one by one. A school of barred-bream are sunning themselves on the far side. No sharks appear.

After a time, the bream turn like wind-chimes in the gentlest of breezes. Five or six silver jacks sweep by. Our spear guns are pointing down but we make no attempt to raise them. A school of tiny fish spills into the glade. A rainbow runner, not more than a pound in weight, dashes along beneath them, then pirouettes upward to snap at those directly above it. The school pours itself into a smaller glade like iron-filings, and feeling safe there, spreads out again.

Peering down, I can clearly make out some forty feet below, each strand of kelp holding fast to its rock, but all around, it's as dark as a midnight church.

A crab swims from frond to frond.

Soon, a lassitude as heavy as sleep envelopes me. Maybe I dozed, then sensed as much as saw, a dark shape near Lambourski. A single point of light touched it, no more than a candle flame on beaten copper, and he fires. The big snapper bolts like a fox through bracken, ties the cord and itself up in a matter of moments, and is dead when we untangle it, as if it died of shock.

Back on shore, Lambourski knocks a few nails through a piece of wood, leaving the heads and points exposed: heads to raise the fishes' scales; points to spray them all over the place. He then guts and rinses the fish, and where we used to saw away at the fins, deftly twists them off.

Seeing us gaping like country bumpkins, he explains, if he'd been going to grill it, he'd have left the fins on, to crispen. *So he wasn't going to grill it?* Rix always claimed, his fish were charcoal-grilled, but how could they be, when incarcerated in an infernal cavern of tinfoil?

With the heel of his palm, he now kneads herbs into cuts made in the skin, saying 'herbs' without the 'h', as if he was a real Italian cockney, and squirts in some lime juice. He unrolls a double-layer of tinfoil, rolls it over his arm, extracts the arm and slides in the fish, as if it was a very expensive garment. Then, having checked the coals to his satisfaction, places the package gently on the grill.

This is the moment we'd always dreaded with Rix, like letting your child go up on stage to be sawn-in-half by some dodgy flash magician. We'd trusted him with our best, but each time he produced something like a burnt sock, or gumboot.

Noticing our concern, Lambourski continues "I don't crease the foil because an open flame will burn pinholes in the corners and let the juices out." *So that's what had been happening. Months of burnt fish explained!*

Well and good, but then starts on how, when stationed in Italy, he'd learned to cook from his grannies. They'd complained with much glee that their husbands treated them like donkeys; secretly thought his fiancée was a hooker (acting out of a demented love), and himself, some sort of geriatric poltroon — capable only of women's work, ironing, doing the laundry and endlessly polishing the buttons on his uniform.

The men were more respectful; saw him as a powerful pimp, with good military connections, but too idle to do men's work and too cunning to need to.

All this proves too much for Warner who, instead of gulping down his usual can of beans and going *glug, glug, glug*, has ended up with this Italian fancy man, rabbiting on about Italian cookery being 'basic honesty with regard to cheese, pasta, the tomato, and picking 'erbs by the light of the moon.'

When Lambourski pauses for a breather, Warner yawns, "All nosh to me," ending with a belch, for rhetorical effect.

Lambourski doesn't break stride, merely glances severely at one potato and moves it an inch, like a cardsharper setting his pitch for a bunch of inebriated rustics, first time at the district market.

This is another thing we Brits, had never understood. Whether Rix placed his potatoes (naked or in tinfoil) on the grill or buried them in the sand under it, they always came out raw or over-cooked. "Would have flummoxed Lévi-Strauss." Barnes said, but don't ask me why.

"What about your wife-to-be?" pipes up Leo, still interested in Lambourski's story, "Wasn't she hounded out of the village?"

"What village? The nearest farmhouse was across a ravine, and two miles by goat track. The thing is, she didn't flaunt herself, did nothing to provoke their scorn, in short, had class. They lavished on her the homage virtue pays to vice." He wipes his brow, "Listen, when she was dropped-off after overtime by the admin driver, and came clickety-clacking up the path, with him carrying the PX bags, a deferential hush fell over the kitchen.

When the old grannies dived into the groceries, they crossed themselves, some out of gratitude to the Virgin of Compostella; others, because it was the devil's work. When I tried to explain how getting the Base Chaplin to talk to the local priest, would only end up getting us excommunicated, she burst into tears. 'How am I supposed to feel?' she cried.

Here Lambourski began to dance round the grill like he was Rod Stewart chasing Tina Turner. 'There's no TV', I told her. 'This is Italy. And you're the star! Enjoy it'. "She flounced up and down on the bed, in fury, till it broke. There were some answering gethumps outside the door. She flung it open and screamed. 'There's a mouse in my bedroom!' Up the stairs they came again, brooms at the ready.'"

"What about nosh?" asks Warner, quite sure Lambourski's forgotten all about the fish.

When he opens the tinfoil, it's all steaming and fragrant. "White to-the-bone", he smiles.

I wanted to ask how he knew, but soon find myself getting left behind, and end up excavating those plump white medallions from the fish's cheeks and thin slivers of flesh either side of the skull, while Warner leans back saying, "Not bad nosh Lambourski. Reckon you'd do alright on the telly."

18 "How can anyone screw-up bangers and mash?"

I wake to find Barnes thrusting two serious looking fish into my face. *Trust him to know exactly how I like to start the day.* "Emperors," he says. "Got them over the sand flats. Plenty more."

"Let's not dally then." I reply and off we go. But I'm not too happy about the name. Sure, they had an impressive antique-bronze gloss to them, but also decidedly un-Roman noses. Ok, the French call the bump-headed wrasse, the emperor (Napoleon understood, of course). The Australians, not usually given to welcoming colonial honorifics, even name a couple of their own fish emperors. In short, anyone can name a fish sergeant-major, el Capitaine, sultan or kingfish – whatever they like – names are cheap, reputations hard to come by.

Barnes tells me they're also bottom-feeders, not good, and browse on salps. *Salps!* Transparent marshmallow-like creatures, which perambulate about, making daisy-chains. *Hardly the sort of adversaries that earned Napoleon his spurs.*

As soon as we enter the sea, we are surrounded by them, rolling around in the surf and all over the place. As we ease into quiet water, every-so-often one nudges me and clings – invisible but insistent – like a child's hand.

Then we see the emperors, thirty or so, no shortage evidently, swaying in a syncopated and dignified procession -- like Cardinals on the way to pay their respects to the pope. Unlike mullet, each feeds independently, stopping in its tracks, dipping down, gulping up a salp, then repeating the process. After watching this a bit, the possibility that they might be simple-minded, in the same way the Hapsburg's had chins, occurs to me. And my only problem will be whether to give the target fish a lead, or fire directly at it. But soon realise that concentrating on a single fish, when the others are popping up-and-down all over the place is no easy task. I'll have to focus down on one and ignore the rest.

Eventually, a big one comes into range. Down it goes, up it comes. And I fire. In the same instant, the silvery underside of a wave heaves over me and the seabed erupts as if stitched by machine-gun fire. I catch a glimpse of Barnes above me on a sandbank, looking none too pleased. All his school of fish have disappeared. I ignore him and skulk off into deeper water.

Sometime later, Lambourski joins me, and soon spots the school not far from the turbulent water we called the shark's breeding ground. (In fact the sharks proved to be the wingtips of large manta rays, but the name stayed).

Lambourski cautiously drifts into range with me close behind, sinks down and with no fuss, fires. Fish and spear disappear beneath the seabed. Phantom shapes rush under us, and we find ourselves propelled out to sea on a carpet of silt.

"It's a rip!" he shouts to the sky, "Swim sideways!"

We end up far out. T-shirts, snorkels and masks, full of murky water. When we return to the sandbank, a worried Barnes asks what the hell we were trying to do.

As I disentangle myself from my sodden and gritty gear, there's the usual witless jabbering on my part. "I thought the emperors had no clothes, but they certainly knew where to find them, ha ha!"

"Bit like Gandhi then," murmurs Barnes.

"Like who?" I say, still shaking the sand out of my ears.

"When he was on the way to see the King, Mountbatten was concerned his friend's get-up might not go down too well with his Majesty. 'Don't worry,' said Gandhi, 'You're wearing enough for both of us.'"

≈

On our way up the escarpment, Barnes and Steve stop by the acacias to photograph a row of hammerkops. Brown, short-legged, heron-like birds (sometimes called the lightening bird of Africa) which have turned up out of the blue, like the miraculous little stream running by their feet. At first they comport themselves with leisurely dignity, doing next to nothing, but stalk pensively about like hooded-friars, reading breviaries. Suddenly, and as one, they stab their beaks into a shoal of small fish and sink back into their cowls.

All is still again. Then, as if it had never happened, or no one could prove it, they move off upstream with a fastidious air of spurious innocence.

"Look at these tiny shrimp" Barnes calls us over. "*Triops.* Gaspar says, their eggs are carried up into the sky by dust-devils and come down in the rain. Can also be conveyed from waterhole-to-waterhole by goats, camels, water-beetles and dragonflies, the latter two using polarized light to spy-out new water surfaces."

"Yes, yes." Says Steve. "But do you see what I see across the wadi?"

Two young bedhu women, willowy as saplings, catch our eye. Each one lifts a jerrycan onto her head with a confident swing of her body and sets off, with a poise and grace that would normally look affected, but not to us.

"Remember that young geologist who got lost?" whispers Steve. "Said the women passed him round, didn't he?"

One puts down her glittering jerrycan and leans forward to call her companion.

A couple of drill-sergeants, either end of the parade ground, would not have shamed their performance, and immediately puts to flight our fantasy of the young geologist's predicament.

The first begins to run. Barnes turns round, opens his mouth wide and shouts. The first thing we see is a four-foot wall of mud, the consistency of school porridge, coming down the wadi. The hammerkops rise like pterodactyls, with cries harsh as crushed rocks.

As the first mud comes insolently by, Steve picks up his tripod, a little too casually. Rix's vehicle reverses past us. Leo and Warner, hanging on to the side, stare at us like we're gonners. "Throw them a rope!" bawls Rix. Leo flings it, but it drops with a hearty plop. Back it comes, spraying us with liquid mud. Barnes manages to lash it to our front bumper. Rix reverses and we advance to a cheer.

"Good thinking lads" says Pitsos, but the others are now staring behind us, open-mouthed. Even as I turn, not five yards before me, the near bank collapses. As the water charges downstream, cave-ins on the opposite side rush upstream, their contrary motions making me dizzy.

In ten minutes, a raging river, a hundred yards wide, and in less than twenty, a steaming quagmire of rocks and drying mud. A couple of dogs flounder in the middle, and an upside-down camel remains stuck in the roots of an acacia. By the time we drive away, the camel's a mass of vultures, thick as crows on a dunghill.

I recall a night on Mount Suda. Along the escarpment, the stars were hard and glistening, only directly above, were there none. The tent roof, stiff with a light frost – cracked like a whip. A second gust uprooted the poles and sent our aluminium plates and foam mattresses flying. We'd just time to bundle a few things under the awning, when there was a head-high flash and a sound like splintering-bone. The drumming roof, split in two, the grass springing alive with leaping mothballs.

Once far off, lit by violet sheet-lightning, we made out a goatherd, plodding along ankle-deep, head-down.

In ten minutes, the sky-overture is ended. Fawn water pours in arcs from the cliff tops as if from gargoyles. Far below, humped waves, like bedraggled sheep, leap onto each others' backs as they race for the exits.

≈

8 am. A week after the flash flood, we're back in the sea. Lively waves slap and chortle against the reef-wall. *But how have we ended up like this, in front of an endless barrier with no way out?* Lured here, in the hope of catching late breakfasters returning down gullies to deep water. Only there's no gullies and next to no fish.

Two sharks come by, way down, but big enough to keep us hugging the wall. All we've seen of prospects so far are two large grouper far below, taking a leisurely gander at us as we trundle overhead. As remote to them as the weekly flight from Jeddah to Djibouti is to us.

A pod of talang queen-fish come in. All complaints are instantly shelved. These magnificent creatures, weaving this way-and-that, like playful wolf-hounds on a multiple leash, give us the whole treatment. As soon as I get a bead on one, it bounds back and another leaps forward. Then another, twice their size, comes by below them. It's imperious ghostly glide – of another order. When it's gone, it's as if the parade's gone by, and the few fish which do appear-- mere litter blowing in the street.

It's getting dark and we can't believe where the time has gone. We're also going to have to accept that the only way out, is the way we've come.

The talang return, but without the one which sent the prickly-chill down my spine. Even as they come in, Warner decides to dive down, to get beneath them. It seems to me an utterly pointless exercise. He's soon out of air and has to come up, which he does, like a toy soldier, presenting arms. When he's almost at the surface, one talang can't resist a last dash beneath him. He does the splits and fires between his flippers. The fish stops in its tracks, turning slowly on the spear shaft.

While Warner covers me, I get half of it into the sack. Luckily the tide's coming in and keeps everything pressed against the wall.

We are about to crawl out by the Greek camp (where the Koreans once found a crate of whiskey), when we see a sight that makes us crawl back in again.

A truck comes along the beach, flicking its lights on-and-off. Then a Coastguard Toyota careens out of the dunes towards it. The men in the truck jump down and line-up to pray. The occupants of the Toyota leap out, form up either end of the line, and begin to pray too.

Under normal circumstances, it would have made our day. But a nervous Warner thinks he hears the creaking of wood, and a moment later, a whiff of kerosene and stale fish hits us. As we try to sneak into a narrow gap in the reef, a searchlight rakes the reef-top.

We can see no boat, but can make out, far off, the gleam of big rollers coming in. The squall strikes and several waves push us into a dead end. No sooner do we get into the swing of things, than we realize we're going to have to get out quick, or become mincemeat. The next time the light passes, we pause only a split second, and then leap upwards. Pathetic it is, but without further fuss or ceremony, we're bundled over acres of turtle grass into the lagoon. *Utterly painless!* And all we have to face now is a bollocking from Rixie.

The tent is half-down and the other half, trying to fly to Africa. "You're late", he says, "Screwed up my cooking again."

We attempt to lighten the atmosphere by grabbing the flapping canvas, straightening tent poles and explaining about the

long prayer time, but he's not registering. "So what's for dinner?"
We conclude lamely.

"Bangers and mash."

"How can anyone screw-up bangers and mash?"

"Take a look."

"Hah! Shepherd's pie. My favourite!" Somewhat mollified by this, he condescends to notice the talang. "A lucky shot. Who got it this time?"

Warner busies himself in the nosh.

"It had a hatful of tricks," say I. "But bollock brain here, just one."

19 The Ethiopian girls

8:30 p.m. The Major and Devrill-Smith have arrived.
Devrill-Smith's immediately off on his beach run, whilst the Major
(whose been threatening to visit for a long time) begins his camp
inspection by falling over a tent peg. *"Ouch! A rebar. Good idea."*
He exclaims, at pains to show his mind's alert, even if his body isn't.
(Each peg being 18 inches of ribbed steel, filched from a building
site, of which four inches usually remains poking out of the sand).
"You must have a good a hundred square feet of canvas up," he
chunters on. "All stowing away on the roof-rack during the week.
Clever."

Rix is delighted by this enthusiasm, and when he's finished,
immediately offers him a drink. The Major hesitates.

"Top class sid", Rix says. "But must warn you, it's uncut."
The Major accepts. "How come?"

"Anyone talking shop or foolish enough to take a swim
before the tent's up, pays a forfeit. One bottle uncut. Keeps out the
jerks. Come, let me show you round." As its no ideal-home exhibit,
he ignores the interior décor and includes the surrounding desert in
an expansive gesture, "Sleeping quarters, ha, ha!" But as he hasn't
been made Camp Fuhrer for his sense of humour, quickly attends to
the major's interest in the stainless steel clamps attached to the extra-
long roof rack.

Not only does he know how to coddle old timers like the
major, but has also become adept at persuading total neophytes to
load up their personal possessions, Tuesday night (by the light of the
moon, if necessary) for immediate departure from work Wednesday
(Thursday and Friday, now being our weekend.)

Then, any last minute request to fetch a towel or check the
mail, falls on deaf ears. Relent, and likely as not, ten minutes later,
we'd find the errant youth outside a jar of ale and checking the
football pools. Or as with Jack one time, staring ashen-faced at a
letter on pink notepaper, mumbling, "Kid sisters up the spout. Needs
cash, pronto."

"A serious matter", Rix had commiserated, "But before any hasty action, may I recommend a long walk on the beach communing with Nature?"

"Cash is the problem, either way, if you get my drift," Said Jack, "How about next week?"

Rix now moves on to show the Major his grill, and I've time to put in a few words about our own efforts at tents.

The first was my own contribution, an effete affair of stitched bed sheets, bamboo poles and curtain rings, which blew away in all of five minutes. The second was Barnsey's fancier item in navy-blue and white-striped canvas, which shredded in the space of an afternoon, flashy aluminium telescopic poles buckling like umbrella struts. The third was the musty old Club tent, charmingly redolent of the circus, goats and beer. And to raise it would have taken the priapic posturing of a team well-practised in the art of caber-tossing. Was never raised, despite Devrill-Smith stoutly affirming, 'Rome wasn't built in a day', then declaiming flat on his back:

> Look on my works ye mighty and despair.
> Two vast and roofless trunks of wood
> lie in the desert. Nothing besides remains.
> Round the decay of that colossal wreck
> the lone and level sands stretch far away.
> Or words to that effect.

Finally a Hadj tent-maker, whose forbears knew a thing or two about tents since the time of the Prophet, stitched us a 16 by 16 ft. awning, with rawhide corners, brass eyelets and clamps to attach to the long roof rack, plus five, eight-foot steel pipes as tent poles (plus a jointed centre one of ten feet.)

Its sewing was a leisurely affair, carried out in old Khamis. Rix went 'ziz' to indicate single stitching and 'ziz, ziz' to indicate double, a procedure closely scrutinized by the household cat.

During a severe blow, the poles could be angled bedhu-style and in a real storm the windward ones dispensed with altogether, eyelets clamped directly to rebars buried deep in the sand. But normally the awning's height and generous spread of shade, let us strut about or stretch fully out and able to contemplate the burning sands without having to participate in the process.

The grill on the other hand, owed its survival entirely to Rix. It started out a small culinary disaster area, mercifully downwind but today consists of a single massive wrought-iron gate, once fronting a Prince's Villa. (Now replaced by one of solid steel, swinging between two granite-faced megaliths, in the New Stonehenge style).

Though the gate is a Sisyphean curse to lift, has survived every other piece of gimcrack ironmongery we've tried. And like any tyrant worthy of the name, crushes whatever is placed beneath it into smouldering submission, in less time than it takes to mix a pre-prandial pick-me-up.

≈

When Devrill-Smith returns from his run, Rix reminds us to be up at dawn to collect wood, but excuses the Major.

What the Major doesn't know and Rix hasn't told him, is that an Ethiopian fisherman's family has been calling in lately at Sand Island and his daughters bathing bare-breasted (as was their custom in the Dhalaks) and ours to wait until their old man waded into the lagoon to fish, then begin collecting wood.

They accepted us walking past, provided we weren't seen to be looking, and for once the lads weren't entirely brainless. Because we took pains to abide by this convention, they made it worth our while, turning their heads away with affecting modesty, scooping up water to let tiny handfuls splash down on profile of firm breast and curve of hip before bouncing up and down beneath the water, to sounds of flowery laughter.

In the morning, even our family men, Lambourski and young Ben, find themselves picking up the same wood twice.

"One has green eyes" whispered Steve, "She's mine."

"No, she's mine," said Lambourski. "Half-Italian already."

Framed like an exotic picture, they remained an easier event to handle than the less contrived sauntering of the nurses collecting shells by Black Mountain.

On the walk back, everyone is bursting with surplus energy. We drop the wood and, spears in hand, spread out to look for crayfish.

Leo comes in, carrying a big fish with the protruding tongue of a serpent: a grouper, which has swallowed a shark almost as big as itself. And brings his total catch for the year, to two, with one shot.

Lambourski now takes command. Leo, the Major, and Devrill-Smith are sent packing to the water's edge with sid, bucket and spade, to dig out small shellfish. Warner is directed to a heap of speckled blue crabs, now orangey-pink, blowing bubbles from the complicated machinery of their mouth parts. "Break them open," he says. "Take out the gills, called dead men's fingers, as they can be poisonous."

"So that's why they tasted like wet chicken-feathers." Says Warner. "But they're still too hot."

Though I like watching Lambourski at work, with his no nonsense approach to the whole process from catch to cooking pot, it's more than my life's worth just at the moment, so I affect to help Warner.

When he was a kid, it seems his mother rarely cooked, simply dumped a puffed-up bag of Smith's Crisps on the table, which he consumed, cockroach fashion; a sort of TV dinner, with mum as the TV.

Lambourski, now takes the biggest squid, which he'd earlier pointed out to me as it lay half-buried in the sand, pale as an alabaster vase with gold-ringed eyes. When he shot it, it had kicked like a rabbit, completely disappearing in brown smoke to reappear in whorls of deep-grained walnut, as intricately tattooed as a tribal mask, pale-blue flames pulsing round its mantle.

He skims off the skin (thin as a film emulsion) with the flat of his blade and shovels the mush of entrails and crushed eyeballs into a bucket. Washes the body till its white as tallow, but freckled here and there with pin-sized dots, blinking off-and-on like an electronic game.

Catching me gawping, he soon has me pouring olive oil over some mashed potatoes, while he sprinkles in fistfuls of crushed garlic. *A long way from basic honesty with regard to pasta, cheese and the tomato.* But I don't say anything, just do what I'm told, which is making some kind of thickener, to absorb the excess juices from the crustacea. *Quite a promotion for the humble potato, if you ask me,* but nobody does.

"Pour the olive oil in slower, dum-dum." He says. "You're not making oily mashed-potato, but a *roux*." Then, because Warner's making such a hash of the crabs, we're both banished down-current to dump the scraps and wash the pots.

≈

How can I do justice to his *bouillabaisse*? For that is what he called it.

We tore into white flesh and sucked juices from carapaces like a bunch of savages invited by another lot, first time ever (and possibly the last), who were doing something never seen before, called cooking.

When we finished, our resident pyromaniac Steve gives the grill the old heave-ho! all by himself, and piles on more wood.

Sid flows and soon everyone is talking at once. On one side of the fire, Lambourski's on about a Mexican policeman in Puerto Angel, who insisted on opening the beer with the trigger-guard of his pistol. On the other, I learn that the town of Taif used to be a sleepy place (most famous export, attar of roses) where scholars, able to recite classical Arab poetry to certain discrete widows, could have a pretty good time.

Soon Devrill-smith and the Major were onto discussing Rimbaud's gun-running in Tadjoura. Warner thinks – or pretends to – that they're on about Rambo, or Wambaugh's *The Choirboys*.

Alas, his derisive attitude to these super-polite Brits, took a long time to change, not aided by the Major's tendency, in moments of conviviality, to incorporate whosoever's tipple lay unattended into his own sphere of influents.

No sooner has Ben finished a tale about a black kid, who lost a toe to a barracuda because of the white soles of his feet, than Steve chooses the moment to fall flat on his face.

"Heatstroke!" barks the Major. "Reconstitute the colloids. Cold water and fish soup, quickly!" Steve is laid out and covered with a blanket.

After administering copious amounts of water, I gingerly offer the fish soup, but he's not having any. "It's bouillon from the *roux*", I plead. "Will reconstitute the colloids. No fish scales. Promise."

"Think I spent too long picking up wood and trying to photograph mirages," he says, weakly.

"Mirages, my foot!" hoots Rix. "Too many hand-shandies in the dunes, watching the Ethiopian girls, more like." (And even hinted, he might tell him about the erotic charm of the Ethiopian love twist, if he survived).

To raise the tone, the Major recounts his own romance with the daughter of a minister of the Church, who used to sneak up on the roof in old Lamu and wait in the deepest shadow, wearing only a buis-buis and attar of roses. Letting the sea breeze and the major's stalking prowess, do the rest.

I fall asleep to dream of a plenitude of girls and fishes, only to be woken by something tapping on my bed. "Warner, is that you?" It hisses, "How about us sneaking over to the Ethiopian camp? Nobody will hear us."

"Don't even think about it," growls a voice. "There's a thermos by your bed. Drink up and pipe down."

Silence, followed by more muttering. "That Major chap is a real wet blanket, isn't he? Come on! He hasn't a clue what's going on. There's more to life than just fish, for Chrissake!"

"Not here, there isn't," replies the voice. "The traditional Ethiopian punishment for female abduction is stretching the miscreant between two palm trees, and when he confesses, releasing the tree and letting him take the strain. Think about it."

Wasted wisdom.

For not much later, I'm woken by the maniacal laughter of a hyena. It's Steve, being towed by Pitsos and Barnes through the moonlit lagoon by his feet.

In the morning, the fisherman's family have left.

≈

Though we weren't to know it, we were never to have bouillabaisse that good ever again, the necessary elements never coming together at the same time:

The Ethiopian girls — to get us up before dawn. An overcast sky — to reduce the glare and bring out hosts of small crustacea. Completely slack water at low tide — to let us spy-out blue crabs, *callictes sapidus* (the beautiful swimmers) breaking the surface far off. And above all, when we got close, no fitful breezes -- to fragment their carapaces into nothing more than serpentine ripples.

After long chases, when they stopped dead in their tracks (pathetically raising gangly claws with none-too-sharp tips and serrated molars dull as a plastic toy's) we felt our first moment of pity. That was our big mistake.

That's when they skimmed away on ultra-light cambered wings to bury themselves way ahead of us, or flicked back into our own sand clouds. Then entirely due to the incredible slingshot acceleration, imparted by long seven-jointed claw arms, slashed our ankles or shaved off a finger tip.

20 Boomeranging sharks

One morning, from just beyond the reef, Lambourski shouts "Quick! Quick! I've a big one!" A horse mackerel. Yet when the boiling foam disperses, nothing, nor time to say *never try and shoot a big fish with a small gun*. Problem is, spear tips also have a habit of seizing-up underwater. Yet if only handtight, any pelagic hunter can unthread one in next-to-no-time.

Pitsos then suggests we make a rule. "Anyone hearing a speargun fire, must come over immediately and offer whatever assistance he can." *Fat chance*. But we agree to try it for a month.

After only three weeks we were in for a couple of shocks. The first (never mind trying to locate the source of a shot underwater) was the pathetic spectacle, the second gun often had to witness. I was the worst. A madman, line all tangled up, speargun stuck down a hole, chasing a battered fish all over the place, and saying it showed I was taking responsibility for my mistake.

The second surprise was even more sobering. The number of times, the person coming over to help saw a shark come in and go off, without the first gun noticing it.

Boomeranging sharks, we called them.

Soon we were seeing sharks all over the place.

It seemed that those we'd seen the very first day, our imagined picture of Leo's shirt-tugger, together with the perfect photos in the Shark book, had all been too complete to allow later mere bits and pieces of shark (impinging on our retinas) to register as shark in our brains.

After witnessing the boomeranging shark, the glimpse of a tail here, the back of a shark tipping over the reef there, began to separate out into individuals with their own quirks and behaviours.

One rare example was the eye-popping superfast large sharks which occasionally whizzed past us at Eagle Ray Point. They were like Formula One racing cars seen on TV, and I reacted to them as if I was in a privileged position (the grandstand let's say), immune to any possibility of their careening through the screen into my living space. To counteract this insane viewpoint, Barnes and Lambourski were not short of suggestions.

One of Barnes theories was that a shark's liver plays a role here, similar to the camel's hump, only in this case it was the shark which got the hump. When its liver was full, everything was fine, neutral buoyancy achieved, and it could travel to breeding grounds (gullies with strong currents), track garbage dumped by cruise liners, and occasionally dine out on a dead whale. But chomping on a surfboard, spitting out a wet-suit, or chasing the odd turtle was mere time-wasting.

The downside was, if the shark missed the rendezvous, it tended to become peckish and irritable. It also tended to sink, and had to keep thrusting itself above the *thermocline* (like having to keep twiddling the taps when lying too long in the bath).

A change in the shark's persona also occurred. The presence of blood, fish oil, squid smoke, etc., became like spirits to an alcoholic, the *ping* of a spear gun --like a beer can being opened, and on rare occasions—the popping of a champagne cork.

Lambourski's hypothesis was even grimmer. He said most shark were *viviparous*. (He too has lately taken to larding his opinions with jargon like *thermocline (*merely the line between two layers of water of different temperature), and *viviparous* (born up-and-about, not in an egg). In the shark's case they're called pups, but pups with a difference, victors of fratricide within the womb. And to him intra-uterine cannibalism was taking care of the competition early on, and the so called shark's feeding frenzy – taking care of it later on.

All in all, their two opinions helped me realize, our superfast shark were probably less dangerous than those mooning about off the reef, topping-up before an important appointment or worse, having just missed out on it.

And to conclude, one odd example remained: suddenly meeting a shark in open water. Whether it was large or small, often depended on one's mood! A small one close up, could be a big one if you were frightened. A big one far off, a small one close up, if you were in a confident mood.

21 Gaspar and the blind grouper

Today Gaspar, his wife and Devrill-Smith turn up. She
brings a cake and he, sid. Apparently he's been having a lean time
lately on the bird-watching front. He'd previously stolen a march on
Barnes by making his best sightings on the new airport landfill,
whereas Barnes (a low echelon employee) has been unable to obtain
a pass. But packs of ferocious dogs have put paid to that, and he's
now decided, he wants to come fishing.

He doesn't seem too sure how to become one of the boys,
or exactly what persona to adopt, and starts off by telling a funny
story (at least to me) about a grenade thrown into a Bierut seaside
restaurant. "Some diners attempted to flee. Some threw themselves
on the floor, others scrambled about under the tables trying to
retrieve it. By the time it should have gone off, the waitresses'
assholes were squirming."

"John, really." pipes up his bird-like little wife in the middle
of pouring Devrill-Smith and Barnes some Earl Grey tea. He takes
off his glasses and swivels his eyes round like the twin-barrels of a
machine-gun, to come to rest upon her mild and suppliant visage.
"You're interrupting my story, dear." He says, and tells us the
grenade was lobbed into a fish tank, where it exploded, spraying
water and fish all over the clientele.

I imagined there'd be the devil to pay later with the Missus.
But Barnes tells me it's all an act, and how one afternoon in
Gaspar's library, he'd heard them billing-and-cooing in the next
room, when Gaspar suddenly boomed out, 'Good Lord, woman! You
mean to tell me we've had a guest all this time? Bring him a beer or
something stronger.' All part a ploy to get him a drink before five
o'clock, which the doctor had forbidden.

During all this, Devrill-Smith doesn't say much, fusses with
his tapes and congratulates us on how fast and far we swim. But who
would have suspected he'd just come back from one of the many
raids on Khost in far off Afghanistan, where he'd been acting as a
stringer for the *The Saudi Gazette*, and seen two men blown up,

82

attacking a Russian 75 mm cannon post. They'd been caught by the second tripwire, the first being fake, a decoy. They'd jumped it and the second one caught them.

The next day, he'd been pinned down in the open, above the wadi in which they'd been hiding. Maybe saved his life.

The Russian gunships came in low. The third one was a new Hind Mi25, armed in the nose and sides. That's when they should have been finished-off, but the crew were concentrating so hard on spraying bullets into the wadi's every nook-and-cranny, they themselves became vulnerable. One after the other, the Mujahadin rose on one knee and fired into the centre of the swirling dust. As a Hind Mi25 is only amour-plated on the underside, the crew probably feared a heat-seeking missile – for what else would anyone risk firing from an open hillside? It spewed out phosphorus flares like a punctured sea cucumber and sailed for home.

Ten minutes later, a Mig came over and strafed the hilltop. Devrill-Smith's companions told him, the helicopter crew had probably reported taking-on small arm's fire during a daring, missile-evading manoeuvre. Not Russia's brightest and best perhaps, but to my mind, better able to take care of their backsides than Devrill-Smith.

Gaspar now tells us, he's interested in those large grouper we bring in, which look like a giant's boots, not that he's stupid enough to think they look like that underwater.

"Correct. They're slimy bastards." I say. "Dry out very quickly, but underwater can bolt through coral like a hare through bracken. You can be chuntering along like Toddy the Toy Train, seeing all sorts of creatures of the field, but to get close, you have to get down and into the hedgerows."

I'm not sure why I'm going on like this, but suspect the fearsome prospect of having Gasper in tow all day has something to do with it. Eventually, he takes off his glasses again, and it's my turn to be glared at. "Is eyeball-to-eyeball with a houbara bustard, close enough?"

"Now you're talking. But you don't have to be totally quiet, else you might spook yourself were one of the big boys to turn up, and give you a heart attack."

"Greenline Gaspar, a heart attack?" As this was also the name of UK's Long Distance Bus Company, it didn't' quite create

83

the buzz intended, and I simply carried on. "Pretend you're a shell-collector and keep the grouper to your front. You don't want to be butted from behind, given the royal run around, and have him end up by the same hole he started from."

"Can't I ferret the critter out?"

"Home base, Gaspar. Leave him till next time."

What am I doing? I've practically invited him! "Er…. What I'm getting at is, if one of us comes across a big one at the brandy-and-cigar stage of his dinner, and fancies he can't lose an argument, sneak up behind him.

"Sounds pretty brutal"

"So is croquet, dear," Pipes up the little wife.

"Well I'll be darned." He says. "Come the day, I'll certainly call you boys over."

Now I've done it. He's invited himself!

"Why did you do it?" Barnes groans later, "You know he's only really interested in logging Ethiopian crane arrivals and spotting the first glossy ibis."

≈

Next time Gaspar turns up, he asks 'where's the best place for looking at fish.' So we take him to a special spot for a look-see.

If one follows the line of four large, just submerged coral bastions (we called the Turkish forts) just beyond the second reef, you will pass several sandy acres, neat as lawns, bounded by florid coral mansions, with a maze of tunnels beneath them.

This is the Beverly Hills of reef society (next to the number one cleaning station, but we don't know that, yet). However, today it's so quiet, we're all disappointed.

No umbrella of bat-fish above the patio, no Tang discretely attending to the horticulture, and no sweet-lips glimpsed circulating through the dim interiors. Then I notice a frozen look on Warner's face. Something I'd last seen years ago on the faces of the Pension Andalus staff, the exact moment the heroine's mother (in the radio soap *Simplemente Maria*) had contracted cancer and the whole Country stood still.

A portion of the reef slips down like a photo in an album to reveal, dead ahead, the great protruding eye and massive form of the biggest grouper, we'd ever seen. It sank down with the serene imperturbability of a docking space-craft before blending imperceptibly into the reef, the phantasmagoria passing as quickly as it had come. It could have swallowed Warner without trouble or trace, an exaggeration of course, but nevertheless started a long serious argument later, whether we'd be able to pull him out in one piece or not.

≈

Over the next several years (yes, years) Gaspar spent a lot of time patrolling the inner side of the reefs, areas of narrow moribund coral channels, requiring great patience to navigate successfully.

One day, when the sun was a fiery chalice, spilling liquid gold all over the shimmering lagoon, a wild halloo from Steve told us that somewhere in its centre; Gaspar had found a big one.

We wasted no time but went dashing over the glittering shallows, dived into deep water, by-passed a triangular minefield of sea urchins and ended up where Gaspar had his spear gun raised like Excalibur. There, above the coral, we saw the top half of an enormous dorsal fin, rippling like kelp.

The black grouper rose slowly like a tethered airship, gills working with ponderous slowness. As it turned and faced me, its eyes filled with amber light shot through with iridescent greens. I backed behind a coral-head and remained there, reluctantly showing a hand, clasping-and-unclasping. The fish seemed nervous and reversed towards Gaspar, then in point blank range, slowly swivelled to face him. But he never fired.

There was a tremendous *thwump!* Sand came billowing up all over the place. Everyone stood up, staring at the cloud as it spread over the water.

Warner comes over. "I'd never have made it, either," He says, pointing to a mass of sea urchins, barely visible in the witches' brew.

We unload our spear guns, find places to sit down and ponder our loss.

"I didn't fire," says Gaspar, "because I thought it was blind." This has happened before. Occurs because a grouper's eyes are like a cat's, and possess a double-layer of silvery crystals as a reflective backing. But, whereas a cat's iris can close down to mere

85

slits in bright light, a grouper's can't, as they have no iris. Instead, granules of fuscine, floating in the corneal fluid, darken quickly in strong light, blocking most of it out.

When this grouper turned to face me directly before the sun, it was momentarily blinded. But when it turned away to face Gaspar, even though its cornea was still covered by a fading milky-grey film (like a cataract) it could see him, well enough.

Back at camp Rix, initially all excited, is none too pleased. "How will you be wanting your Brazilian corned beef, Gaspar?"

"Mmm…" Says he, "You mean there's a choice?"

"Hot or cold?"

22 Barnes' embarrassing slide-show

Barnes gives his slide-lecture to the Natural History Society today (the only opportunity hereabouts for the sexes to mingle socially). We must have told him a hundred times to cut down the number of slides, but when the day came, he simply whizzed them by faster.

Gaspar was meant to show up and ask some prepared questions, but never did. And when it seemed no power on earth could stop the massed battalions of bird-fowl parading past, a small boy stood up and had the temerity to ask an irrelevant question.

Barnes had almost reduced the wee lad to tears, and his Mum was about to give Barnes a piece of her mind, when the Major abruptly stood up and said what a wonderful lot of challenging facts they were getting. "But if you could hold the migrations a bit, ha, ha! Amateur ornithologists like myself and this good family here, would benefit enormously". This was greeted by applause, "Hear, Hears", groans and titters.

In the interval, half the audience leaves.

When the lecture was over, Pitsos and I bumped into Barnes lurking by the water-cooler. "How did it go?" he asked.

"Excellent!" We answered enthusiastically, "By the way," I said (three words too many) and saw the shadow of the angel of death fall across his brow (you know it when you see it) nothing to be done but plough ahead. "Could you spare me? Ok, loan me, one of your osprey slides? Not one of your best, of course." (He had about twenty, with nary a feather out of place). "I'll lend you my *Astral Weeks* tape."

The old Barnes instantly returned and began to hop from one foot to the other as if he'd been asked to make one of the most difficult decisions of his life.

"You don't have to decide right away."

"Maybe I can come up with something," he said. "Sorry, busting to take a leak." And was gone.

23 Nine sharks

It was grey and still, as the reef only is, just before dawn. A shark passed lazily by and was gone. Two came past in deep water, turned into the reef and disappeared. Then, down the gully I was travelling, came a broad-nosed, wide-beamed middle-weight grey. These stolid creatures look as if they've been turned out in basic woodwork class, dipped in government-issue grey paint, and launched without further ceremony.

This one had the entire reef to swim in, but behaved as if it was looking for something, which just happened to be where I was going. It changed neither pace or direction but stuck to both with mulish obstinacy.

Its motor was hidden and nothing appeared to be actually moving, except its entire body through the water. I felt I was being shaken down and, at some invisible Rubicon, one of us would have to give way. A voice in my ear whispered, 'Don't do anything foolish. Even a grey reef shark can turn on a diver very quickly, if provoked.' So I began to pretend an interest in something ahead but slightly diverging from, the path of my companion. He turned too, expressing similar interest.

Then for the first time, I stopped looking at him and looked about me. To my horror, I counted no less than eight greys swimming in my vicinity, and began an octopus-like retreat up the gully. In a pause, halfway, I tried to take my own emotions out of the equation and see what emerged.

The sharks, obviously, had some important business in hand. And this was part of the problem, no hands. So I let my mind float free (even though my body was stuck to the reef like play putty) and imagined a group of lads cycling down a country lane, trying to remember where they'd dropped the tickets to the big game, whatever. And I was but a dog lying in the road. Their road. Or maybe it was even more mundane. They were simply early-morning shoppers, pushing trolleys up and down the aisles, reading bar codes. Here, a holed-up octopus, and there, a pair of philandering rays, *the day's special*, two for the price of one!

When I finally stepped out onto the reef, there were nine of them and they were carrying on, circling down the reef, much as if I'd never been there.

24 Ben's hallucinatory curry

I'm standing close to shore by the reed beds. The sun winks at the desert's rim and as I turn round, lights up the whole western horizon.

My first dive is as quiet as an otter's, and I come face to face with a great bayad. It is silver and the palest soapstone green, the perfect fish for Ben's curry. To come across such a one at the tail-end of the day, and to summon up one last effort, is challenge enough. But this is way too easy.

It turns lazily away and back, no longer reflecting the reed beds behind me. The jade colour drains from its body, which becomes brighter, sprinkled with a ginger-and-ochre dust, tinged with a line of electric-blue. All sorts of thoughts churn in my head.

The fish itself doesn't seem to be moving, but in fact is drifting away quite fast. A split second more and will be out of range. I fire. A spray of silversides washes over me, parting to let it by. It glides away but its movements become erratic. I can see its intestines puffing out from a gash in its side like bubble-gum. It's not going any place.

Young Ben will be well-pleased. We know he's been bringing down his mum's curry powder and green mango chutney (a fetid-smelling paste in a jam jar) for a long time, but we've never gotten him a bayad early enough to cook, as it takes all day.

No sooner have we handed the fish over, and downed breakfast, than we're back on the reef, with Barnes, rod in hand. *How come?*

The problem is our American cousins. They've put up with Rix's burned fish and ring-stinging curries with exemplary stoicism.

They've even sprinkled the obligatory confetti (peanuts, desiccated coconut and chopped pineapple) on Beef Wellington's weekend curry buffets, but likewise to little avail. Its remained a shotgun wedding , no more than the sum of its parts, and never truly consummated until the old soldier Chowdry, egged on by Ali, added a complimentary Kashmiri wedding dish, with the unlikely name 'the full stop' (consisting of a bolus of mutton mixed with herbs, and cooked in goat's milk). But that lay in the future.

Right now, our cousins from the New World, are being asked to welcome Ben's fearsome concoction with the same enthusiasm, the American-Indians did the Thanksgiving turkey.

"If they want something hot, it's usually Mexican, Cajun or Thai, isn't it?" says Barnes.

"Exactly how I see it, Barnsey boy. Another case of Delhi belly or Beri-Beri and a Brit-American split right now, will finish us off for sure."

"Like Suez," you mean."

We do our best. Though I rescue several of his lures from various submarine grottoes, at the end of the day, for fishermen in our position, there are only two kinds, those with fish, and those without.

On shore, Rix, Ben and Leo are huddled over the cooking pot like Macbeth's witches. When Barnes and I see what the once proud bayad has been reduced to, our faces fall further. It looks like the stewed rhubarb from boarding-school days, and that's putting it politely.

"I'm hungry, but not that hungry," whispers Barnes. "The Americans are going to desert us for sure."

In no time, Ben is enthusiastically dishing out great dollops of rice, with the stewed rhubarb on top. We dutifully masticate the fiery mush, slurping it down with oily green-tea.

It's hard to tell when the strangeness began. I remember Warner giving off a series of puppyish yelps as if he was being repeatedly whacked by a piece of four-by-two in a dream. And myself feeling a fire was being banked in my belly, infusing my blood, and gaining hold. I began to drink my bitter tea with rising apprehension.

Ben frowns and pours me a surprisingly ambrosial, new cup. Leo unwraps the purple and bottle-green towel he uses as a turban, and sits on it. "More chutney please, Ben." He says. "A little bit more of that pickles too. Thanks! You've done us proud, me old mate!" Soon we're all asking for seconds. "Me too. Me too," Barnes hoots softly and discards his glasses, his face pink and freckled but pale round the eyes, like an owl ready to embark on some night-flying. Rix's is lit up like a Belisha beacon, and Pitsos's and Leo's glow like pumpernickels at Halloween.

One by one, we roll over and fall asleep.

25 The fish that could close an oyster at 60 feet

Mullet going left.

Mullet going right.

We swim slowly to the right, towards the mullet tunnels.

Only two weeks ago, during the rough weather, Warner got stuck down one, and had to get out of his shirt, underwater. Then, resting on the wave-washed gravely strand of a cave, found himself staring at what looked like a plucked-chicken lurching towards him over the pebbles, mewing like a kitten. It was a baby bat, probably dislodged from the cave roof, during some domestic dispute.

Soon no mullet are coming towards us or overtaking us. It doesn't take that bright lad Warner long to suggest, they may be heading out to deeper water. We go back a bit and head out, too. After fussing about, we find ourselves in some glades near the reef, with coffin-like fault-lines in the rock, but very nice places to lie-up in, should any shark come by.

After a while, a pod of mullet approaches, forages busily, dipping up and down, a misty curtain of crushed shells, falling all around them. They present a right-to-left shot for me and the more difficult left-to-right shot for Steve, the other side of the glade. He shoots first and they take off in a compact bunch, as if painted on a sign towed by a speedboat enthusiast. Steve doesn't leave his spear in the sand for them to come back and check it out, but draws it in. *Flaky.*

Only later did I realize, he had other things on his mind, like why are the mullet travelling in the first place, whereas I tended to see them, more from a hunting standpoint. Those passing through, if fired at quickly didn't disrupt the general flow, but when they milled around, word of our presence soon got out.

Steve leaves to follow one lot, but after a while, comes excitedly back to announce he's found the place where they're going. We swim towards the shore, to a bleak gravely bay, we'd regularly by-passed.

Due to the rough weather of late, a barrier has formed, reaching almost to the surface, behind which is a small lagoon. But no mullet are in it. Steve nevertheless insists there were plenty only moments before. *Flaky* – like I said.

≈

A few weeks later, we are back in the glades. Things look promising, bright fish flit to and fro, but no mullet approach. Then I hear the dreaded crunch-crunch, rasp-rasp of hundreds of parrotfish behind us.

If I don't mention them here, they might slip my mind altogether, as the subject of sheep might a Kiwi guide, chatting up a couple of happy-go-lucky hitch-hiking blondes.

From pasty-pink and pale-blue to macaw-gaudiness, they swarm over our reefs, often giving them a rush-hour character. Today they stream towards me and part as if I was the local bag lady, and they, Fifth Avenue shoppers.

And to this day, the biggest still act like prima-donnas, treating us as a great occasion for the dramatic exit — the rear-end aria — defecating clouds of coral sand all over the place.

At times we can simply be minding our own business, going with the flow, when some big butt whacks the water with its whole body. *Whoomph!*. Every sensate creature within ten meters, gets a wake-up call, uptight clams hunker down, and irate spear-fishermen, back-off.

At first we took it personally: the classic put-down of the country cousin by the city slicker. But as they were so many, soon realized, if we got stroppy, we could end up *persona-non-grata* on every reef from here to Qunfudah.

After spending a considerable time watching them from a distance, I've learned a few more things about the *whoomph!* Sometimes, they don't do it at all. At others, they do it with mind-numbing regularity, and at others, with no apparent rhyme or reason. I'm beginning to think, Steve's hypothesis might have merit. Their behaviour is predictably unpredictable, sometimes random, sometimes not. And equally annoying to deep thinkers and non-thinkers alike and, as Steve has suggested, especially to shark.

So far, none of us have seen parrotfish and shark together on our reefs. But it's early days yet. At night it's a different story, at least for the big ones. They wrap themselves in clingwrap and hope for the best.

26 The biggest boom since the Klondike

For many months we've noticed an eerie glow over the escarpment at night, with kites wheeling in it. And at times we can hear a distant hum from below, as if from a great city.

Now the word's out that the Wadi Ghawan is open to traffic.

One weekend we drive out to the escarpment and enter the cutting, right where the brick wall once stood. An acrid smoke of diesel, cattle dung and freshly burnt rubber, rolls over us. Our wipers clog. We add water and they end up trowelling mud.

Multi-wheeled behemoths, lit up like Christmas trees, dance halls, Mexican bordellos, or whatever takes your fancy – come grinding past, claxons braying.

At the very first bend, a truck lies on its side, half-way down a scree. In the haze far below it, we spy the occasional glint of more windscreens. The view only completely opens up once, to reveal two (once maroon and silvery-grey) Suburbans from Northrop, sensibly spaced, before a pick-up crammed with Somali long-tailed sheep and sacks of charcoal (could be wives) slips in between them.

At the third hairpin bend, traffic shudders to a halt. A three-tonner, loaded sky-high with orange-and-green foam-rubber mattresses from Czechoslovakia, is slewed across the road. A man with dust-thickened eyebrows lies on his back and grins up at us as he wedges in breeze blocks, while a tiny Yemeni dances about on top, trying to stop the mattresses floating away into the valley.

After the second tunnel, its lights already smashed by a high load, the hard-packed surface is crossed by almost impassable trenches, which the Greeks are bridging with reinforced concrete – in their own good time.

Here, as if participating in some mythic journey, we're offered a choice: the way of the Greeks, or the way of the goats along the wadi floor, into which great boulders are rolled at intervals.

All around us drivers are shouting at each other in unknown tongues, heat-warped cassettes squawk like Donald duck, or moan like drowning men in deep water. Datsuns and Mazdas, bursting at the seams with Egyptian road-workers and hard-hatted Turkish pick-axe men, pass Peugeot estates, full of frisky-buttocked Florence of Arabias, who think they've found the promised land.

Various 4-wheeled-drives, driven by dour Scot's engineers, flubby-faced alcoholics and ex-Nam vets, edge past minibuses, carrying workers from Hotchief, Phillips Holzman, Bechtel Corporation, British Airways and Lockheed. Half the world it seems – in the biggest boom since the Klondike.

We pass a camel couched by the roadside, with no head, and escape by the German dynamiter's camp, where Rix's friend, the iceman, knows a way out the back. We hit the badlands in the afternoon, and the beach, by dusk.

Over several trips, donkeys as if from nowhere, gathered on the hairpin bends, grew gaunt, and died where they stood. The camel's body swelled up, and an Egyptian eagle, more persistent than its rivals, pierced the carcass and attracted a quarrelsome group of Griffin vultures, who pulled out the entrails and engaged in macabre dances and tugs-of-war.

Whenever we turned that corner, a vile stench hit us, and for weeks afterwards, there hung over the lower wadi a sweet odour, as if from a tropical market.

In time, the camel's hide dried out over the rib-cage, and a new lad thought it was a road-worker's-temporary shelter. "Pop your head in and offer them a Vimto." Said an old lag.

27 How fish hide in open water

7 a.m. Pitsos and Gaspar call Warner, Steve and me over. "Come and look at this. No need for flippers."

There are hundreds of small fish, like dark shadows all along the shoreline. When we get close there's the usual panic and confusion. Left and right, and behind us, they go. A moment later, our toes are nipped, the confusion's ours and the joke on us.

In fact, Pitsos and Gaspar, have been trying to get us to study small fish for quite a time. But we haven't come all this way to do it first thing in the morning, especially when big ones may still be out-and-about.

Yet here am I, the very next day – before breakfast – nose-to-nose with six, inch and a half long barracuda, and small fry, each no larger than a grain of rice. The little barracudas are so quick, all I see is a wink, a twirl of silver, and they're back at their former station. The school of fry hardly moves.

The next time we find the little barracudas; there are only four of them. And they've turned their attention to a rather rambunctious school of baby jacks, but don't seem to be getting anywhere.

Gaspar however, is delighted with these snippets of information. Apparently, schooling fish only develop the scatter response, a specific number of days after hatching. The young barracuda likewise, only in their case, it's to chase scattering fish. If these are too experienced, they themselves may end up in trouble, like right now, as a mix of dizzy immature tiger fish and sly bonefish come in, looking for prey of suitable size.

Next week, we come across only three pencil-length barracudas in the turtle grass, but it is now us, who have changed. From being large harmless stage furniture, we've become potential predators, and they don't want to know us.

Since then, we often come across large schools of silversides in the lagoon, with one or two, two foot-long barracuda in attendance.

These almost static duets often stay throughout the morning as if sharing an after breakfast siesta. Their shimmering beauty gives them the aura of exclusive clubs, to which we've bestowed names like The Laguna Crevalle Country Club and The Young Silversides Sports Club. But when approached, the barracudas ease round to the other side of the school. And if we tried a fancy pincer-movement, they simply faded away.

I often wondered why the schooling fish put up with them. Maybe they hoped the barracuda's presence would protect them from any marauding bands of larger flighty jacks.

But apart from these vague thoughts, our interest would have probably stopped there, had not Gaspar come up with some questions, and special sid.

It was the colour of whisky and aged-in-wood, or rather with bits of aged-wood floating about in it. When these were removed, the amber liquid was as soft and smooth as a Dufftown bap!

"Puts an entirely new complexion on things." We said. "Fire away Gasper! We're all ears."

Gaspar too changes his tactics, begins to flatter us by asking questions and saying he needs a bit of help from experienced people like us. He is particularly interested in how the different fish we've come across, hide or escape in open water.

We answer briskly enough: starting with flying fish, tail-dancing garfish and pipe fish, which hide in the apex of small waves, and slide from one to the other. We even include those tiny critters, which look like flecks of kelp, until you actually touch one.

Soon we're showing-off about fish we've only heard of. One which projects a small light downwards (using its own swim-bladder as a reflector) and emits a soft effulgence, exactly equal to the light striking it from above, so erasing its silhouette, when viewed from below.

Then Barnes mentions a unicorn fish, not even from the Red Sea, but New Zealand, which produces smoke like a squid. This prompts Steve to bring up an even more exotic squid, which, he maintains, not only uses light to erase its own shadow, but like a torch beam, to probe into nooks-and-crannies.

He's summarily crushed by Gaspar, who says, he doesn't want to know about hunters' techniques, but only those of the hunted, when in open water. And is very disappointed, despite our erudition that we seem to have forgotten the commonest.

We scratch our heads. But where can fish hide in open water? Or does he mean simply bolting and zigzagging?

"They find another fish to hide behind." Says he.

We think about this for a while, and ask if he's seriously suggesting that the ballooning, contracting and rushings of a school is simply caused by one fish trying to hide behind another.

"That's probably how it began," says he. "When was the last time, you felt you might become another creature's dinner?"

"Last time we saw a big shark."

"There you are. Your asshole tightened and your bladder loosened. Two contrary impulses gripped you, to huddle and to flee."

Fascinating though this stuff is, I must have somehow dozed-off under the influence of the new sid, because the next thing I remember is Warner's jabbing me in the ribs. "You're jeopardizing the sid supply," he hisses, "Gaspar's just asked you a military question."

"A what?"

"How do you turn round when marching?"

My army career is not something I dwell on too much, but on noticing Gasper making two simple sketches in the sand

and , have instant recall. "The first, the thread-back, is best for a quick turn-around. The second, the pivot, is for wheeling, when you have more space."

Warner gives a thumb's up sign.

"What did you do, if suddenly attacked?"

Instant recall again. "Scatter! Immediately dilutes the target area, and minimizes bumping into each other."

"Excellent." Says Gasper, "Any problems afterwards?"

"Where to reassemble. It would be nice to scatter and stay in the same place, but that's impossible, isn't it?"

"Is it?"

He draws another picture, which looks like instructions on a packet of Durex for the mentally challenged .

"What's that supposed to be?" Says Leo.

"Called the fountain," says Gasper. "When a pelagic hunter attacks head on, the school often streaks away, then doubles back like a peeled banana, leaving its pursuer hurtling into empty water. So what does the barracuda do next?"

"Takes a rest." Says Steve. "Remember the big barracuda, which inched forward over the turtle grass, and the silversides turned round at the tips?"

"You mean the buffalo-horn manoeuvre" Says Warner, and draws a three picture sequence ⌐ 〇 ⊃ ⊚ in the sand. "The barracuda ends up weather-vaning then retires."

"The double circle's called a vacuole!" Says a delighted Gaspar. Warner gives a slightly pissed grin and balances a glass of sid on his head. "Yes, oh master," he murmurs, slowly raising his outstretched arms into the horizontal. "Your every wish is my command." Gasper ignores this and continues. "So what does it try next?"

Steve steps up to the plate. "Comes in medium pace, as if going for the centre of the school then rips along one edge. The fish bolt and there's a chase."

"Attracts trouble and wastes too much energy." Says Pitsos. "You remember that joke by Mr. Morita, the Head of Sony?"

"No."

"Well, he and a business buddy were strolling in the countryside, when they saw a Tyrannosaurus Rex. Ran away as fast as they could, but before they got far, his business partner suddenly knelt down and began putting on his Adidas running shoes.

'Don't do that!' Cries Mr. Morita. 'Nobody can outrun T Rex.'

'But I don't have to outrun T Rex,' replies he. 'I only have to outrun you.'

"Betrays his own kind, you mean," says an astonished Steve.

"Well, that's the joke obviously, but I guess he's also suggesting there might be a better way to sort things out. And perhaps, after millions of years evolution, the fish have come up with one."

So, it's back to the drawing board for us, or rather to Gaspar's first diagram in the sand ⟨XX⟩, the thread-back.

We stare at it awhile. All of a sudden, Steve exclaims. "I think I've got it." A bit later. Ok, quite a bit later, I see it myself. *A relay!*

As the barracuda approaches, each fish at the top of its turn takes the baton of vulnerability and hands it to the next. The school begins to spin, but the individual fish remain pretty fresh and alert, while the barra's the one who ends up, bushed.

"What does the barra do now?" Gasper pursues relentlessly.

"Beats me." I say.

"Come on Dundas, I'm talking to you as a fellow hunter of some repute." And tops me up a couple of fingers, maybe three. Luckily Warner comes to my rescue. "The barracuda tries to find a target." But even in my addled state, it doesn't take me longer than two, ok, three seconds, to see that *not* making oneself a target, is precisely what schooling fish is all about, and say so.

"Right on!" pipes up Pitsos, "Remember that famous American radical around the time of Angela Davis. El … It's on the tip of my tongue. El ..."

"Elvis." Says Steve.

"Not Elvis. Eldridge. Eldridge Cleaver, the Black Panther. The LAPD put out an all-points bulletin on him, and picked him up in Oakland, Watts and several other places. Then realised it was too good to be true, the black grapevine having already told the soul-brothers to dress up like him. He escaped, lost his revolutionary zeal, but not his sartorial flair. Ended up along with Huey Newton (who already had his own sportswear-line) being praised by Senator Buckley, and advertising Y fronts."

"I was right about Elvis, too," Puts in Steve. But as I've lost the thread of his conversation, have to ask Pitsos what's going on.

"I think he's talking about Elvis's impersonators," he says. "In Elvis's case, it happened when he'd passed on. Like Che Guevara, he lives on in another realm. But I'm willing to bet another bottle of this excellent sid, Gaspar, if he ever comes back from Hamburger Heaven or wherever he's go to, Colonel Parker won't let him back in the line-up."

"I think we've all had enough". Says Gaspar, and caps the sid.

≈

In the morning, the long ribbon of schooling fish is still in the shallows. Feeling I owe Gaspar one, I've just spent a tough half hour staring at the mesmerizing herringbone pattern of silversides, and the visible digestive tracts of juvenile jacks till I'm really dizzy. Then spend more time tracking one twitching little critter, until I realised it wasn't alone but one of several taking turns, stretching their gill arches and jaw muscles, yawning in fact. And would have had me doing the same -- had I not this darned snorkel in my mouth.

I was about to give up, when I saw it. A bright vermillion squiggle! It had me staying put until I'd counted to fish number 98. Only a small black smudge this time, but I had my answer. Parasites!

I leapt out of the sea to greet my public. Barnes was nowhere, Gaspar still asleep, and Leo checking something under the Toyota, not a good time to disturb him. But by beer bottle beach, Jack and company have just arrived. They're all agog at having met some nurses on the way down who told them, their own beach was becoming too crowded. Apparently, Jack barely had time to shout 'Not ours.' before they were whisked away by their driver.

Jack listens to my own announcement with ill-disguised impatience, then suddenly exclaims, "Supposing she'd asked, 'What do you boys do on your beach?' And you said, 'Studying marine ecology.' 'That's great! What species?' 'Tiddlers and parasites.' 'That is so cool. Can I bring the whole gang over?' " Followed by moronic laughter all round.

I go looking around for Lambourski. And find him raking out the grill, but all he says is, "One more reason not to eat the buggers."

On the swim out to Pitsos, I realize I'm going to have to jazz things up a bit if I'm to get any worthwhile response. But when the sand lifts from the seabed in the channel, a strange thing happens. I have a vision of my old science teacher, Father Bernard (or Bunsen Burner, as he was called) covering the blackboard with clouds of chalk dust, until he'd reduced both sides of his theorem to their essential simplicity. On this occasion, Joule's famous equation, illustrating the equivalence of mechanical work and energy. Even today, it's a shadowy concept, but then it meant absolutely nothing.

He turned round and scrutinised our faces with an optimistic smile. Then, had a heart attack. Not a killer, but we knew he'd been badly hurt.

To this day I can still see Fatty Donovan, our brightest and best (albeit form Four, class C) screwing-up his face to exhibit sudden fake enlightenment, then real concern. It was also the first time I sensed the inner struggle of those men who, in attempting to scale the heights, find their reach exceeding their grasp, and realized Father Bernard's mentor was as much the man of faith, Saint Bernard, as the monk, Mendel. And himself, no more merely calculating our chances of passing 'O' Level Physics, than I counting fish, or Mendel peas. But really believed, behind the exasperating façade of our interest, lay souls to be saved, or why did he bother?

In the relative calm beyond the channel, Pitsos was watching a moray playing with a small black grouper. "So what's up?" he says.

As he's often mentioned that there's more going on between morays and fishes than meets the eye, I don't hesitate to put in my plug for the barracuda, and it all comes out in a rush. "I think, the barracuda's early morning duet with the schools in the lagoon is a deal, a sort of Sergeant Major's drill-and-health parade. He breakfasts on sloppy-dressers, misfits, mutants and malingerers. In return, the school gets a great workout and practice in state-of-the-art synchronized swimming."

Pitsos shakes his head vigorously, and I can tell he's impressed. Only much later did he ask if I'd actually seen a barracuda take any such fish.

"Not yet" I said.

At this, he's even more impressed, and I felt compelled to ask why.

"You could have lied" he says.

I can honestly say that up to that moment, it hadn't occurred to me, and added. "Still have to tell Gaspar."

Here, surprisingly, he counsels caution, "Remember what happened to Watson and Crick, when they first thought they'd discovered the structure of DNA?"

Being put in such company I took to be normal piss-taking, but also vaguely remembered Gaspar's anecdote about how an exchange student, called Sanger, had noticed two graduates walking forwards and then backwards in the quad, and thought them an odd couple. And in Gasper's own jazzed up version Gaspar had said "that same evening, Crick got his zipper stuck, while taking a leak in The Eagle Pub's bog" (or The Rose and Crown's, I forget which). Anyway, when Crick had sorted that out, he returned to his companions and told them, he'd discovered the secret of life. As one writer well put it, 'since he was by no means the first person to discover the secret of life in a pub, and wouldn't be the last', no one paid much attention.

In the morning they got their superior, Bragg out of bed, to look at a dodgy model of DNA with a twisted carbon double-bond – a Chemistry 101 boo boo, no less! "Almost lost the plot, didn't they?" concluded Pitsos. "Funding cut. Further DNA research vetoed."

"Frankly, in my case, that would be a relief." I said.

One eyebrow goes up. "No more special sid."

"Forget I said it."

No need to inform Barnes either. He's already left for Texas beach to look for the nurses.

≈

We were settling down to sundowners when the lads return.

It's immediately apparent there's been a difference of opinion.

"Your fault," says Jack.

"Yours," says Barnes. Jack pours himself a large drink with a frustrated air, "Not so." he says. "You're the one suggested we talk to the nurses in the sea. Then you tried to pull a fast one."

"Only because their driver wandered off and we had to move quickly." says Barnes. "But when you came over, you just stood there with that uptight gormless look on your face, like you'd forgotten your glasses."

"Ha, ha! Didn't need glasses to see what everyone was gawking at." Says Jack. And turns to include us in the conversation, but we're already in it. "Had one leg cocked-up on the bumper, like this, and was wearing his granddad's World War II R.A.F cavernous shorts, big enough to hide a Lancaster bomber, but not his bollocks."

"So what? They're nurses. See them all the time."

"In the women's ward?"

"Wouldn't surprise me in the least. Desperate men, desperate ventures."

"Speak for yourself. Then you pretended you didn't know me." says Jack.

"To be honest, you didn't enter into it. Time was running out and we were trying to finish an experiment to see if the sun setting over the Red Sea, got smaller when one turned one's head upside down."

"Sorry?" We chime in. "Are we missing something?"

"You sure are," says Jack. "When I came back, he had all the nurses lined up on the beach."

"Three." says Barnes.

"They were bending over with their bums in the air as if he was about to give them the old knee-trembler."

"Grow up," says Barnes. "It's you who are arse-over-tit. Why not listen and try to learn something for a change?" Turns to us and continues. "Trees, telephone poles, the game of Africa, everything in our world, subtends a smaller angle towards the horizon, except the sun and the moon. Not being in our world, they stay the same size, so sometimes look bigger when touching down on the horizon.

"If you want to check that this phenomenon is not just to do with the atmosphere acting as a magnifying lens, you can stare at the horizon, slowly turn your head upside down and actually see the sun getting smaller."

No reaction from Jack, so Barnes goes on. "The older one, Elaine, happens to be an optometrist. Said that men have red and green colour-blindness slightly more often than women, and wanted to see if men (more the horizon-scanners), saw such setting suns differently to women (more the berry-pickers and baby-carriers).

Jack's jaw drops.

"They were eating it up like jam on toast," Barnes goes on, "till bollock brain here, comes charging up the beach like the bull from the sea. Rose erupted in giggles, Anne turned red, leaving only Marcia to science. A total waste of time."

"So what happened?"

"The driver came back – that's what." Says Jack, "Told us it was a family beach and we all had to leave. So I said 'Whose family?'"

"You didn't say nowt. You couldn't say boo to a goose."

"Calm down lads" says Steve. "All is not lost. I've got their phone numbers."

Soon they've forgotten all about their argument and are trying to arrange a future meeting under the auspices of that well-known hothouse of sexual intrigue, The Natural History Society. When this meeting was cancelled (men and unrelated women, no longer permitted to meet in certain   venues) another was planned. This time at Ballast Needham.

We all went. A row of hospital screens divided the room. Many young people showed up and only a twentieth of the original slides were shown.

When Barnes finished, groupies gathered round the slide-projector to discuss ornithology and buy Steve's posters.

But success went to their heads. They immediately set about organizing a Society outing with Jack in charge of transport, who then ran into difficulties trying to find the last eunuch in the Kingdom to chauffer the ladies. Then he went on leave (Kid sister up the spout again), but not before selling a Peugeot he'd been repairing for one party, to another; borrowing the Major's wool suit and wearing the ring in case the best man absconded with it.

When he returned, he was posted north to Tabuk on half-pay. Most people felt he'd gotten more than a fair deal, except himself and the Major (who found at the new Airport opening, his suit no longer fit).

When we drove him to the airport, Barnes said. "You're way too much the gentleman, Jack – if you don't mind me saying so." Jack didn't. "Always rushing-off to help the ladies".

"At least I tried to get a bit of social life going, which is more than can be said for most of you dozy gits. So don't say, I didn't, eh?"

"Promise," said Barnes, "Least we can do."

28 The favourite music of the permit fish

On lazy days – and most days are lazy days now – Pitsos dallies in the grouper's playground, spread-eagled and staring down, just to cool off.

Gone it seems, are those exhilarating hours spent dashing about outside the reef, where the breezes were freshest and plenty fish streamed past. Sometimes we have to stir up smaller fry to bring in the big boys. Never before have I experienced such a mix of tedium and surprises.

"Bit like the Stock Market." says Gaspar, who now splits his time between bird-watching and the cleaning-station, where he often appears to be asleep.

One morning, we happened to be crossing the lagoon's shallows, when we came across a nursery school of young pompano (or very young Permit) and drifted over them like dead men.

Because of our good behaviour, they let us perform the service of sun umbrellas. Somewhat intrigued by this, we dallied awhile. As we let things take their course, more came around, about twenty in all, and began to circle us, rising and falling in a gentle wave-like motion.

Pitsos, who's already spent several mornings among them, said they liked music, if anything coming out of a snorkel could really be called such. The *Tennessee Waltz* was their favourite, but anything more vigorous than *You are my Sunshine* sent them into deeper water.

When he told us in greater detail, I began to realize something more interesting might be going on. So early one morning, I agreed to put up with his rendering of the *Tennessee Waltz* and *You are my Sunshine* and became for a while, a wall-flower at the dance of the young pompano.

First I hung off, well out of sight, tucked into the kelp and determined not to move a muscle.

As the sand settled by a Nissen hut shaped coral head nearby, I saw it had a tunnel through it, and was staring at this, when the pompano approached. I don't know whether I moved or not, but one on the outside of the school, switched direction and soon several were going clockwise, and some anti.

I remained quite still, and after a while, my studied indifference became a source of irresistible curiosity. First one, then another, swung out, came up to me as if on a dare, then darted back in. When I eased deeper into the kelp, they fell back into their previous circling and gentle wavelike motion.

None of this registered in any significant way, until Pitsos asked if we knew that the doyen of American sports fishing editors Malcolm McClane, had once written that permit were the rarest game fish in the world in terms of how few were caught as opposed to how many anglers cast for them. Indeed we didn't. And this increased our respect for them.

We soon began to see really big ones sweeping past the tip of Sand Island, like the white keels of racing yachts, their fleeting yet purposeful passage of a quite different order to our own reef-hugging perambulations.

≈

One day, Pitsos and I were tapping the tips of some staghorn coral to coax in a school of jacks, when a single permit swept in like a huge white bird, poised completely motionless above an ivory dome of brain coral, darted down, picked off a crab with extreme delicacy, and was gone. Its creamy off-white side glinting a pale buttery gold, when the sun hit it. And beneath a domed forehead, its eye, bright and bird-like, had none of the haggard world-weary look of the larger jacks.

Another time, we were idling across the bay with a couple of saddleback in the bag, when we came across five or six large stingrays laid out on the sand, like carpets for a sheikh's picnic.

As we knew by now that many small rays were Olympic-class gymnasts (capable of executing forward flips to stab their prey), we swam some distance off. There, I dove down to scuff-up sand to attract any passing jack, and found myself staring into two raised eyes, in the corner of the biggest carpet of all.

My natural buoyancy deserted me, and I could do nothing but imagine being slam-dunked onto its barbed-spine. The creature, undoubtedly affronted by my injudicious posture, began pawing the ground. Then, cushioned on clouds of sand, rose slowly like one of those early space rockets, which look as if they're never going to make it, wobbled, and a complete failure in the rocket department, loped slowly away.

The next moment, I was in the middle of a school of big permit. One rocketed past me like a well-executed soccer penalty then another flashed by, no more than a white blur. One moment they were performing like an audacious circus act, the next, gone. And that was strangest of all. They didn't stream away with the abrupt simplicity of jacks, following their leader. They continued to criss-cross, but each time, a bit further away, and there seemed less of them. Only much later were we to discover how this was done.

29 Um Ladj

Um Ladj's great deserted bay had gone steeply down into deep water. A few yards offshore there had been nothing, no fish, just a blue haze. Then one of those enormous barracuda had turned up out of nowhere, and left likewise.

We'd just made the mistake of cooking our earlier catch in sea water, when a small dhow, or sambuk, sailed into the bay. Two old fishermen came over and offered us a couple of watermelons. It was the feast of Eid el Fatir, and ever since, Devrill-Smith has almost considered them to be holy men, sent by God.

Now, a year later, they've miraculously turned up again. It's a pity Devrill-Smith's not with us as he understands their lingo, whereas Rix often simply pretends to.

Most of the time, they're a bit shy and say little. The first evening, they gave us some fish and Rix offered them some Burbank potatoes.

The second evening, after a long pause in the conversation, the older one suddenly whispered, "Whiskey, whiskey." A moment later his side-kick repeated it. This was no joke, even if it was meant to be one. We acted like we hadn't a clue what they were on about. Offered them Vimto, a potato in shiny tinfoil and a gander through the Major's binoculars, which was accepted. When the older man's side-kick clunked into the full moon's massive bulk and fell into that river of fireflies the Milky Way, we too fell off our logs out of pure nervousness. And in the end all ended up a pretty relieved bunch of happy campers.

In the morning they were gone before sun-up, leaving us a couple of milkfish for breakfast.

≈

Later, crossing the badlands, looking for pitfalls and bustards, there pops up out of nowhere, two little lads about ten or eleven years old, one staring straight ahead, mouth open wide, the other, dribbling. They are both smartly got up, so somebody close by is no doubt, keeping an eye on them.

When we offered them Vimto, the senior pulled the junior back, then, thinking better of it, thrust him forward again. The latter took a swig and his eyes filled with delight. Then they took turns, and soon both were blowing bubbles.

When we looked back, they were still staring at the patch of innocent air we'd so recently vacated, until our dust plume galumphed over them like a great brown caterpillar. "Somebody's not going to be too pleased," mumbled an unhappy Rix. "May have blown relations with the neighbours."

In the wadi Adam, the acacias are in bloom, the air full of the hum of insects and the swooping glides of bee-eaters. At sundowners, Warner does his dance. One leg up, slap and skip, other leg up and repeat. Some tribes have their rainmaker – we, our mosquito-dancer. Only one problem, there's no mosquitoes. "Unreliable", says Pitsos. "Neurotic", says Barnes. "Sad", say I. Except, we've all spoken too soon. That night they come out in droves.

For our next trip, we borrowed the store's army surplus mosquito net, draped it over the vehicles and lashed it to head-high branches. These snapped in the wee hours. And we found ourselves, cocooned in acres of heavy double-mesh muslin, being attacked by the ants' rapid deployment force (which the Major had warned us about), and now telling us, we were the stupidest, fattest, caterpillars in all the world, for not checking what the superstructure would bear before making our bivouac.

We soon learned that the middle portions of these wadis, often chorused from dusk-to-dawn by mosquitoes and airless as cupboards, were entirely different beasts to windy beach and gusty escarp.

Lambourski wasted little time in coming up with a more oriental approach: airy nylon nets, light as silk, which soon had us poncing around, attaching ring to thorn in a prissy ritual half-way between pik-a-stik and Japanese flower arrangement, and ending up as ready to commit hari-kari as Japanese brides with ruined trousseaus.

One evening Leo, completely fed up with this continuous buffoonery, rose like Rodin's Thinker from his rock and beckons me (net bundled in my arms like a foundling child) to follow him.

He walks into the clearing between two walls of thorns, reaches up to the end of one of the springy out-riders which sprout from the very crown of the tree, and attaches a corner of the net to it.

Advancing a bed's length, he does the same to a second corner. Crosses the glade and repeats the whole procedure. Then on his orders, I release my burden, which floats up into the air like a spectral coffin under which he now slides a camp bed.

At night, after making sure no portion of the net touches the ground, we retire under gossamer sails, gently stirred by a breeze passing through the trees' topmost branches. And, chorused by a threnody of mosquitoes, are born across the River Acheron into the land of Nod.

Each dawn, the sun stalks across the wadi and wakes us to the sound of cicadas. At first, it's nothing more than the clicking of a single fishing reel announcing a nibble on the bait. Then *Zing*! It's taken! And in no time, the entire grove is in the grip of a mad machine – driving the whole day forward.

Some mornings, we're visited by an old henna-bearded bedhu, who harangues us unmercifully about some perceived wrong, he holds us personally responsible for. Mohammed, his friend, informs us tactfully that he's blessed by God.

One day old henna-beard found us preparing our spear guns. Thinking he might go bananas, we sloped arms and sang for him a chorus from *The Yeoman of the Guard*, which went someway to convince him here were two, perhaps even more blessed than he.

Another time Mohammed, after tutoring Rix in goat calls and how to sling-shot them on their way, asked if water flowed forever in our Country. When Rix more-or-less affirmed it, he got soundly rebuked, and told us it only happened in Paradise.

Here we sorely missed Devrill-Smith, somewhat of a dab-hand at explaining mini-skirts, Scotsmen's kilts, praying at the North Pole and such sundry considerations. Without his input, Rix's explanation of English drizzle could have been Lambourski grating parmesan cheese; as difficult to grasp as flash floods had been to us.

One day, watching Barnes at work, Mohammed plucked up the courage to ask if he could have his picture taken.

When Barnes turned his Polaroid on him, he went catatonic. Barnes waited till he thought he'd been snapped, then as he leaned forward, pressed the shutter. When Mohammed was handed the photo and saw nothing on it, we all received funny looks. As he saw a man slowly appear and lean forward as if to touch him, he rose abruptly and, calling his goats about him, made off quickly.

We passed him not much later, striding manfully through the scrub, holding the photo, arm's length before him.

30 The Phantom on the foreshore

Dog days. We are four tiny figures moving under the immensity of a cloudless sky, over a dead flat plain. In the shimmering heat above the sun-baked sabkah (once a lagoon, now a beach) the reef's nothing more than a flickering white tape half a mile back. It could be bleached bones for all the wetness it conveys, and the camp, a bleary hallucination, half a mile ahead.

My grouper was luck. I'd been watching a small inquisitive squid, hoping to see it blowing water at the sand to expose prey or even give itself cloud cover, as I'd once seen a barracuda do with its tail. Then the grouper had turned up to watch. Apart from the grouper and a few squiggles of ink left by the squid's departed brethren, and clusters of small fish no bigger than oak leaves, we'd seen next to nothing. Then the permit had turned up, and Warner missed it.

Leo and Rix squat down to wait for us. They are parked near one of those small neat piles of shells dotted over the flats, and hoping perhaps to see a hermit crab house-changing party. Lambourski says they've been left by an octopus, but many shells are still occupied and we've never found the octopus. Maybe, knowing the tides, it's already floated away, or made previous arrangements below.

What switches the flats to lagoon here, more than the modest tides, is the push and pull of the monsoon over the Arabian Sea, which raises and lowers the water in the bathtub of the Red Sea by very small amounts. Yet in three of four months, will be enough to put many of the flats we drive along, underwater. Even looking around now, it is hard to believe that in a few hours, the sea will have returned to these creatures.

"Any luck?" Leo and Rix signal with the time-honoured sign of arms-wide and questioning faces. "They want statistics," mutters Warner, "I still can't believe I missed."

"This time of year, we're lucky to have seen one at all," I say. "They should all be in the Fahrashan Islands breeding, shouldn't they?" I'm not sure if this is strictly true, but the best I can do under the weight of this cursed sack, whose contents keep stabbing me behind the knees every step I take, and am only carrying because Warner's got that extra load of self-loathing, which is so often the empty-handed fisherman's lot.

Though the permit had looked to be in point-blank range, it couldn't have been, because after the shot, the spear and line (lying on the sand) didn't even reach to the tall vase-like sponge, behind which it had been lurking.

"Was it cold when you dived for the spear?" I ask.

"Yes."

"There you are then! The cold water lens effect. Makes the fish look even bigger." It sounded good to me, but he's not impressed.

We slump down sack and tire, and Leo hands round the water bottle, frozen solid when we set out.

Over time we've tried marking the good spots for fish in the lagoons, by lining up rocks on shore with odd-shaped dunes and points on the escarp. But the chiaroscuro (light and shade) of the dunes, changed by the hour, and by midday the escarp had usually disappeared in haze.

We'd also taken to hiding a frozen water bottle on the way out, even looking back to guess how the place might look in the setting sun. But frankly, by the day's end, such niceties were usually beyond us.

We pour water over ourselves. The sudden coldness restores a sense of perspective and clears my head. Warner even pours some over the grouper, which gives a hearty thump.

I point to the shells. "Any action?"

"Not yet."

"Let's rest a bit and watch." We lie down, wet rags over our faces and fall asleep.

It seems only a moment later that we are woken by a strange drumming through the ground. In the distance something approaches, tall as a row of poplars one moment, sleek as a line of stretched Cadillacs, the next. Then, sliding in and out of the glass walls of heat, in the strangest manner imaginable, comes a line of camels. Not just camels, but a fast moving mounted group, with black figures running alongside, who leap up by means of looped rattan stirrups to gain a brief vantage point.

Other men, rifles across their knees, on swift rangy beasts and wearing the towering Kifiyah headgear of woven palm, shaped like an upturned vase and tall as a bishop's mitre, swirl by. And there are regal women too, mounted on the finest she-camels. Yellowish eyes and white teeth flash in our direction as they sing along to their beasts, which seem to have a fluid and indomitable rhythm they do not wish to lose, for if once broken, might never be regained. Then they're gone, swallowed up by the rippling heat.

Were they the harem of some highland sheikh from the Yemen? Later we learned they were just that, but originally from the dark-skinned lowland Zaranqui tribe, linked for many generations to the dreaded Danakili across the sea.

At the time of Pliny, around 50 AD, the famous Captain of the *Periplus*, bound for the Himyaritic Kingdom of the Yemen, saw on these very shores, the fires of the fish-eaters. This captain was a Greek, born in Egypt, but also a Roman citizen. We do not know his name, nor that of his ship. The *Periplus* is merely another name for a ship's log, but in this case has become a treasure trove of reliable information on the many places he'd visited.

I'm mentioning this here because the fish-eaters must have also witnessed the arrival of the first camel-riding nomads into this region, 'turbulent, predatory, elusive and unassailable' as depicted by E.V. Bovrill in his classic *The Golden Age of the Moors*.

To us the equivalent might be the ant-like speck of a stealth-bomber, approaching over the Nevada flats. Its after-image barely grasped, before vanished. And to our local bedhu, the heart-stopping roar of a fly-past of F 16's, might better fit the bill.

"Every age has its top dog," said the Major. "Red flags waving and benefits proclaimed. With the first steam car, it was 'no more horse dung in the street' and to our friendly goatherd Mohammed, on seeing his first high rises shimmering in the desert, 'How will the occupants avoid the goats pissing on them from the floor above?'

"Impossible to know where the next shit's coming from." The Major had conceded.

Before we reach the shade of the tent, Pitsos comes out with binoculars, a can of apple juice, and declares, "We've seen the Tihama Road lads. But doubt we will again."

31 Paranoia

Dappled shadows on bright sand. The canvas awning drums like a trusty sail. Draped over it, is a British Lightning's landing-parachute (inch-wide cloth strips, stitched into a large net) and found on the landfill at the end of the new runway. Gives us shade, helps prevent afternoon tent lift-off, and can be used to batten-down stuff in the back of the vehicle when we're on the move. Yet it's the stupidest idea we've ever had.

Dozy soldiers at roadblocks jump when they see it, as if it was hiding a mounted machinegun or was a fishnet swimsuit on a well-endowed model.

After making us take everything out and finding nothing, they're pissed-off, as if asking 'why is she wearing it, if she hasn't the goods-she's-pretending-to-hide-under-it, in the first place?' A fair question in this land of mirages, rocks and women in burquahs, which has, no doubt, troubled many a hermit since Simon Stylites first sat upon his pillar.

An officer comes out, scowls at the mess and picks up a can of tonic. "What's this?" He asks.

"Tonic," says Rix. I thought for a moment, he was going to expound on its health benefits then thought better of it.

The officer lifted up a corner of the net, "And this?"

"Parachute"

His face went hard. "Military," and it wasn't a question.

"Very old," said Rix, and being congenitally unable to resist his usual histrionics, wrinkles his nose. *Don't get smart Rixie, not now please. Cut the cackle* – well it sounded like cackle to me – with the officer's boot not six inches from three bottles of uncut sid in the bottom of the ice box.

I tried to think of the parachute as a fortuitous distraction, and was fully prepared to admit, the British Lightnings were over-priced, over-complicated and even compare them unfavourably to the F-14's, only omitting to ask how the latter had helped the Shah.

Then the officer lost all interest, dropped the net as if an offensive undergarment, saying, "Don't let me see it again." And dismissed us with a cursory flick of the fingers, straight from central-casting.

After two bends in the road, Steve whispers, "Think he knew about the tonic?"

"It was Schweppes, and he probably went to Sandhurst," says Barnes.

"Hardly end up in this neck-of-the-woods then, would he?" says Steve.

"Don't know about that," murmurs the Major, up to now as silent as a tomb. "The Yemenis are smuggling in arms, and the Saudis bombed Hodeida only last week. Things are looking up, ha, hah!"

When Gaspar returns from his bird-watching, we offer him the parachute as a bird-blind, but has difficulty in seeing the funny side of being caught under it with binoculars and bird book.

"Bury it," he says.

"Not so easy," says Steve, paranoia reasserting its grip. "A camel might dig it up, get entangled, break a leg."

So back to the dump it went.

≈

Shortly after this episode, milk cartons appear in the cooler tray instead of tonic.

Steve considered tonic too much a security risk, and in an effort to placate us, tells us his dad used to drink milk and vodka (called a moo moo) in the Australian outback, though I've yet to meet an Australian admit to it. Contrary to what might be expected, it proved as smooth as a pina-colada, possessed a bouquet of crushed almonds, and packed the kick of a rutting camel – without any of the slobbering drooling sputum and bubble-gum blowing, needed to impress the ladies.

After one glass, it had Gaspar telling us, without being asked, how we broke down our own mother's milk. Apparently, this milk molecule is built like skylab, and takes an enzyme as strong as a bulldog to break it into the simpler sugars, glucose, lactose, etc. "Enter two young Frenchmen, Jacob and Monod", Gaspar carries on without stopping, "chronically short of funds and researching yoghurt, either end of a corridor in the Pasteur Institute (the third member got squeezed- out). They asked an English friend, Bragg , if he could help them with his fancy microscope, by examining the bulldog's enzyme in action. Bragg gave it a bone dipped in glue, and managed to photograph it in mid-bight.

The canny Frenchmen were more than grateful, for they realized that no mere babe-in-arms could possibly afford to keep such mastiffs in vittles like some English Lord, and posited a miniature French poodle as the activator. They were right.

"As soon as a milk molecule splashes down, up jumps this little fellow from his doormat, to reveal a sign, 'Kennel workers required immediately.'

A stream of helicopters patrolling above, full of DNA inspectors, repairmen and construction workers, then lands, disgorges a posse of kennel staff, and in no time, bulldogs are charging out of the kennels and snapping up the milk, like there's no tomorrow."

Then with hardly a pause, Gaspar introduces an off-the-wall American lady, considered eccentric for little more than climbing the wisteria whenever she forgot her keys in the upstairs office. "Yet when many scientists were still gazing in awe at DNA's spiral-staircase, she was already giving a paper on Jumping Genes. And in the silence which followed the obligatory flutter of applause when she'd finished, was distinctly heard to mutter. 'If they can't understand it. Then bugger them.'

"When she later received the Nobel Prize, she said Monod had become like a son to her. 'Smart Lady'. Said Gaspar."

After only the second glass, in order to explain something to Leo, he's imitating a peahen addressing her chicks, and we listen in amazement as he cheeps, "You may think I'm coy and complaisant, curtseying and saying 'No, Your Majesty, Yes, Your Majesty'. And letting him donate his little bouquet in my ladies' chamber. But don't forget, long before Chinese Emperors wore silk and Maharajahs built palaces, we were helping him weave his splendorous tail and complete his Bayeux tapestry.'"

'But mama,' cheep her chicks. 'It's the pizzazz, shimmer and glitter, we really dig. Not musty old heirlooms."

"Exactly, my sweets. Go for the bright-eyed and bushy-tailed. But in this case, it happens to be no rented tux or hired limo. It's the finest up-to-the-minute health spreadsheet you'll ever see, and money in the bank. The gene bank, the only one we've got. *Tweet, tweet!*""

I mention this here as fair warning, for when Gasper decides to deliver his own dreaded story of hunting.

32 Knocked over on the reef

Today a large white-tip comes along the reef, sweeps past us like we don't exist, turns slowly in a long arc, twists abruptly to the right and dives down into the depths. A moment later, it comes up behind us and repeats the whole manoeuvre. We retreat out of its flight-path to watch what's going on.

It appears to have come across a school of silversides trying to enter the lagoon, and is using the ring-craft of relentless circling, to prevent them doing so. It comes by again, hugging the reef top, using dead ground like a low-level attack aircraft, passes over the gully, dives down and disappears, presumably along the base of the reef.

Impressive though these tactics are, it seems odd that a shark needs such a long distance to manoeuvre in, unless it's also mapping out an area where visitors aren't welcome. Eventually we lose patience, and fancying the shark might too, slink off.

As the weather freshens, more schools of silversides muster along the reef. In the afternoon, near where Barnes was fishing, tuna come in. I slip quietly into the water, but don't move away from the reef.

Flashes of needle rain go this way-and-that, and am privileged to witness the tuna, wheel and advance in close order, stacked like artillery shells, one on top of the other. The silversides open up and double back, leaving the tuna hurtling into open water. *Gaspar's fountain in action!*

I wait for them to return. The school shifts, darkens, rushes ahead. Then I see nothing but the wobbly face of Barnes above, shouting "Shark!" and I am out real quick.

We both watch the broad-beamed, blunt-nosed greys come in one after the other, chomping down on silversides. I stare at them with that foolish grin people wear, who've had a close shave with danger, but must savour it again to appreciate more fully the precarious nature of their existence.

Later in the day, Lambourski reports seeing a big shark further down the reef. As we didn't actually see it, it didn't fully register. Then, when we did, it wasn't where we expected it, but came cruising between us and the reef.

We closed ranks and all watched it, which was a mistake, for in that moment were sucked upwards by a wave behind us, and unceremoniously dumped on the coral. This had happened before, when we'd been dragged across the reef towards a huge wave. But that one had fallen not a yard seaward of us, and we'd been lifted up and carried into the lagoon on a luxuriant bed of foam. This occasion was somewhat different. I was smacked into a coral head, got tangled up in my line, and just had time to see Lambourski trying to stand up, when Warner came spinning in beside me, his wounds mainly psychological. But Lambourski has twisted his ankle.

We clamber over to him and together, lift him out of the swirling brine.

Spear guns, flippers, snorkels, masks – all are gone.

Two weeks later we found one spear gun, 200 yards down the reef.

Back at camp, Rix plunks down before us a full bowl of steaming ring-stinging curry. "Get this down you me hearties," he says. "It'll swill the bilge from your scuppers."

Lambourski promptly throws up.

33 The Korean fish's eye

We remake our spear guns with help, considerable help, from the Koreans.

Next time we return with a big Korean fish, the distance is so great, we don't take the spears out for fear blood might bring in shark.

Being so close to the fish and specially its great eye, is like having a reporter's camera thrust into one's face and being obliged to answer awkward questions like 'Why are you killing me, just for the sake of a meal?'

'For the same reason that you were chomping down on silversides the other day," I reply. "Good chow.'

'But you're a human-being, much better able to exercise choice over your vittles than I am.'

'And if you were only a fish, you wouldn't be able to ask that question.'

'Touché.'

And realize it's a conversation I'm having with myself. But as no actual public or pontificating prelate is party to my thoughts, I cut myself a bit more slack and wonder if Barnsey's own attitude isn't so bad, after all.

When his girlfriend, who loved all God's cuddly creatures, introduced him to her mum, and he was about to decline one of that imposing matriarch's tuna-fish sandwiches, he received a glance from his affianced, telling him, now was not the time for playing silly buggers, so silly buggers he did not play.

Suddenly there's an almighty *Thwack!* --Time to stow the gab and halt the metaphysics -- for the fish is diving down towards the reef! We just manage to wrest it up, retie the lines, and after soundly abusing each other for not paying attention, push on towards the shore.

I know that in Nature's school of hard knocks, pain has a specific job to do. The playing-possum stage is to lull the predator into complacency, and the pain, Nature's kick in the pants so-to-speak, to make the prey bolt or fight back.

But causing unnecessary pain is *our* problem, and nobody can say, three spears stuck into a fish, doesn't hurt. And what about being pulled out of the water, and left to die? "Is it like being suffocated, or like dying in the snow? First the dumbing down, then the letting go". As Steve told me, Emily Dickinson once wondered.

Dr. Livingstone too, while sojourning between the jaws of a rather irate lion, said he felt no pain. Yet *The Daily Telegraph* only the other day, quoted two Zimbabwean hunters in similar predicaments, saying they experienced plenty. Perhaps the Reverend, after a life spent helping his fellow men, simply felt he deserved a rest. And though the pearly gates weren't exactly how he'd envisaged them, so be it. Whereas our two hunters, having no such intimations of immortality, and probably no government pensions, weren't prepared to call it quits quite yet.

I stare into the velvety orb of the fish's great eye with all the concentration I can muster. What I then say is between me and the fish, but not a flicker of an answer do I get, no little curved reflected-window, either. Maybe, the corneal fluid being denser than air and of a crucially different density to seawater, has something to do with it. Whatever. It's like looking into a deep well of nothingness.

But that can't be true either, for somewhere within, a movie is up-and-running, which I will never be able to experience unless I become a fish and return to tell the tale. A question I later learn, Chuang Tzu put to his friend Hue, over two thousand years ago, while watching fish from a bridge over the river Hao.

So I end up telling the fish, I'm making no promises now because, though I know how to say something suitable, I'm quite capable of doing the opposite at some later date.

After the Koreans move up the coast, whenever I spy a large Korean fish, I mutter "emergency rations" as we pass each other by. I hope with not too unfathomably different feelings of relief.

34 The Blue People

I am halfway across the lagoon, thinking of this-and-that, when I find myself staring at three great permit, unmoving in the water.

Dappled sunlight plays over them, enmeshing their backs and flanks in a golden net. I stare at them a long time. Then I turned very slowly towards an outcrop of Gorgonian coral, partly to get it between me and them, partly to anchor myself, and partly to let them know, I had no interest in them.

When I glanced back they were gone, and felt instinctively they'd been waiting for just such move on my part, before making their own.

It's also hard for me to accept that the camouflage offered by open water and the sand flats, can so often be as effective as that furnished by bracken and underbrush, to similar land creatures.

In a copse or underbrush, you can stare long and hard at the very place, say, where a game bird's breast feathers curve away and should darken, but don't. So you see nothing special until some tiny motion or shift in focus, makes the plump brown bundle spring out of the layered flatness.

But here, the observer is challenged differently. Between the waves and gently billowing sand, there is no question of staring long and hard at one spot because everything – including oneself – is in some sort of motion. Sand and seabed slide this way-and-that, while small waves fling down their nets of light on all and sundry, effacing the permit's outline, breaking its mould and leaving but an unframed mirror, reflecting the empty sea.

Thus the barracuda patrols almost unseen and the permit comes and goes, as if by magic.

≈

Today the wind is fresher, the waves choppy, and a great number of sea birds are about. As we swim to the second reef, we notice a mother-of-pearl gleam coming and going under the surface. Whatever it is, it draws us forward in stops and starts.

Just beyond the drop-off, hundreds of horse-eye jacks are pushing forward all the way down the reef face and left and right, as far as the eye can see.

Thwack! Thwack! Thwack! Three fish straight away! An osprey tries to grab Leo's as he surfaces. Other odd things follow. While putting the third one in the sack, the first calmly swims out and away. Never mind, we're back at the reef face as fast as we can go. Already they're beginning to thin out.

Thwack! Thwack! Two more. Back to the sack and return. Now it's mainly stragglers, eager to catch up. Pelicans crash around us like a bunch of angry old ladies with umbrellas. Two more hits and a miss.

Back to the sack and another shock. It's been ripped open, nothing left but a gaping hole.

Back we go to the reef. But now there are considerable spaces between the groups of fish, and the last shot misses. There's a commotion some way ahead, but common sense advises caution.

Swimming in through the lagoon, we find the remains of one jack, bitten clean in half. So after all the excitement, we've ended up with a grand total of two and half a fish.

≈

That same afternoon, driving through the badlands, I clearly see in the clouds of Pitsos's raised dust, the hallucinatory forms of hundreds of horse-eye jacks, swimming across our front.

Then, who should pop up, but Tweedle Dum and Tweedle Dee, clutching their possessions and staring to their front. Rix checks that his rooster dust-tail won't envelop them. And as we draw closer, Dum starts to dribble and Dee to quieten him. I worry they might be epileptics, and perhaps the Vimto cause them to blow more than bubbles.

"Vimto's pretty harmless stuff," says Steve, "Maybe you're muddling it up with Vim or Gumption."

"Made by the same Company probably."

"Could be."

Nevertheless to be on the safe side, we offer them cold water and a piece of chicken. For some reason, probably the excitement and stupefying heat, I envisage Dum getting a bone stuck in his throat and being left with only Dee to help him.

"Relax. They're not idiots, you know", says Steve. *Could have fooled me.*

But after drinking the water and scoffing the chicken, they wrap up the grease paper and place it neatly in their bundle.

≈

After a good night under the acacias, we reach the Wadi Ghawan at dawn. What a surprise! Smooth, black, spanking new tarmac hisses under our tires. Gleaming yellow lines and sparkling cat's eyes, guide us round the curves. Over-sized, immaculate pale-blue signs announce Khamis and Abha in two languages. But there's no traffic. We could be coming into L.A from Vegas on interstate One Five at dawn, as Lambourski once said.

We enter a time-warp. Striding along in the half-light comes a small band of the Blue People, citizens of their own tribe, herbs in their hair, silver daggers in their belts, and arms casually looped over long-barrelled antique rifles. Some stare into the middle distance, into a landscape in which we happen to be in the way. And this enhances their aura, already established by an apocryphal story, in which a Khamis barber, ordered to give one a haircut, had his throat cut in return.

Suddenly, out of the mist high above us, looms a phantom Shangri-La. Prince Sultan's new palace. Hamadryas baboons insolently strut along its walls, above which, incongruously peep the green tiles of Korean-style roofs.

Through large wrought-iron gates we glimpse across spacious mosaiced forecourts, austere futuristic buildings of granite and royal-blue glass. And an isolated one of such astonishing beauty, we drive back to take a second peek. For the rest, it's the usual wealth (with a capital W) proclaiming with as much discretion as it can muster, 'we're not playing catch-up, but leapfrog.'

35 Cichlids and finches

The morning is peaceful; the only sound, the occasional whistling of the kettle.

Barnes shows me a postcard, postmarked Gibraltar, with the picture of a baboon on it. It's from his niece, a precocious if giddy child (whom he'd told about our baboons) informing him that feeding the weakest member of a troop, merely indicates you are below it in the pecking order. 'So watch out!'

It also reminds me to send the hospital's wheelchair cowboys another postcard with a bigger shark on it. (And if I sent no more, let them choose whether I'd forgotten to, or simply met my just desserts!)

Then Leo, out of the blue, asks 'what's the most intelligent fish?'

"Cichlids". Say Barnes and Gasper in unison, suggesting they've been perusing the subject together. However, Gaspar wastes no time in opening the sid and taking up the running.

"They're small freshwater fish," he goes on, "which originated from one ancestor in the African Rift Valley lakes about 120 million years ago. And those who keep them today, often consider them more intelligent than the neighbours.

"Anyway, the Rift Valley lakes were pretty much to them what the Galapagos Islands were to Darwin's finches. For example, some finches blown on to one of the remoter islands, would have died out, had not a few managed to lever open the scales of fallen spruce cones and extract the seeds. Then in conjunction with breeding enough offspring with genes for crossed-beaks, became over time, a cross-beaked species.

"In the case of the cichlid fishes, their lakes were formed by the same kind of upheavals as produced the Galapagos Islands. Whenever the Mountains of the Moon (in today's Uganda) erupted or froze over, the cichlids were shunted from lake to lake, (they don't like rough water, just as the finches don't like rough weather) and eventually consolidated in Lake Kivu. Here they evolved, not the beak of a parrotfish, but a small elevator muscle in the back of the throat.

"Not for them the glory of Pavarotti's voice but something just as important," says Gaspar, and digresses completely -- no doubt under the influence of the sid -- to tell us how his banker uncle, once noticing his portly spouse weeping during one of Pavarotti arias, offered her his handkerchief. And, on realizing the truth of the old adage 'none deceive so well as first deceive themselves,' told Gaspar how he'd paid off his mistress the very next morning, citing a heart condition.

"But the cichlids also ended up with a meal-ticket for life" He goes on. "They could snack along with the very best, breathing and swallowing at the same time!

And if not invited to dine, happily dined alone, squirting water into overlooked nooks and crannies, siphoning up the contents, but not above engaging in long tugs-of-war with obstinate worms, and the eye-pods of over-curious isopods. Or if hassled, cutting and running, spitting out carapaces to delay pursuit, and unwrapping the goodies later. Yet in time of famine, they happily scavenged in schools, all pulling outwards, without snapping at each other as hyenas do.

Of course, numerous tricksters abounded, and perhaps even a few thinkers. Konrad Lorenz claimed he once saw a cichlid grab a worm, and take the young into its mouth. After a while it blew the lot out, swallowed the worm, then took the young back in, "There's also a species where the female takes the eggs into her mouth as soon as they are laid, and the male has evolved bright red spots on his tail. Coming across a female hiding her eggs, he sidles up like Antonio the Spanish Dancer, and gives his tail a shake. *Ole!*

Thinking the spots are her eggs, the female darts at his decorated appendage, and as she does so, he discharges his sperm into her mouth. *Ole!*

"In some species, family values and parental care are as assiduously indulged as in Renaissance Rome. Some are born great, some achieve it by force of arms, and some have it thrust upon them. With the Gold Midas, the one born gold is dominant even if the runt, whereas with the Thai Swordtail, the male has to fight his way to the top. With the Anthias, 'remove the male, and the female has the mantle of maleness thrust upon her, plus all the gaudy colours and elaborate caudal streamers needed to boss a harem.'

"In other species, sporting traditions prevail. Couples challenge each other to boxing matches. If the male is simply too pathetic, the female saunters off with a well-advertised capacious yawn.

"Among the usual reprobates and outlaws, there's a cannibal pirate who cruises about in cryptic colouring. On sighting its prey, it hoists not the Jolly Roger, but the prey's own ensign. Comes alongside real-friendly like, and chows down. Some bite only to the left and some to the right, don't ask me why.

"Some females have evolved semaphore: five black stars mean I am guarding my young and will not tolerate interference; one black mark, I am busy spawning, and two bars. Help! I am desperate and have nowhere to go. There's even a male, who believes chivalry is not entirely dead. When frightened (dropped into a bucket with not much water), immediately adopts female colouring.

"And here's a final question," says Gaspar, "that Barnes and I have long pondered," (causing Barnsey to blink like a ventriloquist's dummy). "How come the cichlids, which flourish among Nile perch in so many Rift Valley lakes, failed to, when a well-intentioned colonial officer, dumped a batch of mature Nile perch into Lake Victoria in 1954?

Maybe it was the first time ever, mature Nile perch arrived in a lake *without* a concurrent rise in water level - which would have allowed the cichlids to escape into the surrounding countryside."

36 Our mullet were no cichlids

Our mullet were no cichlids.

Often we'd set out to look for them then forgot what we were looking for. It took me a long time to realize, their interest lay in the very nature of their boringness. More of which later. In the meanwhile, because the glades were less visited by mullet than we'd hoped, we moved to a new ambush position further up the coast. The problem here wasn't so much the long slog over the lava, but that the set-up was too good!

In the new place, with its narrow arcs-of-fire and fancy curtains of kelp, the mullet got a bigger shock on seeing us, than we them. Their information zipped straight from lateral-line preceptors to bolt muscles lying alongside; whereas ours went from eye, plus a brief trip to the brain, all the way down the spear-arm to trigger-finger, by which time the fish had long gone.

Pitsos said we should try and let the mullet get used to us first, and Warner and Steve that we should pay more attention to our backgrounds as seen by the mullet. To this end, they even splurged on some puce-coloured cut-price polyester shirts from the souk, with the inspired pattern of crushed rocks. But when buttoned up, looked such a right proper bunch of twats, we had to take great care no one on Beer Bottle beach saw us.

So here we are back in the glades, on our best behaviour and hoping the mullet will be less intimidated by our new outfits than they were by our Singha beer, UCLA and 'You'll Never Walk Alone' T-shirts.

There's also another reason. We've thrown a couple of dice on a checkerboard drawn in the sand (depicting our hunting area) and this is the square they've fallen on. The idea being to stop us visiting our favourite places too often, and their becoming the fish's least favourite ones.

Steve claimed he got the idea from Nanook of the North, not in person, but from Nanook's last stand, when his desperately small hunting party had to decide whether to stay put or move on.

And the sacred bones were caste, enabling them to go to their destiny without fear of later acrimony and recriminations.

We soon forgot this wise procedure because, I guess, we weren't in dire straits and maybe mislaying the dice had something to do with it.

Today, after a considerable wait, a pod of mullet approach, forage busily just out of range then retrace their steps.

The old ennui soon returns, and Steve goes on swim-about. Then a shadow falls over the sand inside the glade and expectations rise. It's probably a barracuda or a grouper but as neither Warner nor I can see what it is and daren't move, there's little we can do. Then it's gone.

Steve returns and reports, no mullet seen, no pond, no barrier even.

We are about to exit the glades, when a walleye sallies by. This fish is no relation to its feisty American namesake, where I've heard two are sometimes caught on the same line, the second grabbing the lure out of the gill-opening of the first.

Our walleye looks like the front half of a lead-grey fish and the back half of a bottle-green one, glued together .We've named it for its habit of eyeing us askance, like a horse which has just unseated its rider and intends to keep it that way, almost as if it had but one defensive gene, saying 'Stay three meters from all strangers son, and you'll have no troubles in life.'

Thinking it might be a good test case for our new shirts, we forget all about the mullet, and study its antics closely. It meanders about; keeping about three meters away, goes over a ridge, then comes back fast.

Instantly, Warner and I are primed for action. We inch forward and peer over the ridge. Three meters from us is a big snapper (probably the owner of the shadow) facing the other way. When I fire, the spear goes in the gill case and comes out the mouth. As I lift the fish up, partly to show off and partly to stop it sliding off, the shaft snaps, and it's gone in a flash.

After my usual sequence of tantrums, two items go down in my diary: 1. Fish look bigger underwater, but grow heavier out of it. And 2: If I'd remembered what Father Bernard had said about Archimedes in his bath, this last part might not have happened.

"But don't forget what happened to Archimedes," adds Barnes sympathetically. "During a lull in the siege of Syracuse, he was so focused on a theorem he was drawing in the sand, never heard a centurion order him to stand up. The indignant soldier then hurled his spear and killed him on the spot."

37 Jaffri's house

One morning, an old man with a wispy beard, comes riding by on a donkey. He's shaded by a battered umbrella affixed to pommel and wooden stirrup.

Rix, never averse to learning something from the natives – be it plunging his right hand into a pot of ghee or learning to plough behind a camel – hails him over for a cup of tea.

His name is Mohammed Jaffri, village headman and beachcomber, (the village being none other than those nine or so beehive huts we saw on our first trip down).

Rix offered the donkey one of his scones, which it wisely declined, but buried its head thankfully in a bucket of water, and stayed there.

Before Jaffri left, he invited us to visit him. When we did, nothing about the hut's modest beehive exterior had prepared us for the interior. The domed ceiling was plastered and whitewashed, and the lower portion beautifully decorated with paintings of interwoven leafy branches, from which were cleverly suspended, a host of kitchen utensils, dried herbs, dates, mirrors, camel bridles and trappings, amber worry beads and big yellow Yemeni honey gourds.

Three swarthy crones were cackling away in front of an unplugged TV, like chickens each claiming to have laid an egg larger than the others. Devrill-Smith told us it was a discussion about whose turn it was to collect the donkey shit, an important fuel item.

After mint tea, served by his daughters, who moments before had been running like the wind outside, skimming a frisbee, and a discussion whether it was better to bring the camel to grazing or grazing to the camel, his son arrives in a Datsun pick-up, wives and supermarket-trolley in the back. And himself, descending, brolly in one hand attaché case in the other.

When he drove us back to the trail, he told Devrill-Smith, his daughters had been most impressed by Rix's method of finding his way around.

For a man with a carefully nourished reputation for getting lost at the first opportunity, this aroused our keen interest. "How?" we asked.

"He'd park the Toyota," Jaffri's son replied. "Then climb to the top of the highest dune. Sniff the air like an oryx scenting moisture, blow his nose twice into a cloth, and examine it carefully, before returning it to his pocket. And when he'd descended, always knew which way to proceed."

38 Long day's hunt

We are seated witnesses of a most magnificent panorama. In one vast arc to the northeast, the lava sweeps up from the sea to three dead volcanoes on the horizon.

To the East, an osprey comes fussily low across the face of the sun, now bursting over the desert's rim. It's flying to its nest in one of the new pylons marching over the lava beds, courtesy of the Koreans.

Closer to, the tranquil surface of the lagoon is broken in several places by the turbulent swirls of hunting jacks.

I slip under the water, and head towards them. Very soon, I am in the centre of a carousel of sombre lantern-jawed goliaths. As they press around me, I have one moment of hiccupping fear like a motor-cyclist might feel on the wall of death, when his engine splutters. Then they open up like metal plates coming apart, and stream away on a common impulse.

With their great down-turned mouths, they looked as sad as Alistair Simms in *Good-bye Mr. Chips,* or if you missed the movie, the deeply-lined faces of King Faisal, or Somerset Maugham. One weary from balancing the books, the other from writing so many, and the fish from harbouring so many secrets from the deep

A shout from Pitsos breaks me from my reverie. He has a barracuda, and needs a helping hand as it's swooping this way-and-that, but otherwise doesn't have too much fight in it. Size for size, jacks fight harder because they expect to be pursued and fully intend to escape, whereas a barracuda seems unable to accept anything is faster than itself over a few meters. Having a shaft of steel in it, merely adds injury to insult.

Warner and I hang off lest anything else comes by, while Pitsos tows it back to Black Mountain. It takes us a while to find a shady pool and a rock large enough to cover it. Even then, a cormorant, drying its wings and hoping to pinch an easy meal from an osprey, expresses interest.

We're hardly back in the water, when half a dozen plump fighting-fit, silver crevalla appear weaving in-and-out of focus, just beneath the surface. They're soon all about us and we're powerless to do anything, except shoot each other.

They return open-mouthed. Small fish scrum around us for protection, spraying this way-and-that. The jacks snap up the escaping fish like intercepted passes and bolt over and under our spears. One jack returns and leaps an invisible hurdle, just where I am aiming. A year back and they wouldn't have had the nous to do this.

A cobia turns up, coming into the shallows like a racing corvette. A rare visitor, I see its horizontally-barred side, dusky-yellow, grey and green, as it passes between me and the rocks. I am going to get it and swing as if upon a pompano, but giving it more lead. It swooshes off. It's first speed, no speed at all.

We pass over a large turtle, eating in a dignified manner – a real dowager at the Ritz. She takes care to show us, by the way she raises her head and looks down her nose (perhaps she raised it in order to look down her nose) that to her all forms of haste are unseemly. We slow to a decorous paddle. Then with a couple of alarmingly rapid stokes of her flippers, whizzes away like a well-caste frisbee, into the wide blue yonder. Many creatures here possess two speeds, one in character and one out, the former to lull you into acceptance of it, the latter to catch you – or escape from you.

In a matter of moments, the sea loses its motion and becomes hazy. We decide to cross the deeper water to the outer reef. It's against the current but we have no choice. It is Rix's birthday and we're going to need a fish, both he and Lambourski can really get their hands on.

The big reef announces its presence in the usual manner – by the cheerful glitter of schools of fusiliers.

Three pompano come darting out over it. Like birds over a cliff, they hover a moment, back off, fly round and come back again. One comes our way. I get the impression that the other two are watching for our reactions. Then they all go off together.

At the same time, more jacks rise slowly up, head-to-tail from deep water. We try to keep still, like skydivers set in correct configuration. A school of smaller and livelier jacks now bursts through them and streams brazenly towards us, but thinking better of their sudden boldness, go into a tizzy, scooting all over the place. The bigger jacks back-off, and that's that. Many incidents like this – over which we have next to no control – occur at intervals during the day, making it both interesting and frustrating.

Things soon quieten down and there's less fish about. We wonder if we've scared them away. In time, we surmise it was probably due more to our manner of arrival than what we did on arrival. By perambulating slowly over the roof of their world from a distance rather than slipping in over the reef-top, a lot more fish had had their curiosity aroused. Then, finding no particular benefits to themselves in our antics, simply continued on their various ways.

We've been slogging along against the current for a good few hours, and have had enough. We turn around.

What a change! We drift effortlessly along and can take in everything at our leisure. Ghostly coral heads loom up and glide by. A crown-of-thorns starfish and a colony of rapacious snails, encamped on a denuded patch of brain coral, pass not a yard from my spear arm.

Thicken up this brew like a *roux*, boost its viscosity, colour it red, and we could be white corpuscles, leucocytes (killer cells), out on a hunting spree in the blood. But this isn't correct either, because the leucocytes are the home-side and we're the intruders, if not invaders, antigens, no less! And the blood's larger macrophages, now become our nemesis – white-bellied sharks looming out of the dark to devour us.

I glimpse in passing, a cluster of sea urchins, and deeper in a gully, the black eye-spots of small grey snappers. They could be cold viruses with their own microscopic insignia, and wedged so far into the cell wall, even leucocytes couldn't reach them.

These reflections, so briefly entertained, are swept aside by a boisterous swell, which is soon going to dump all of us on the reef if we're not careful. We ease further out.

A big snapper weaves up, turns round, darkens from dusky-rose to deep copper as it moves out of the sunlight, then unbelievably, panics. Instead of making for open sea or diving, tries to bolt into the kelp. Only against organized pelagic hunters would this have made any sense, so I guess this is what we appeared to be.

Warner keeps after it and fires. It shakes the spear out of itself like a boxer who's taken a surprise early blow, and Pitsos has his spear in it before it has gathered its wits together. We land it, not three meters from the spot it had originally been headed.

The wind is growing stronger and the sea rougher. Even the ospreys, patiently patrolling above the reef, and keeping an eye out for frigate bird and cormorant, are finding it difficult to make any headway.

Over by the camp, Rix too, is having a spot of bother. The wind's uprooted some of the tent poles and they're cavorting about like a bunch of tipsy skeletons.

We go back for the barracuda caught earlier, but it's gone. A couple of bedraggled cormorants look down on us. *Too big for them surely.*

They're also creatures in transition, similar to penguins. In the cormorants' case they swim under water rather than fly, and their water-proofing has to be reapplied each day.

But if they didn't take the barracuda, who or what did? *A bit of a mystery here.*

When we finally stagger into camp, we have to shout above the mayhem, "Happy birthday Rixie! Brought you a present."

"Just as well," he says, as he fusses past us. "You'd have got fuck-all, had you come back empty-handed." Then he sees it. "*Wow!* Thank you! Who got it this time?"

"Dinglebat here." Says Leo. "The only one of us with any piss-and-vinegar left in his bottle."

"Teamwork," mumbles Warner.

Rix guffaws. "That'll be the day. But come and look." And directs us to a jaggedly opened tin; Pitsos's prized reserve Virginia ham from Czechoslovakia, which we dutifully file past like mourners viewing a dearly departed, now become a greyish-pink lump in a bath of melting aspic and looking like a heart-transplant, nobody wanted.

When the wind finally abates, and Rix's new potatoes and peas are reduced to the usual mush, Lambourski simply lays the fish on top, which is a great idea, as it absorbs all the excess juices.

Everything disappears with much smacking of lips. But the wolf-pack scenario of us swooping down on big snapper off the kelp, so vividly envisaged during our repast, is never to be realised. Dad's army had peaked without our knowing it.

39 Deep waters

One bright morning, Rix dumps some dusty tomes from the newly defunct British Library on us: Isaak Walton's *The Compleat Angler,* Coleridge's *The Rime of the Ancient Mariner*, Doughty's *Arabia Deserta.* Even some worm-eaten Russian Classics and the Tide charts for Karachi and Jeddah, 1938. Not exactly the cutting edge of contemporary thought.

Though we fell asleep many an afternoon with these weighty tomes on our chests, the literati amongst us enjoyed reading about young Isaak on the banks of the Avon, making fishing rods from springy willow, swapping trouties for the occasional pail of milk and singing duets from John Donne and Kit Marlowe with the local dairy maids. Like us accompanying Neil Diamond and Jim Morrison on the ghetto-blaster but without the dairy maids.

Isaak Walton was both a man of his time and ahead of it. His *bête noire* was the otter (much as ours was the shark) and were depicted in his woodcuts -- as mean-looking as sewer rats. But with regard to religion he waxed more philosophical, even penning a ditty:

> Many a one to his Country, his religion owed
> And in another would as strongly grow,
> Had his nurse or mother taught him so.

More relevant to our concerns, he noted that 'King Edward I's statutes of 1616 for the fence months (closed season) were both praised and ignored, and everybody's business had become nobody's.'

Leo even dipped into Coleridge's hallucinatory and jaunty *Rime of the Ancient Mariner* to see where Rix got his nickname, emerging with but two criticisms: the punishment (for shooting the albatross) didn't fit the crime, and the ending was open to too many interpretations.

Steve, who could recite great chunks, thought these examples were deliberate. The albatross could mean a thousand things – from a creature of solace to sailors lost at sea—to a bird of ill-omen, not above plucking out the eyes of drowning men. And in Coleridge's particular case, may have referred to a single foolish act, a small opium pill, taken too often (on poor advice) and for far too long. So much so that his solitary voyaging became real and eventual return home, death-in-life.

Only much later did we ourselves find an albatross to which we could raise a respectful toast. One heard in the dead of night by a father while sailing his son (and son his father), round Cape Horn:

> I was blowing on my fingers when my
> heart suddenly jumped at an eerie, flat slit of light
> to starboard, an orange band like a dragon's eye.
> Then it started to rush at us. Heart beating fast I
> realized it was the moon rising between the
> horizon and a black ribbon of cloud. Exactly then,
> there was a blood-curdling scream to port. Of
> course it was an albatross.
>
> Out there with my son and with all the
> layers skimmed off, I had crept to the centre of the
> intricate web of my expensive education. Alone
> with the vast ocean, I found far more pleasure and
> use for it, and far more unity with my distant
> fellows, than in the hum drum application of
> keeping afloat in shallower waters of witty
> conversation at the Century club or embassy
> parties.*

"But how does Rix fit into all this?" Leo still wants to know.

"Now you're entering deep waters," murmurs the Major. "Cricket. They say he was dropped as wicket-keeper from the second eleven, last posting, because 'he stoppeth only one in three.'"

*Quoted from a fine book, *My Old Man and the Sea*, by David & Daniel Hays.

40 Late on Reef 1

Darkness doesn't come down on a reef, it comes up. Near at hand, as if bathed in river mist, it is a warren of peeping eyes: cardinals, goggle-eyes and squirrel fish. Further off, dim schools of grunt are waiting to make their way head-to-tail, to the feeding grounds, where big groupers wait for them in the turtle grass, now in darkness.

A shark glides by.

I am out too late and am not hanging about a moment longer. Just as I turn away, a dense school of blackfish, almost rectangular in overall shape, approaches, a rag bag of winter leaves, strangely agitated at the edges, and I recall Macbeth's:

> Light thickens, and the crows
> Make to the rooky woods.

Peer inside and get a right shock, part of it is a big swimming moray. As the ghastly bundle comes past, its head reaches out, and takes its time pulling the rest of itself down a hole in the reef.

On my way inshore, I'm greeted by the oafish leer of a puffer fish in a lumpy moth-eaten leopard-spotted coat, like an over-the-hill hooker. There's a flurry of sand and a large grouper bolts past my face.

Thoroughly pissed-off now, I peer aggressively into every recess and burrow along its retreat. By a stroke of luck, I see its speckled form lurking in the back of a cave and fire quickly. But it is only a somnolent school of small black-and-white fish, hoping for a quiet night.

Coral can be ugly, but its occasional companion, appropriately described as 'an algal mucilaginous matrix known as palmelloid,' is uglier. Sometimes we come across small coves covered in its octopus-like brown furze, which when prodded turns liverish-pink or a dirty mossy-green, as if the whole area were some dim-witted creature.

I cross a zone bordered by palmelloid and not protected by outer reef: Colossal junkyards, strewn with broken bones, organ pipes, reindeer's antlers — their velvet streaming from them like Spanish moss — and long lines of misshapen heads, stacked with manic neatness.

And all the while, I'm searching for that patch of moving ugliness, which is the grouper itself. If I see it, I must wait till it slips undercover, then before it looks out, try to execute Warner's incredible lightness-of-being leap onto the top of its hiding place, but without that final wobble, even Olympic gymnasts are permitted. The idea being, I already know where it's gone but it doesn't know where I have, and will be consumed with curiosity, until it finds out.

The next part is odder. I must forget all about fish and think only of a giant potato. When I see a portion of one emerge, I must fire instantly, no good arguing *is that a grouper looking out? Looks more like a giant potato. No it doesn't. Yes it does.* It will be gone, in different garb, different direction, or simply be waiting for me to investigate, then swim over my back.

But nothing moves in this graveyard, so I push on. I want to get back – but I want to get back with something. I know I'm going too fast: that easy pace which shrinks distance without my being aware of it and warns the very creature I'm looking for, trouble's on the way.

I begin an argument with myself as tedious and as finicky as any old married couple's. 'You missed the grouper, because you were in too much of a hurry.' 'No, because I allowed myself to be distracted by a puffer fish.' 'But you know that's its job; to perambulate like a barrage balloon in front of caves.' *Enough!* Slow down. But even that must be done slowly. Stay focused. Go the last mile. But as there's only a few yards left -- somewhat pathetic.

A stream of bubbles, suddenly released from a blade of turtle grass, actually give me a fright! Though my thoughts rumble through my head like tanks in the street, I am, in fact, progressing as apprehensively – as a mouse. A cowrie shell pulls its dowdy mantle over brilliant leopard spots – getting ready to go out – or turn-in for the night? Haven't a clue. I am as ignorant as day one.

A coarse-grained hump appears by a Nissen hut shaped coral head, I've seen somewhere before. I fire, even as I continue a mental process, I can't afford to finish. A grouper galumphs away, but stops with a jolt, open barb pressed against his side. I have him!

We both rise, dripping, into the glare of the setting sun, the fish's black pepper-and-ginger spots turning the colour of sand, wishing itself invisible, too late.

As I walk back, I think with a young boy's glee, how many trips down these watery paths have I taken and how slowly the dross of experience has accumulated before Lady Luck deigned to smile.

41 Charles Montague Doughty

Charles Montague Doughty's *Arabia Deserta*, has become our favourite siesta reading, guaranteed to ensure a good snooze.

At a time when English explorers and their ilk were increasingly being cast in the heroic mould, it was refreshing to be introduced to the first whinging Brit, and one who made it a point of style to let the natives give voice back.

Over the years, he's taken a lot of stick for writing in Chaucerian English, but that maybe because much was composed on the back of a camel. No distant steeples or church bells to console him, only the muezzin's call from minarets on the hot desert wind: endless horizons, verticals becoming horizontals, psalms mantras; heroism, submission. And all travellers, having entered into this world of self-forgetting, on being awakened to receive no more than a teaspoon of water, gave thanks to God. But not Doughty. As likely as not, he'd proclaim it not fit to drink.

Another of his sure-fire techniques was to wander off into the Nejd or some such neck of the barrens, get lost, and at the most inappropriate moment, announce he was a Christian.

Inevitably, he ended up guest of the local sheriff. If this didn't suit him, the sheriff was made to realize, here was a case which must needs be seen to be believed, and was bundled-off to the Sheikh. The Sheikh would have normally clamped him in irons and have done with him, but simply had to let the Dhoula, (the much 'unesteemed' representative of the Turks) have a peek.

The Dhoula was no fool either, and realized, here was a gift best returned to sender. The British Consul in Jeddah took up the baton and did what they do so well, packed him off to England with no fuss, where, in relative obscurity, he was able to compile his final list of complaints into his masterpiece, *Arabia Deserta*, which Richard Burton, the greatest mountebank and scholar of them all, called a right well-told tale.

Lawrence of Arabia called Doughty a masochist (a case of the kettle complimenting the pot) but Doughty didn't use words merely to embellish tales of derring-do, but rather to heal the sick (in this case, himself), shed his stutter, cure his shyness, cash-in his social ineptness, in short, get a life. And that he survived the plot, does his hosts – no little credit.

42 Coastguard visit

We wake to a musty smell in the air. Hundreds of camels! All over the dunes and moving north. Flowing through the desert, affirming Flaubert's intuition that the 'exotic', in his case Egypt, with its bellyful of colours, hollering, groaning beasts of burden and robustly defecating donkeys, were but novel adaptions, yet to be understood.

We just have time to make out the black tents, way over towards the foothills, when a herdsman appears atop a dune, and almost jumps out of his skin.

Rix tries to persuade him to have a cup of tea, but he's having none of it, and is off.

As Doughty himself once wrote: 'Every tiding is presently wide blown in all the open tents of a nomad menzil and there is no idle tale that will not ride upon the tongues, light as leaves, of the witless bedhu, to drive the empty hours.' Rix is worried the herdsman will tell the Coastguard, he's seen *Israe-elis* on the beach.

In the event, he's right. At 9.20 am the Major, listening to the BBC's *Music with Mathew*, drops his binoculars and informs us, the Coastguard's coming. We kick over the mugs and hide the sid.

They arrive in a small sandstorm, to see a bunch of chaps at morning ablutions. A lean beak-nosed officer, in weathered fatigues, and King of Jordan headgear (chequered table-cloth, secured by a double cord, maybe once used to hobble camels), leaps out and greets us with time-honoured formality, while remaining outside the shadow of the tent. He requests passports and our Red Sea pass. As we scurry about, his eyes dart here-and-there like a barbary falcon watching a covey of sand grouse in disarray.

Having checked our details, taken-in the set of our rig, and deciding, we seem pretty much bedhu-at-heart, does his party piece. Lays the pass (English version) on the bonnet of his vehicle, and before his gaping entourage translates it slowly into Arabic, reading from right to left.

Then, wishing God's peace upon us, is away like the mercurial hawk to watch once more, the passing of the herds.

The Major chuckled over this incident almost as much as he did over Herzen's account in *My Life in Exile*, when the Tsar's first bureaucrats-cum-secret police, reported on the local flood:

Number of drowned	4
Reason for drowning	2
Total	6

But our problems with the pass aren't over yet. Everyone understood that anyone turning up on the beach without his name on one, could be for the chop. But what about a name on the pass and no such person present? Somebody who'd simply been unable to make it? Lt Mufti considered this was someone who'd scorned the Governor's munificence and benevolence, and should be punished too.

So what about a name, discretely whited-out? Alas, this was more serious still, involving a disappeared person, and required thorough investigation.

"But who would ever try to disappear himself on this God-forsaken coast, I ask you?"

"You," said Barnes.

"Touché," said I, remembering Ali's offer of a goat smuggling boat.

43 'Like locusts we'll come, and we'll go'

As more roads advanced into the Tihama, so did wealth. If you've never been able to afford litter, litter becomes the first sign of conspicuous consumption. The ostentatious glitter of drink cans began it, squashed and piled high outside modest beehive huts and collected by the local Yemenis.

Then came marble-fronted mosques, roundabouts, wayside phones (patronized by the canine community) and volleyball courts (used for threshing). TV aerials sprouted through domed thatch, and genetically engineered sorghum, of a blinding greenness, waved over the once arid desert.

When the bedhu first ventured out of these voracious dunes to picnic on the fresh tarmac, they were decimated. So came speed bumps, catapulting goats and female family members all over the place. Then came traffic lights, and rules not in the Good Book – enjoining males under eleven, not to drive. And of course, more of us: blustery red-faced infidels with naked thighs, and Vimto never cold enough.

Enterprising locals waited for us where the road ended. Pulled us out for a fee. *Like locusts we'll come and we'll go. But God's Will abides.*

Over time, more and more bedhu began to stream along the highways into Jeddah, Mecca and Medinah. Scorned the jungle of high rises (designed by commission men in Geneva), preferring to siesta in the shade of overpasses. And at night to spread themselves under the stars on charpoys (stout wooden beds, bound with date palm) drinking mint tea and passing round the hubbly-bubbly.

It seemed to us that many were becoming gypsies in their own land. Gone for them it seemed, were the sleepy wadis of the Hadramaut and Hejaz, where each day flowed easily into the next, season into season (up to the escarp in summer, down in winter) and 'all the needs of the day met within walking distance of the black tents'. But, as to what they thought was to come, we were clueless.

44 Shaban

One day, we try to get through to the great bay which the old fishermen called Shaban. Big dunes go right down into the sea but we keep slogging on because Ben, our man from the Seychelles, can't swim.

The heat grows so intense, it comes right through our sandals and we turn back.

On the way, we get led astray by the low floating flight of a lesser bustard, which alights on some sticks. As we approach, we see they are two skeletons side by side, knees raised. No hint of how they came to be here do they give. But their sojourn as the dead, turning slowly into sand in this windswept place, seems as appropriate to us, as gravestones in a country churchyard.

Rix warns us never to touch the dead here, as if fearing Warners's knees-up-Mother Brown dance (due to the heat) might be prelude to some inappropriate ritual.

We plod on. Ben, usually so quiet, tells us why he's never learned to swim. Once, playing in the sea, something had touched his leg, and he'd found himself staring at an open eye. An Indian man had suffered a heart attack and was rolling around in the surf.

Shortly after driving off, we come across a string of bedhu girls crossing the dunes on their donkeys. They raise their hands, half in outrage, half in glee and hurry their beasts past us, that is, closer to us. But we know by now, they aren't above falling off and claiming, we'd run over them.

The next time we visited the area, the dunes had shifted and the skeletons had disappeared.

45 Like the tongue avoids the teeth

Windy today. We go out a bit from Eagle Ray Point. Tall dense sea grass, heavy as haystacks, heaves beneath us. Schools of small fish watch us then disappear into it like flocks of birds into standing corn. We retreat to the reef and advance horizontally against the current, using the kelp strands as rope.

I'm about to pack it in, when I find myself almost committing the indiscretion of trying to squeeze past an immense grouper, staring lugubriously seawards; its heaving gill-case, opening and closing in time to the swell. At the last moment, it turns a single eye on me, as big as a traffic light, and *whoomph!* I hear its bones working as half the kelp bed disappears. *Suppose it had been a long-tailed stingray?* Enough is enough.

Speaking of the devil. Back on shore, Rix is standing with one leg in a bucket of hot water. A small stingray, in water not more than four inches deep, had flipped over and stabbed him in the ankle as he was picking up some apples bobbing by a broken crate, labelled Produce of Lebanon.

A pair of Demoiselle cranes come whistling by overhead and land in Flamingo inlet, now filled with driftwood and edged with foam like a giant meringue pie gone wrong.

We go surfing in the big waves coming through the channel, and wonder how the reef-fish put up with being churned around against the reef, day after day. "Like the tongue avoids the teeth" says Leo.

≈

Back up the escarpment, we pull on more clothes, as there's dew on the junipers and a chill in the air.

In the compound, the Recce Hall's deserted, save for the assistant cook, Chowdry, asleep under the ping-pong table. A pane in the big window is also missing. *Strange.*

Walking past the villas is like peeking into the moribund fish tanks of an under-funded municipal aquarium. Two are empty.

In the third, a figure with earphones is energetically jigging about in one corner, as if suffering an atavistic urge to fly.

In Colonel Cufflink's villa, a group is watching a cat lapping up milk. The medic's villa has a Christmas tree, stable and manger, the lot. We bring him a bag of apples and tell him, Rix might be needing some repairs. "Never a dull moment with you lot," he says. "There's people here going out of their way to get themselves fired before they've rubbed two pound notes together. More than my job's worth, I can tell you."

Then Marsden bursts in with something looking like a hatbox. "Ah! The reef-rapers are back, I see! Happy Christmas!" And he's off. In the box is a football, which the medic seems happy to have received.

Later we learn, the recce hall window hadn't been shattered by a football coming over the wall, but during a big punch-up. Someone had snitched on Motor Pool employees, flogging tyres before they needed replacing.

I try to slip in our villa's back door to avoid any more conviviality, but find my way barred by an arm, one end attached to a full tankard, and the other to Rix. "Merry Christmas!" he says heartily. "Get that down ye me handsome!"

"Thanks. But no thanks, really. The medic's waiting to check your ankle. No, thanks. Honestly."

When I've drained the fearsome brew, he shakes his head sadly. "Dundas, you've the will-power of a nit."

46 You want to be saved from dying of shark-bite or not?

Dust devils skim over the land, small squalls pass over the lagoon, hissing like mechanized street-washers. Occasionally they drench us, totally obscuring the surroundings. Then it clears for miles, and hard to believe it ever happened.

The almost season-less months continue to roll by, and the months to become years. When the last leave is too far back to recall, and the next too far ahead to contemplate, we feel like a troupe of actors touring the boondocks. Same old back-drop of open sky, same couple of stage herons in the foreground, same rag-bag of T-shirts to pull on, and same twinge of stage-fright, as we teeter over the reef's drop-off.

But that said, the very routine has moulded us, feet, arms and legs, without our really appreciating it. New arrivals are amazed, how far and fast, we swim underwater.

It went to our heads a bit, and combined with Jack being delayed in bringing back new spear guns from UK, led to us being conned into helping Washington with his beginner's Scuba Course.

During the week, we gave newcomers snorkelling tips in the new pool. They were white as ghosts, keen as mustard, beat the water like paddle-steamers, and we were utterly unable to explain our flipper motion to them. It remained as foreign to them as roller-skating to cats.

Most of them were computer whiz kids, completely over-qualified, with knife-edge creases to their pants and the look of Latter Day Saints, but knew a dead-end career when met head-on. The main problem was that they were expected to keep the restless bedhu glued to their chairs most of the day, instead of first finding out what interested them.

After a few weeks the whiz-kids left, with no fuss.

Then men in white coats arrived to review qualifications, and investigate why the attrition rate kept going up in tandem with the astronomic pay rises. That is, with us receiving pay-packets we

155

didn't deserve, and had us spending more time on planning how to spend them, than on the job.

Then the experts changed tack. Old timers (whose quirks would have normally entitled them to medical attention of the fancier sort) were now deemed to be exhibiting traits not dissimilar to the latest combat aircraft, unstable in level flight, but resilient under prolonged and varied stress. And in some cases, displaying symptoms of benign addiction to contract work, in short, of belonging. And, (mentioning no names) not a few found themselves being discreetly slipped into the newly vacated slots.

In the meantime, Washington distributed his Scuba Course book to us for free. It had a Foreword by Prince Charles, two pages devoted to putting on flippers (so I was finally able to twig why mine kept splitting) and two large photos captioned 'a typical lagoon' and 'a typical reef', in case you got them muddled up after a session on Beer Bottle beach.

Washington also promised, nurses were coming, and swore it had been cleared right to the top. After two weeks we reminded him and he told us, James and Dean were both qualified nurses and life-savers. "You want to be saved from dying of shark-bite or not?"

Then, even in that innocent age of air travel, Jack, by wandering round Heathrow with our new spear guns as if they were a new set of golf clubs, so intimidated the air hostesses, they had them sent to the baggage hold.

When they didn't reappear at Jeddah, Jack went to Lost and Found. This was an old aircraft hanger stuffed to the rafters with camel bags, bursting suitcases, and apparently doubled as the airport hotel for a noisy entrepreneurial breed of Egyptian rat. So he settled for cash-in-lieu and sent us the refund, less expenses.

47 The ocean as womb

So here we are, back in the Red Sea. But instead of splashing about in the shallows under sunny skies with a bevy of nurses and showing off our new spear guns, we're greeted by the B team: a motley collection of undersized grey snappers and grunts, with several goatfish snuffling about beneath them.

They're soon poking their noses into places they normally wouldn't -- as if we were their protectors. For this reason I've always held that a key prerequisite for a successful hunt is to drop off the B team at the earliest opportunity.

This morning the goatfish are the first ones to grow nervous at my resentful posturing. Their delicate colours, as neatly laid out as on a shy student's palette, first day of art class, begin to become muddied. Then, when a mist descends on the water they all move off, but the lads decide to follow them.

They go left, I right.

A very small shark turns up. There's something particularly humiliating in being followed about by a *very* small shark (I even check it isn't a remora). And it takes me a while to accept that it's the sort of thing that could happen to anyone, as when President Carter was attacked by a rabbit, and Bush Junior concussed by a pretzel. But as it seems to think I know where I'm going, the result is we're both soon lost. Eventually, it loses all faith in me, and pisses off.

The next moment I am in a miniature Sargasso sea, full of squirmy creatures going in for sex and procreation in one act, the ocean as womb. Full of fish eggs in clusters, clumps of transparent tapioca and jelly-bean snakes, some over a meter long, all seemingly perambulating purposefully about.

Most are semi-transparent, no doubt to avoid detection, but by the same token, rendering themselves more vulnerable to ultra-violet light. And probably helps explain why they've chosen such a dreary day to congregate.

Some appear to be salps. Though their eating habits are basic (they clog up if food is too plentiful), their life-cycles are sophisticated. One generation perambulates about in daisy-chains, whereas the next prefers to hitch rides on ocean currents. This generation then rests up in fecund calms to breed, changes sex, and travels on to seek new partners and adventures. I'm told the species is older than Methuselah, and long before we came down from the trees, were criss-crossing the world's oceans, and avoiding the empty spaces 'where feasts were few and famines plentiful.'

Eventually, I spy the others making their way back. Lambourski clambers out first, draped in glistening bandoliers like Pancho Villa after crossing the Colorado River. He empties the sack on the reef and out spills a scattering of salps, a red snapper, a large dark brown saddleback, violet-specks still flickering, and a bream.

Before Warner condescends to tell me how the B team led them to the only clear patch of water for miles around, I have to submit to a bollocking — for being a snob. Then all he says is, "Like Piccadilly Circus, it was. Even Leo got a fish."

"But where was it?"

"Not sure we could find it again. It was like Aladdin's cave. Didn't last long, either." So that's that.

Suddenly we hear a shout from Pitsos, whom we've forgotten all about, "Big permit! No twitching!" And he's gone beneath the surface. We jump back in, and swim through the soupy goo to deep water.

The sea erupts over a wide area. Scores of thin dorsal fins and scimitar tails, break the surface. For a moment, I see ghostly white banners waving, deep down. We hear a strange sound, but can't say it exactly lends enchantment to the ear, as it turns out to be Pitsos humming the Tennessee Waltz through his snorkel.

"Hundreds of them," he says. "Like being dropped into the middle of a troupe of ballerinas during May Day celebrations. Just when I was beginning to think it was a bit of alright, the Great Leader must have given an order. Everything speeded up. I turned round to see what caused it, but there was nothing. I turned back and they were gone. Just like that," And clicks his fingers.

48 Matavai Bay

We're sitting on the reef watching sea birds whipping by, and tugs-of-war between small green wrasse, while Steve tells us more tales of his dad's travels.

He's done America and had our Country Cousins rolling their eyes. I wish I could remember the interesting things discussed, but it's the silliest I remember, don't ask me why. He arrived in Grand Central station, and gave the black porter a handful of change. The man dramatically tossed it onto the marble floor, proclaiming, "You're in the big city now!" And so thrilled him, he jogged the whole way to the Bowery, or so he claimed, where his brother worked in the Catholic Worker Soup Kitchen. When he knocked on the door, the man said "No soup after 11. I've told you before." He almost got arrested in Chicago because a nail in the seat of the Greyhound bus, had ripped his pants, and didn't notice, till the windy city told him. And in LA, he believed the man who informed him, the Westwood Mormon Temple was Frank Sinatra's house.

Today, his dad's on his way to Aussie, and he's dropped off in Tahiti with two mates, honest Aussie lads, who believed they could get bit parts in the current *Mutiny of the Bounty*.

This version was rumoured to be a murky drama in black-and-white, with the natives looking much as they did in the daguerreotypes and copperplates of old; and themselves hoping to be part of a small band of murderous tars, flint-locks at the ready, lured into the forest by hallucinatory glimpses of dusky maidens bathing in shady pools. But ended up, confronted by a single crone who promised them the acquaintance of more lasses with shivering hips, clad only in tree bark, if they returned with a bag-of-nails, apiece. No problem. But if they brought muskets, or company, they'd be barbequed by men tattooed like pythons. Fair enough.

Whether this was script or fantasy, Steve doesn't say. In any event, his dad finished up being sprayed with brown paint and rowing the longboat all day, while one Aussie sat in the stern, wearing a cocked hat, assailing him with unseemly banter about the cat-o-nine tails and walking the plank.

Then, there was a change of plan. The film was to become family entertainment, highlighted by a great dance at Matavai Bay on Bastille Day, when the sun also set over Moorea's loftiest peak.

But cost overruns soon brought down the Moguls from Hollywood, and time-wasting debates, whether bougainvillea arrived with Captain Bougainville and rotten teeth with the ship's crew, shelved. False teeth, once in then out, were in again. Then it was declared, though the Pope had fig-leafed Michelangelo's David, Hollywood would never brassiere Africa (and why should Sweden be permitted to corner the bare-breast market?)

The Artificers of Taste ended up with the same obsessive concerns as the City Fathers of Holy Rome: Nipples. Not in their case whether Adam had them, but were these dusky maidens, with their strangely white breasts, to be allowed to flaunt theirs?

The City fathers had finessed their problem with tendrils of the vine, and now the moguls' minions did theirs, with skin-coloured bras, leis of frangipani and safety-pins.

A few minor irritants remained. All sea-fronting palms with aluminium bands (to prevent coconut crabs climbing up) had to be hurriedly painted matt grey, to stop them glinting in sun. (This was in the days when some of the public complained, they'd seen an impatient centurion glancing at his Timex watch.) Then on Bastille Day, a chief banned from the V.I.P stand for being in bare feet, returned with sandals painted on, to resounding cheers.

The great day's festivities passed without a hitch. Then as the last of the tamure dancers wound their graceful way under the palms and the drums finally fell silent, Tarita came down the beach to paddle a pirogue (taboo for unmarried women) across the lagoon.

As the sun's rays were scattered over the heavens, the Bounty came past in full sail. Over the taffrail, Fletcher Christian was brooding. On raising his eyes, he caught sight of Tarita, and something of that look, which may have set the original tragedy in motion, passed between them, or would have, had not two snorkels, closely followed by two goggled-gentlemen from Geelong Surf Club popped up between them. They clambered onto the reef and began to leap about, waving and cheering the Bounty on her way. But when abused by loud- hailer in no less than three languages, popped quickly down again.

49 The Russian Listening Post

Before returning up the escarpment today, we take a quick run down to Gizan.

There's a change around Black Mountain. Someone has shaved the top off a nearby peak and is building a villa.

The new road south has enough lampposts on it to light an Olympic stadium. It also runs just close enough to the pristine beaches to give one an annoying sense of future urban encroachment, but no doubt to the locals, one of more comforts to come: shady kiosks, warm kebabs and iced sherbets, specially for the ladies after permitting the sea to take such liberties with their persons.

Further south, the highway bypasses Gizan, and a terrific stench hangs over the desert like an invisible fog. We turn off briefly to look at the market.

In an immense open hangar, loads of grey mullet are being swung in the air, dumped and go slithering over the concrete. Powerful hoses spray heaps of gape-mouthed grouper and barracuda up-ended in tall baskets, some bent like starting handles. Here was all the boisterous activity of booming commerce. We accepted that it gave employment to Jaffri's extended family and many more, and that we were a tiny bunch of visiting elitist sportsmen, but wondered how long it could last, gaped impotently and drove away.

Because of the tremendous increase in leisure traffic and as no road had yet made it over the lava beds, the Corps of Engineers laid down a hard by Black Mountain.

Over time, the inshore current shifted, and where there'd been white sand and clear water, thousands of pebbles now groaned underfoot. Conscientious families buried their garbage well back from the beach, but camels and small foxes rooted it up. In time, the whole international camping area, became a hell-hole of goat's gristle, flies and tattered pennants of grey plastic.

The Russians built a Listening Post directly across the Sea, in the Dhalak islands. Graders appear on our side, reburied the garbage deeper, and laid down vast tracks all the way to Ras Ahmed, erstwhile domain of turtles and wild sea grasses.

A Saudi Listening Post was established on the Point. And inland of Black Mountain, behind an impressive wire-mesh fence, one or two pink and blue cabanas, sprouted on the austere face of the lava.

North of the last lava beds, lay our own area of sleepy lagoons and windswept dunes, as yet undisturbed, and seeming more precious than ever.

50 The great barracuda becomes our Totem

8 a.m. We gaze at the sea. A few pelicans are out, and one or two waders, bobbing, side-stepping and dashing about on the kelp top.

"The school's about a hundred and fifty yards long, from the edge of the Grouper's Playground going north," says Lambourski. "About three or four yards wide and not more than three feet beneath the surface."

"You're having me on," says Devrill-Smith.

"No great mystery. The pelicans come by every morning, regular as clockwork on their way to Shaban. Only if they see a good school here, do they bother to plonk down. Unlike their Mexican cousins, they're more scoopers than divers. The fish know this and keep just below scooping range. The pelicans then disperse themselves along the whole school, so if any portion gets stirred up, one at least will pick up on it.

"Their chief is opposite us, has a white patch on his back and tends to follow us around. When travelling, he doesn't always lead, but likes to lie in another's slipstream, a bit like a wily Mexican burro using a younger one's tail as a fly-swat. Also, the porpoises, we saw earlier, were playing rather than hunting, so I'm guessing not too much big stuff is around, yet."

No sooner has Lambourski finished showing off, than a commotion starts way off on the left. The pelicans fly to the place, and by the time we arrive, are going round and round like bumper-cars at a fair.

When we arrive, two powerful looking horse-eye jacks are rushing up and down beside an unravelling school of fish, which twists this-way-and that like a tormented sea-serpent.

Pitsos is about to have a go at the first jack, when a barracuda turns up. Warner could have shot the jack there and then, but thought Pitsos was going to. Pitsos thought the barracuda might grab the horse-eye once he'd shot it, so nobody did anything.

The jacks leave, the barracuda fades into invisibility and the pelicans take off for Shaban. And when the B team turns up, we shamelessly leave Warner to deal with his fan club, and head into deeper water.

I should mention here that our attitude to barracuda hasn't changed much since Pitsos was on about 'the dancers of Yap not eating them, lest they acquired the dumb stare of the fish', and the following incident occurred. Barnes, returning from an evening's bird-watching, was greeted by unusual confusion: Steve whinging that someone had left a milk carton in the sun, myself complaining, the fish tasted peppery, and Leo waving a smoke-blackened fork about, urging him to get stuck in 'before it was all gone.'

Then Warner rolled over clutching his belly and Barnes yelled, "Stop eating, everybody. It's Ciguatera!" When Leo carried on eating, Barnes attempted to throw his plate into the sea. And when Leo tried to explain that he'd just passed 'the true friend's test', Barnes finally got the message, and threw his plate into the sea anyway. At the time, I thought it was the funniest thing since Mr. Bean.

However, none of this was on my mind that sunny morning, as we moved into deeper water.

The lagoon sloped gradually down till we came to a sudden drop-off, revealing depths for which we were unprepared.

Long beams of almost vertical light flickered in time to our flipper motion as if from high windows, with ravines and gullies far below, bathed in an eerie blue light.

Steve and I saw a dark form edge into the light. Then I noticed Lambourski about twelve feet down, and a few yards away, a tremendous barracuda. He trundled past it, as if pretending it wasn't there. I could sense his trepidation, and perhaps the barracuda did too, because it began to advance. Only then did I remember, he didn't shoot them, never mind eat them. The fish continued forward as if Lambourski's new diver's watch, glittering like a Christmas tree bangle, now sparked its interest.

Then Warner advanced and as it weather-vaned towards him, fired. The barracuda hadn't made more than a foot before Pitsos's spear smacked into it, mid-riff. It spun inside a vortex of foam, as they dragged it backwards inch by inch. Never before had I seen our lot perform with such chilling efficiency.

Back on shore, Steve took some photos. Although it needed two of us to lift it off the ground, exultation quickly died down. We were now so much masters of that inert mass of flesh, it signified little, other than a living creature, which once patrolled the blue sea with all the cold beauty of a freshly drawn sword, no longer did.

Later, Lambourski grilled us barracuda steaks (touch of butter, garlic and squeeze of lime) and seeing no ill effects, actually joined in.

Since that day, we've never again confronted those aloof totemic presences, which loom up to inspect their domains, then fade away. But when Warner asked me what I meant by totemic, I hadn't a clue. Yet from somewhere inside me, came an answer of sorts.

In shooting the great barracuda, we'd essentially called its bluff. And though such confrontations were no longer dangerous, the consequences were. We'd simply require another challenge, and so on.

It was the 'and so on', which worried me. And whenever we saw one after this, this was the message it conveyed.

51 Warner suffers his first attack in the Red Sea

Warner rarely gives advice, but today must have been too much for him. Like an itch one has to scratch, he says, "You take far too long." Fair enough.

He's brought in a good-sized talang, one of four; the other three having come around me, then sped away. I could have said that one is sometimes easier than three, but it wasn't just that. As they came in, caudal scutes bristling (stubby turbine blades in front of the tail), they looked magnificent and so easy to shoot, I simply said 'Next time, next time,' till of course there was no next time.

I notice this excuse in my diary: 'If I like looking at them, more than shooting them, then obviously I can't do both,' which I guess is another way of saying, being greedy for both sensations, I'm simply reluctant to make up my mind.

That afternoon, we were trundling along about ten feet above the reef, when Warner, up-ended himself to check his mask. At the same instant, a large peppery-speckled grouper came rushing along the rim of the reef and, like a pig-with wings, went straight for him. I felt sure it would bolt away the moment it saw me, but instead, grabbed his ankle like a demented mastiff, didn't like what it had got hold of, spat it out and bolted back into the deep. Warner bobbed up and down. "What the futstt!" he spluttered.

Only later, when he saw the large red brushstroke across his ankle, did he realize he'd suffered his first attack in the Red Sea.

In the evening, the wind rises. The fire rips and flares, and picks out a small dhow looming out of the dark. In it are the two old fishermen, who visited us not long ago. They tell us there's a storm on the way, and we should move back.

In the confusion of our retreat, Steve poured what he thought were the last drops of wine into the remains of the chicken stew.

When Rix offered our guests what Steve no doubt imagined to be a tasty *coq-au-vin,* he got a whiff of kerosene and whipped it back.

Devrill-Smith, mortified by this unseemly breach of etiquette, rose immediately to bring over his reserve rations. At this, the older man leaned forward as if to utter some deferential and time-honoured civility, but instead murmured. "Mafi Kerosene. Whiskey."

Devrill-Smith, who had no idea this was now pretty much a standard joke, appeared so shocked, the older man lowered his eyes and his side-kick, forwent repeating it, reached for the binoculars and began an earnest scrutiny of the scudding clouds. Later Devrill-Smith saw in this incident, the discriminating hand of Allah, whereas Steve considered it more the work of a mischievous Djinn.

When our two guests departed next morning, Rix offered them the talang, which even he admits he's never got the knack of cooking properly, but knows they like to cure by hanging from the mast on long journeys. In return, they gave us some sultans and small tasty grunts, known as *yam yam*.

52 Locusts, termites and ants

We settled slowly into the Tihama's seasons. In March, brief sandstorms whipped along the coast, white-capping the sea yet leaving it, beneath the surface, clear as a snow-fed river.

Calm days came in high summer and we expected it to be clear too, but parts of the lagoon became feisty brews of micro-organisms, hot as bath tubs.

One of the constituents was *Paramecium bursaris.* Under the microscope it looks like a miniature hairbrush and when it runs out of food, simply sunbathes, its green parts taking their energy directly from the sun. Another constituent was *Trichodesmium erythema*, which turns the sea rose madder, possibly giving the Red Sea its name.

More important were the vast algal mats which spread themselves over the tidal flats and when decomposing, gave off *dimethyl sulphide.* Its molecules can form the nuclei of raindrops, and some say, the scent helps guide migrating seabirds to the crustacean and algal-rich areas, rather than the dry and dusty ones.

None of us slept any more under the awning, and one evening I happily copied into my diary Peter Fleming's brief exultation from *Travels in Tartary:* 'Have no further need to sleep under the obscurely irritating confines of a roof.' (That is, when he wasn't running-off to the Consul.) And next morning, my own brief conceit was capped by a two minute drenching, which however, left us dry again in ten and equally surprised.

That same evening, something began wriggling in the ground beneath us. Small grasshoppers hatched out, whizzed about energetically enough, but didn't appear to be going any place.

We lit a lamp and placed it on a dune. After a while, two small frogs appeared out of nowhere, and proceeded to dine on quick-fry, ricocheting hoppers.

Gaspar produces some sid, and tells us how these little critters evolved millions of years ago on the banks of many a wandering Nile. Hatched every three, five or seven years (as in the bible) and in increasing prime-number intervals, eventually leaving predators like birds and mice, little hope of locking into 'the years of plenty.'

After several moults, and the right vegetation, the hoppers may reach a critical mass. Then, if they bump into each other enough, become party animals and bite each other's shanks. The incentive to move accelerates, and they morph into that wind of stones, the awesome airborne cavalry of the locust swarm.

In the African Rift Valley, there's a lake whose ancient name means 'death to locusts' because of its strong contrary winds. In a Moroccan cave, they've also found old paintings of a locust God, and in the Canary Islands, one of the oldest locust figurines in the world, prompting speculation they may have played a part in man's early migrations: manna from heaven to some, and the devil incarnate to those of a more settled disposition.

But our own pathetic hoppers hardly rate in the Tihama's social calendar compared to crab-night, when they come down the beach in their hundreds, build sandcastles to attract the females, and swim-off in the direction of Sand Island. Or beetle night, when we're sniped at from dusk-to-dawn by invisible pea-shooters. And Mooney termite-wedding nights, when termites flop about all over the place, shedding wings like graduates clothes at the end of a frat party.

The newly-mated queens waste no time burying themselves and laying eggs. And their progeny are soon knawing driftwood (which their bacteria digest) and extending the termitry, urged on by pheromones, pumped like martial music through the queen's new corridors of power.

Soon, partially zonked-out bed-chamber attendants are dispatched with a sophisticated mix of cocktails to tackle problems of design and strategy.

Some workers build towers and seem to know when to start the arches. As a lot of termite architecture above ground is concerned with temperature regulation, its design and style depends upon a lot of factors: its east-west orientation, the sun's elevation, wind direction and speed etc. An even more complex mix of inputs may be involved, with regard to the positioning of exits in the event of attack, and in the last resort, when to wall-in the queen herself.

In Africa, some termites go down thirty five feet or more, bringing up water to irrigate fungal plots. The fungi link up with neighbouring root systems, and help bind sand-and-silt together, protecting the trees from being swept away in storms and flash floods.

"But all work and no play, makes Jack a dull boy, eh Jack?" says Gaspar suddenly. "And soon enough there's another termite wedding breakout."

Jack, I forgot to mention (most of his debts paid off), is paying us a social visit. Though he's promised to be on his best behaviour, at this very moment he's in the process of getting a praying-mantis tipsy. It's swaying about on the rim of his mug like a holy-roller at a rival prayer-meeting. And Gaspar's not amused.

But *surprise, surprise!* Jack picks up the offending insect and deposits it carefully on a dune by the lamp -- where it's promptly gobbled up by a frog.

That taken care of, Gaspar powers on: from termites to ants, to acacias, only stopping once, to disentangle a hopper from his own hair. "What I'm getting at", he says, "Is, if ants and termites work so well with bacteria, why not with each other *and* the acacias? They do. Ants and termites do it by not getting in each other's way, ha, ha! Ants work the day-shifts, and termites the night (they have tender skin and must avoid drying out).

Bacteria engage with all parties. They help the acacias, by fixing the nitrogen under the soil (unscrewing its triple-bond). In return, the acacias give the bacteria access to surplus carbohydrates and gum-arabic. It's a deal, analogous to being given cold beer for fixing the fridge.

The ants raise mushrooms, and carry round bacteria on their undersides (as antibiotics) to prevent fungus intruding. If the fungus gets the upper hand, they don't boost the dose, as we tend to do, but dump the crop, and start over.

"Some fungi attract ambrosia beetles, who deposit spores in holes they bore in the trunk. When the spores fruit, their pungent truffle-like odours attract gourmet rodents, who burrow into the humus, aerate it, deposit faeces and urine, and generally improve the compost."

"Sure," says Jack, extracting a hopper, frog-paddling across his sid. "And the ants get high on magic mushrooms, and listen to termite rap."

"No joking", says Warner. "Remember the ticking we used to hear at night sometimes, coming from those elevated subways on the acacia's trunk?"

"Don't get too carried away," cautions Gaspar. "I'm not saying, it's Woodstock or one big happy family, it isn't. Ants and termites march to different drums, and sometimes go to war. We can't hear the ants' martial music, because they employ a caterpillar combo, whose vibrations are too small for us to pick up on. But when the caterpillar's sucker feet clasp certain hollowed-out branches, the sounds are amplified. And when a caterpillar's ribbed antennae strum in alarm against its thorax's chitin leading-edge, the ants immediately rush to its aid. Speed is vital, because a single caterpillar, rearing-up and displaying menacing eye-spots, is only a short-term deterrent to a social wasp intent on laying eggs."

"But what's in it for the ants?" asks Jack.

"Good question." Says Gaspar generously. "Once they've seen-off the attacker, the caterpillar extrudes tiny papillae (like a cow's udders) which, when stroked, produce an ambrosia, the ants find irresistible."

"Just like here and all, then," says Jack. "The Saudi family-tree employs us to assist in its defence, pays us in petro-dollars from underground while we hunker down behind high walls, distilling our own ambrosias, and only upper-echelon employees are allowed sex."

Suddenly, with a roar like a passing train, something comes out of the night and races across the lagoon, charges up the beach in a whirlwind of ghostly white sand and stops dead in its tracks. Lies there like a flatulent sea slug. But nothing emerges. Then it rises, roars back over the lagoon, parting the kelp over the reef, giving it a scalp massage, and disappears the way it came.

"Holy Moses!" Says Leo, "That's one noisy toy, I wish they'd kept in the box."

53 "What a great hunter you are!"

I liked to feel that in our spear-fishing, we were returning to our prehistory as hunters, but in a novel environment. Barnes was pretty much in agreement, though he expressed it somewhat differently: we were tourists, with spearguns in place of cameras.

At this time, as I wasn't even sure whether pygmies were people or chimpanzees and wasn't about to ask Barnes, I decided to look into this matter of early gatherer-hunters myself. And soon had my work cut out perusing ancient tomes from the defunct British library.

I learned that pygmies were the little people of the forest, who held its soul to be benign, provided they lived there half the time, and shared what they had with it. If they didn't, they might be better-off, but no longer be pygmies.

In a special forest clearing, an old crone was allowed to bollock a seriously incompetent alpha, and then organize the young women to make the large hunt net. If the hunters failed to make good use of it, they forfeited the pleasure of the young maidens' upper thighs. And all this, long before the Greek play *Lysistrata,* and the famous Herero women of South Africa refused to bear the children of men who'd accepted German oppression.

The pygmies traded with the Bantu (the blacks), generally deferred to them, and pretended to be scared of their shamans, while taking secret delight in showing their children, it was not exactly so.

The Akoa pygmies sometimes hunted elephants, but only after the long pondering of auguries and careful planning.

With the Mbuti pygmies, it was only one elephant and the task of a single hunter. He followed it and covered himself with its dung. When the situation felt right, he moved under its belly, stabbed deep once, then in rapid succession, like an attack of hornets. If all went to plan, the elephant raised its trunk, taking care not to stamp its feet, and headed for water. The hunter then returned to camp, holding his spear pointed downwards all the way. The elders could then tell which organs had been hit and whether the elephant would live or die. If the latter, it would be tracked. When found, its belly was usually hugely distended.

Another hunter then cut out a small patch of skin, layer by layer. Tiny portions of the raw meat were passed around, and none too tasty at that. When the final plug was removed, the intestines ballooned-out and were bitten into by the successful hunter's youngest son. It was a gross and disgusting moment, which also released spontaneous outbursts of *schadenfreude* (pleasure at another's discomfort) and also compassion, those little twin leaps of the heart which keep us human. And as we've all probably met the little brat who has to tell you who his dad is, gave everyone the option of holding their noses should he later choose to exercise bragging rights. After the mums rallied round and cleaned up the little tyke, a great feast was held to give thanks, not to the hunter, but the elephant.

On the other side of the world, in similar forests, lived the Dyaks, who never uttered the name of the prey they were hunting, but like the pygmies, gave great parties, which we duly noted.

But my notions about the Yanomani of the Amazon were probably completely wrong, thanks mainly to Napoleon Chagnon's take on them.

We all knew, the Masai of the African savannahs were herders, who hunted for status, but not that in hard times when they had to gather, became Dorobos, whom they liked to pretend were another tribe."

We knew the Eskimos of the furthest north, had to hunt for everything, as there was next-to-nothing to gather, except on carefully timed occasions, shellfish in tunnels under the ice.

Their God's prognostications were brief and to the point. 1. Shit happens. 2 Worse shit happens. And they survived by a mix of compulsory patience, pragmatism and a sense of humour: 'Lend wife for knife, and end up with wife and knife, ha, ha!'

All this we learned from the writing of a Victorian-era Frenchman, who knew how to pass the piss pot round an igloo in the dark.

Our favourite tribe was the Ik (we pronounced it Yuck) from Northern Kenya. They'd been driven into impossibly harsh terrain for hunting and herding (but not hiding, other's cattle). And had developed a philosophy beyond live and let die: relieve the dying of their last morsel of food and run off, giggling, at which the dying person joined in, not wishing to be deprived of the last laugh. *Hard to believe.*

The Aborigines of Australia weren't on my map. When six and a half, a sweet old missionary had given us a slide-show on Africa, and caused great hilarity, when he put the rhinoceros in, upside-down. And we were thrilled at being invited (for a nominal contribution) to give baptismal names to pickaninnies. Saints' names were encouraged, Winston and Victoria permitted, but not Sambo.

I read that the Kalahari bushmen made tiny fires, and wasted nothing. Were sharers by necessity, but not above avoiding that obligation should opportunities arise.

They were extremely thoughtful about their prey, but failed to get a handle on their worst predator, humans. They were partial to leisure, discussing a really good murder, and spent a lot of time filling the world around them with a complex network of relationships, in which little was excluded. It was a magic world, pretty hard for us to understand today, where the stars, praying mantises, and even the wretched thorn bushes, had animate life, and could express the most sensitive and sociable feelings.

But what particularly grabbed me, here and now, was how they had much the same problem with their steenbuck (a small antelope) as we did with our purple-and-brown groupers on the far reefs.

Sometimes these grouper were sitting duck, and at others impossible to hit. The bushman's steenbuck too, sometimes stands quietly besides its hiding place, and the bushman, who has come to shoot it (in his own words) 'finds there is a steenbuck person behind him who, feeling he is looking nicely at the little buck, makes him act nicely and prettily too. He fits the arrow to his bow and aims to shoot. The steenbuck person behind him pulls his arm and makes him miss. This is the magic of the steenbuck. It has a steenbuck person to protect it.'

If I understood this aright, the bushman's world was animated by an ethical power all around him, and worked something like this: If he missed the steenbuck (never mind how careful he was) he wasn't meant to hit it. If he did hit it, that was okay too, provided the steenbuck's spirit was subsequently released, as ritual prescribed.

We, on the other hand, were in a slightly different position. We could hit our purple-and-brown grouper, and still be wrong. Do everything right and still miss.

So my idea was to combine our approach with the bushman's. That is, decide if it was the right thing to do. *Did we need it? Was it a mature fish? Were there any shark prowling around, etc?* But once in range, no more dithering about, just pull the trigger. I called it the Zen approach, as it sounded good.

The next stage was to put it into practice.

≈

The day this took place, started well enough. When Warner and I arrived at Eagle Ray Point, waves were buffeting its smooth rock walls, so we hung about in the kelp. Soon five large, hunting pompano arrived, no doubt hoping to pluck crabs off the rock face. We moved behind a basalt pillar, expecting them to pass before us, but they never did. We tracked back along the reef then swam out to the next one, hoping to meet them again.

After a time, I noticed Warner gazing seawards, probably suffering from that adolescent spear-fisherman's malady, the big-fish syndrome, usually caused by nothing more than a big fish rising from the depths, peering briefly at you, before returning whence it came. But the damage is done. You've become infected with expectations, which a single moment of sober reflection would deem unwarranted. And foregoing which, you neglect the food-gathering task and frequently return to camp, empty-handed and disgruntled.

I draw up to Warner, all prepared to bring up the ticklish subject. He flips up his mask and I can sense something's on his mind. "This is utter bollocks!" he says, "Let's try somewhere else." Without more ado, we haul ass out to the third reef.

No sooner do we arrive at a narrow pass than we're greeted by not one, but two big green groupers.

We waste no time. I select one, Warner the other. I run through my Zen approach precepts: They're mature fish, no shark about, and so on. It's all systems go.

As I close the gap on my fish, I hear an imaginary Pitsos whispering encouragement in one ear. *'No mucking about. Move in. Shoot!'* And in the other, a grouper person, *"What a great hunter you are! Your spear's not a foot away. Talk about shooting fish in the barrel. Go ahead maestro. Fire!'*

Contrary forces drag my flippered-feet one way, my spear arm another, but the saddleback is master of them all. And we remain for an indeterminate time locked in a dance as formal and intimate as a tango. Then things take a turn for the worse. I notice Warner gliding in on his fish below me. One moment he's there, the next he's flipped head-over-heels by a wave passing overhead, mask going one way, snorkel another.

When I retrieve his gear, he says indignantly. "Punched my lights out, it did."

On the long slog back, despite our having picked up two bream in the lagoon, he's strangely quiet, and his head is set at an odd angle. When I suggest that both the wind and tide in the channel might have changed at the same time, he blurts out. "And the groupers weren't dark brown, either."

"A total balls up." I have to admit.

≈

Back at camp, we hand over our catch almost apologetically, but Lambourski's well-pleased. "How about steamed-bream in goat cheese with Chateau Khamis, June vintage?" *Two months old! A tribute to the Major's patience, but obviously not his own, as it's already half-finished.* "We've already had a nip", he adds quite unnecessarily. "Have a swig! My kid's had his annual hospital check-up, and is now, one hundred percent."

"Congratulations! Why didn't you tell us? Might have been able to bring you back a big saddleback."

After hearing our tale of woe, he offers Warner another swallow. "Do your head good. Don't worry, there's plenty more." Warner drains it, drops it in the sand, mutters something about missing the *nutty piquance*, and takes no further part in proceedings.

As Leo and I put paid to the next bottle, I ask Barnes if he thinks the green and the brown saddlebacks, are each a different species, or merely colour variations. Apparently, it's a subject he, Pitsos, and Gaspar have long pondered. "The green, being the most sea trout-like, "he goes on," are probably the first to colonize distant reefs and the lagoons of remote atolls. The dark brown, verging on purple, hunt in a reef's deeper gullies. And the orange ones with black spots (often called emperors), lurk in the tunnels of the reef face."

"Thank you Barnsey," I say. "You've given me a lot to think about."

But he's not done yet. "The two you met today (he called them 'the couple'), were probably sequential hermaphrodites, an advantage, since any single fish on an isolated reef, doesn't have to wait for a member of the opposite sex to arrive. Any two can breed up, swapping roles, and becoming a formidable hunting pair, to boot."

I thank him for illuminating the darkness of my ignorance, but he's now noticed a black-headed gull among the herring gulls which shouldn't be there, and I'm left staring at my favourite, old one leg, court the wind, bluff his companions then drop a piece of bream guts into the dry kelp, minimum safe-distance from us. There he begins to preen, ending up like us, an aficionado of sunsets. Only when the rest of the screeching gulls move down current, does he tuck in.

On picking up my book, I come to this passage:

> The old bushman Magae spoke with a
> tremor in his voice. He could not understand why
> they must not shoot the animals which they used to
> eat for food and which the white man does not eat.
> Why he asked. I could only answer because we
> like to look at them.

All of a sudden, I feel the urge to honour the bushman, father of us all, as he brought the eland out of the pitiless Kalahari to feed his tiny band. (Barnes tells me it was more likely to be a gemsbuck, the Eland being too heavy). However, he soon enters into the spirit of the thing, and is waxing eloquent on the Mbuti pygmies' skill in hunting their own forest game: the Lendu, Sindula and Sondu. And this sing-song bestiary, far from irritating me, as it normally would, makes me feel we're one big happy family.

Lambourski brings over the bream, simmering in cheese, forked tails sticking out, and all lightly garnished with specks of wood-ash.

I recall the words of Isaak Walton, Vol. II. "Come, good scholar. This troutie, all twenty two inches of it, when flushed with marigold on its belly, looked pretty enough, but methinks it looks better in this good sauce".

Warner opens one eye then closes it.

"Think he'll be alright?" asks Leo.

"Be right as rain in the morning," I say. "Head-butting's something of his speciality, but in this case the shock, is mainly psychological, like scoring an own goal." Sure enough, in about two minutes, he's tucking in with the rest of us.

"What about the Zen approach?" Pitsos asks me later.

"More work to be done, I'm afraid. Have to read Vol. III. *Zen Approach to a Windy Day,* ha, ha!" And raise my glass to toast the bushman.

Old one leg, alarmed by my sophomoric elbow-raising, takes off.

≈

Next time we come across the saddleback in the pass, our Zen teachers don't want to know us. "Sensible move," says Warner, and I remembered that Natural History was to him, studying the opposition and their skill, his measure of respect for them.

54 The end of a super highway

"Heard the latest?" Asks Marsden, turning audibly on his new leather barstool.

"But no doubt we will," says Pitsos. "So let's have a couple of sid-and-cokes and a Kamikaze, and you'll have our undivided attention."

"This will really put an end to your Red Sea capers!" says Marsden enthusiastically. "The Wadi Ghawan Road has gone."

"What do you mean, gone?"

"Washed out. Kaput."

"Bullshit! We've just been watching the news on the new TV: The Royals waddling around like emperor penguins, exactly as they always do, a fire in Tennessee, the first half of a ski-jump ending in mid-air. McEnroe shaking hands with somebody, and floods in Mozambique. Absolutely nothing on floods in the Kingdom."

"According to Islam, the world is divided into two zones", Marsden continues dryly, "*dar-al-harb*, the zone of strife, and *dar-as-salam*, where peace reigns – or haven't you twigged?"

"How'd you find out?"

"Grapevine me old mate." He hands over the bottle. "An ex-RAF Flight Surgeon, just back from a helicopter over-flight with Dr. Metwalli, told me, all the bridges are down."

≈

Two weeks later, we turned off the new coastal highway on the way to Gizan, to take a look. There was little enough to see. A bleak gravel mound spread itself over the wadi. The sides, though dense with stricken shrubbery, were pleasantly drowsy with the cooing of turtledoves. We soon came to a stretch of undulating tarmac, lifted from some place further up the wadi, and gently laid before us as if by an amused, but powerful Djinn.

In the distance we see the pitted stumps of concrete pillars, but no bridges. In the shadow of one, stands the gaunt figure of a goatherd like an Old Testament prophet gazing at yet another vanity of man, with an updated caste of dodgy characters lurking just off-stage: over-confident engineers, rip-off middlemen, impatient authorities, plus the contribution of smuggled goats. (The last, fine for pruning old growth, but disastrous for new shoots).

We didn't dally, as we didn't particularly want to meet old henna-beard, who would no doubt, hold us personally responsible for the whole mess.

≈

A new super-highway to go up the escarp, was begun at Mutlag (between Wadi Adam and Al Lith), and the Wadi Ghawan returned to its former sleepy ways.

And the old one, 'like driving between LA and Vegas', as Lambourski once put it, disappeared under a carpet of spice-scented milkweed and the pink blooms of rock-breaking *Adenium arabicum*, where God had so summarily swept it.

55 "How does the barracuda close the gap?"

10.30 AM. A single cloud hangs over the sea. Under it, a dark blue shadow floats like a sleeping whale, a large school of silversides.

"Clever," says Gaspar. "Let's go check the little critters out."

We've already been swimming for several hours and it's not what Barnes and I had in mind at all. "Hang on a mo," says Barnes. "We don't even know whether there's a barracuda with them yet. We could be flogging a dead horse, and off on another wild-goose chase."

But Gaspar is made of sterner stuff. "If we see a barracuda before we've hidden, it'll probably mean it's already seen us. Just what we don't need."

And instead of traipsing out over the lagoon, he starts working his way along behind the reed beds. Every so often he looks up at the cloud, probably calculating the path of its shadow across the lagoon, no doubt using some advanced mathematical formula involving the sun's trajectory and wind speed. I get the feeling we're going to have plenty of time to mull things over.

I'd also never gotten around to telling him about barracuda targeting malingerers and parasites, because it had been too hard to get close.

Over time I'd lost interest in the problem; put mullet, silversides and juvenile jack all in the same basket and forgotten about them. Now I saw my mistake. Young jack, mullet and barracuda, grow apace. Silversides get left behind. A great barracuda, requiring a square meal of silversides, will need new tactics.

As we chuntered along, I also recalled the first day, we met shark here. However many there actually were, hadn't been enough to stop the corralled prey school from unravelling along the kelp. And, as any couch-potato knows today, it often takes several tuna, seals and even orcas, to keep such a school up-and-spinning like meat-loaf on a spit. So how could a single territorial barracuda hope to control the ends, middle and underbelly of such a school, by the power of one?

When we reach the place Gaspar's selected for his spy-out, the school looks even more impressive, ballooning and churning from within like a small erupting volcano.

We watch the sun climb slowly into the sky, but no barracuda appears. Then I remembered asking Gaspar, when we ate Ben's first curry, if he thought, shooting the bayad first dive of the day, was unsporting? And he'd joked. "Not in that particular case, for who knows what fate might have befallen us all, had you spurned such a chance to savour his mum's voodoo chutney, ha, ha!" And gone on, "Normally when you begin the day, by all means play to a fish's strength. but come midday and no dinner, play to its weakness".

So, come midday, I say to Gaspar. "We'd better go try and get something for dinner."

"Right," he says, "You know where to find me."

Barnes elects to follow me and off we go.

Not wishing to yield these bird-watchers and putative hunters any more control, I say to Barnes. "No more mucking about Barnsey. We'll play to the fish's weakness." But it's difficult to know if he's impressed by my resolve or not, because his mask's half-fogged up.

In the reed-bordered glades towards the reefs, clusters of tentatively circling trumpet-fish appear mysteriously beneath the mercury surface. In the last glade but one, a suety-looking leopard shark, sprawled half-way across a flattened reed bed, is pulling up great clumps, like there's no tomorrow. While we gawk like a couple of pedestrians at a building site, a blue-fin, more curious than us, glides out of the sand clouds and gets itself promptly speared. As we work our way back in the gathering dusk, another shadows our progress the whole way in, like a will-o-wisp.

We drift towards where Gaspar should be, but it takes a while to find him. When he comes to life, I'm about to tell him that I believe he once stood eyeball-to-eyeball with a houbara bustard, when Barnes pipes up. "Any luck?"

"A big one." he says. "Appeared just like that, must have followed the school all the way in. When they turned around, it backed-off. Why would it do that I wonder?"

I was going to suggest, playing to the school's weakness, then for the life of me, couldn't remember what it was.

On the long slog back, it came to me. Schools have a tendency to grow too big for their own good, no single fish wanting to be first to leave or last left behind. *But we've already been down that route, haven't we?* The school can double back (the fountain), circle opposite ways (the vacuole), thread-back (the relay), skitter on the surface, and so on. But if there's enough different predator species attacking from above, the sides and below, the school can only spin faster and faster, tighter and tighter. They're doomed. Maybe explains why the lone barracuda, backed off.

Dusk comes quickly. We stop for a rest and slump the fish down. As the waves sweep in, ghost crabs dance up and down the beach, sprinting away in great arcs. Then a bigger wave swamps the lot, like pebbles in a stream, spins the fish round, and almost snatches it back. As the water is sucked down, the wet sand flashes along the beach like a great mirror, then darkens. Eye-pods pop-up here and there, keeping an eye on things, fish-wise. And Barnes asks out of the dark "How does the barracuda close the gap with the silversides? That's the problem."

"Maybe it doesn't", says Gaspar. "Let's the school do it."

"How?"

"Very slowly."

"But the school will simply begin the buffalo-horn manoeuvre," Barnes and I chime in, "like the Zulus did to Michael Caine at Rorke's Drift."

"Much slower than that. Think of grass growing, or a pet boa-constrictor."

"A pet boa-constrictor?"

"Don't keep gawking at me like a couple of country yokels. If you don't get out of your stick-in-the-mud human viewpoint – you'll never get the answer. Remember how the Pygmy stalked the elephant?"

"Covered himself with its fresh dung."

"Exactly. So try and use a bit of imagination."

184

"Flipping hell! And Pitsos says we use too much. Calls it stepping into Thoreau's rainbow." (Apparently young Henry, once saw a man standing in the end of a rainbow, and imagined himself doing likewise. So he said, he had.) *Can't be done.* Tried it myself, skipping about in Rix's sprinkler. Ended up doing the hoola-hoop with the rainbow as the hoop. The new site-manager chose the moment to come by. Thinks I'm another of those English instructors, practising for Swan Lake.

Gaspar ploughs on. "A boa-constrictor doesn't necessarily start by squeezing; often preferring to take up the slack. Sometimes, even professional handlers don't notice it, go red in the face, and the spectators think it's part of the act. And you know what the silversides have become like?"

"I hesitate to think."

Now he's really mad. "There you go again! No imagination. They're like those frogs, some people say, don't move in slowly heated water until it's too late, though I've never seen it, nor intend to."

"Frogs now is it?"

As he has our full attention, he ignores this. "The barracuda continues to lie there, inert as a log. When a wave eases the silversides into a gully, it's eased-in too, but being heavier, drags a bit. Likewise on the way out, maybe ends up a tad closer. Eventually, it passes the silversides' critical bolting distance without them noticing. Slips under the photo-electric beam of the supermarket door so-to-speak. The individual fish are unable to respond unless the barracuda moves fast, but then it's too late and they're too close. They've become the consistency of a large fish-burger!"

"A large fish-burger? My God! I believe you've got it."
We'd seen it, but had forgotten!

Back at camp, I hastily searched for the old diary entry about the big barracuda which spent the whole day by a compacted school of silversides. It was headed *Non Event with Barracuda*, I guess because it was in the early days, when adventure meant action, and courage meant not admitting fear, not what you did when you had. But there it was: waiting all day for its meal.

≈

A couple of weeks later we are relaxing on the reef, having a few beers and watching a grouper in a deep kelp-fringed pool. Its greenish ink-spots and dark bands, fading and reappearing, till no one is sure if it's a grouper or not.

Steve is soon talking about the film *Awakenings,* we saw the other night, about a sleepy sickness epidemic, where patients remained in strange fixed bodily positions, sometimes for years. The doctor was played by Robin Williams and the key patient by De Niro, (which most of us had expected to be the other way round).

Did we remember when De Niro couldn't move, "and the doctor suddenly threw a crumpled-up piece of paper at him and he caught it?" Steve asks. Indeed we did.

"Well, there's a related syndrome called *Tourettes,* which Dr. Sacks, the doctor in the original drama, also writes about, where patients can string swear words together as if going for the *Guinness Book of World Records,* and sometimes end up in terrible convulsions.

"Also mentions one intelligent lad, who, on good days could deliver almost un-returnable table-tennis serves, and run full-speed through spinning swing-doors. But on his bad ones, went into a catatonic and zombie-like state."

Then Steve starts implying that there's a relationship between this and the silverside's behaviour under certain conditions.

"Hold on a mo, Stevie," says Pitsos, who's been paying more attention than the rest of us. "Are you seriously suggesting, a Tourette's sufferer, whizzing through swing doors, and delivering almost unplayable table-tennis serves, is in an analogous nervous state to a darting school of silversides when in top form? And vice-versa, a Tourette's sufferer on his bad days, is like the same fish held in thraldom by a big barracuda?"

"Yes."

"And that once the barracuda passes a key distance, no individual fish in the school, has what it takes to make the first move?"

"Yes. But if something, a bit further away approaches very fast, they may react quicker than De Niro.

"We'd better see what Dr. Sacks had to say in that book you've been reading, Stevie boy," says Pitsos.

≈

186

In the medic's copy of *The Man who thought his Wife was a Hat*, we find two sentences dealing with the more severe symptoms of Tourette's sufferers: "We see here", writes Dr. Sacks, "genuine ancestral traits and behaviours which have been summoned from the phylogenic [evolutionary] depths which we still carry in our genes." And: "They are ancestral chemical pathways which are still retained in non-adaptive form, showing that man's descent is indeed a billion years old."

≈

A few weeks later, we're relaxing on the reef again. Lambourski takes out the beer and puts three gutted milkfish in the sack.

We open a bottle. And Steve's takes up the old notion that human tears may have evolved from a fish's way to expel excess salt and boost lubrication. A sort of sniffles gone on a long evolutionary journey, taken over by the sneezing and spitting marine iguana, gone beyond the trevally's altruistic burst of gold, and even more audacious than the moth's dizzy random fall when a bat's radar locks on. To end up with our own tears, the 'it's all too much response' to overwhelming grief and joy, but able to evoke instantaneous empathy. And as the vulnerability it signals is usually genuine (crocodile tears excepted), eventually producing legislation to protect widows and orphans!

And Steve's sheer effort to get this notion across to us dozy dumdums, almost has us crying in our beer.

The sun is now beating so harshly on the sea, I lie down on the cool seaweed, peer in, and get a shock. The back and tail of a large shark passes between two abutments on the reef. We decide to call it a day.

≈

Next morning the lagoon is totally calm.

In the sun-sculpted waves of evening, fish may jump and skitter, but it's almost impossible to see what's going on under the surface. But this dawn, I can see not only several shimmering schools with barracuda in attendance, but all the way to the seabed.

As I gaze into this three dimensional seascape, and perhaps as I should have done long ago, imagine myself asking one of the silver-liveried doormen (a semi-retired Sgt. Maj. Barracuda, no doubt) how the school's aura of exclusivity is maintained, considering all members of the species seem to be invited.

"With utmost discretion, Sir." he replies most deferentially, before fading, Jeeves like, into invisibility.

Of course. *Silly me,* black-balling here, only takes place after membership is granted. Not the sort of Club, Groucho Marx wanted to join. Nor was it the one the Chagos islanders of Diego Garcia thought they belonged to, before the Queen was conned into signing them into exile.

They are low-lying islands, smack in the middle of the Indian Ocean, undisturbed by cyclones, and inhabited for ages. The British thought Diego Garcia would make a great airbase; kicked out the islanders and rented it to the Americans. Dennis Healy, Foreign Secretary at the time, considered it one of the most despicable acts of his life -- and man enough to admit it.

"Must write a letter to the Queen about it," I say to Gaspar.

"That'll be the day." He says wearily, as we set out on our next excursion.

56 Coral

Schooling fish were complicated enough, but at this time, I didn't even know if coral was a plant or an animal.

Its day-to-night changes were baffling, from intricately designed rock gardens, with pretty fishes flitting above, to spooky night time gloom. And sometimes, from rows of empty daytime vases and sealed pots, to bristling night flower markets, bursting with extravagantly plumed and prickly creatures, whose closest neighbours, Barnes informs me, were often sponges. But forget the homely bathtub sop and fibrous back-scratcher, many were like lumps of ugly play putty, stuck higgedly-piggedly on the reef furniture by a disturbed child. *Did they simply say, 'Excuse me, I need this parking space?'* Hadn't a clue.

In time I learned that the coral polyps, like most city dwellers, live in apartments, isolated yet attached to their neighbours, but happy enough to pass nutrients and messages one to the other.

Inside the polyps, live algae, like household plants or pets. They are symbiants, exchanging oxygen and extra carbohydrates for the polyp's own waste nitrogen and phosphates, normally scarce in tropical waters. But if neglected, or lacking adequate sunlight, may take off on their own. And if overfed, may inadvertently suffocate their coral hosts.

Some ocean currents plunge down 'like cold cream in a coffee cup', and in the tropics well-up, to nourish, smash, and replenish coral reefs.

Many reef fish feed better in the gentler locally circulating currents, but if they spawned in great numbers there, such places could quickly become the killing grounds for opportunist pelagic predators.

Some bream, for example, move to deeper zones, above which the currents are so strong, no coral grows. Only when they've gathered in sufficient numbers, do females travel up to the surface and males compete to fertilize the eggs. After many such sorties, eggs well on their way, the bream don't hang about, but return to their home reefs and atolls, to feed again.

To spawn successfully, sedentary coral needs to take into account, wind speed and direction, current strength, tides, temperature, cloud cover, you name it. They've had thousands of years practice, but if things change suddenly, may be caught out.

The crown of thorns starfish, though a bit more than a coral pruner and browser of surface algae, is normally little bother as a predator. Triton conches, bump-headed wrasse and even dainty painted-shrimps, can deal with them. The latter tickle their toes, causing them to lose their grip and become neutrally buoyant. The shrimps then tip them over and chomp down, as if on one of Ali's pizzas (he's now gone into private business), and that's that.

But the infamous crown of thorns massive outbreaks, as we now know, are an entirely different matter. They crawl all over the coral in their thousands, leaving it bleached and looking dead.

As no actual poison or bleach is used, whether it is actually dead, is probably best left to the experts, but that didn't stop an energetic public response. Lobotomize them? Give them formalin injections? Fund university research – undergrad jollies on tropical reefs? All had their merits, and the devil lay in the details.

Both crown of thorns larvae and coral larvae spend their youths travelling the ocean currents in an apparently neighbourly manner. But the former have learned to tolerate decreased salinity, a wider temperature range, and graduate more from the University of Hard Knocks — even night-school. They have a bundle of diplomas to prove it, with names like blastula, brachiaria, opinaria etc.; headaches to remember, but nothing to the ones the mature starfish can later give to the coral.

The problem usually explodes into the open off estuaries and fringe reefs after heavy rain, especially when accompanied by run-offs from plantations and real-estate developments.

What the crown of thorns larvae appreciate here, are not the run-offs themselves, but the algae feeding in and on them. Though high risk, high return areas, full of opportunistic predators, the crown of thorns larvae are nevertheless able to bulk-up very fast and in huge numbers, then hightail it to the reef.

Whereas the coral larvae have settled down on the reef and become regular home-bodies cast-in-stone, only peeping out at night to feed, the crown of thorns remain mobile. They rest up in crannies by day but prowl round at night, and are able to climb their erstwhile travelling buddies' fences, attacking them in their homes and sucking out their vital juices.

Even the coral's own algae, primed to desert as soon as things deteriorate, appear to be caught off guard, and are gobbled up, too.

On behalf of the coral property owners, our question now becomes: How can these massive outbreaks, not be stopped, but rather, pre-empted?

In my simplicity I thought of whale sharks (who gather off Djibuti like municipal street-cleaners), basking shark, manta rays (who never bask) and even the plankton-eating mackerel which so assiduously patrol our own reefs. But as we can hardly just order them up, that's as maybe. So how about some facts?

Here we happened to find a small item of particular interest to Barnes, the angler, and myself, the spear-fisherman.

In Australia in the sixties, dedicated researchers observed large numbers of emperors, *lethrinus chryostomus,* feeding on crown of thorns larvae. When the emperors' own numbers declined due to their becoming the preferred prey of a new breed of reef-anglers and spear-fishermen, the crown of thorns numbers went up.

Maybe if Barnsey and myself, don't scare away too many of our salp-guzzling emperors, they'll be better able to help our coral, when the crown of thorns larvae come by.

57 Rock-hard land is soon gone and we're in hilly ocean

'Nothing gives warning of the approach of morning,' I read in the sand-filled worm-eaten paperback, *Song of Malaya*, 'till a faint breeze wafted from the sleeping earth stirs the leaves with a sound like a rising curtain. Forthwith the te-te-goh bird of the two twilights scatters its three notes upon the air.'

For a moment I am nostalgic for rain-drenched woods, full of birdsong, and feel deprived. But this deprivation is precious too, intensifying the silence, broken only by the occasional slap of a small wave on the beach.

Though our local vocalists wouldn't make up a twentieth part of a forest's morning chorus, each one sets its seal on a different part of our world: the parched caw of the fantail raven over the high plateau, the wolf whistles of Tristan grackles tumbling above the escarp's rim, and the early morning repartee of the weaver birds before their nests – like bacon sizzling in every doorway.

Then I hear it, or perhaps it was there all along: the faint-fluting coda of the hoopoe-lark, coming from as much in my head as from the burning sands.

Lambourski, being absent today, I've been detailed to make the chilli con carné. I've finished soaking the beans and am inspecting them: for mould, black spots and bad characters in general, but can't remember whether I'm meant to add the minced meat to the beans next, or the beans to the minced meat.

As I reach for the cooking pot, I sense Warner watching my every move – like some nervous sea-creature waiting to squirt something at me. Sure enough, out it comes.

"Lambourski said you're meant to drain-off all the fat, before you add the beans."

"Thank you. Didn't know you'd become a gourmet. Your old man must be turning in his grave." I pour off the fat, and leave the beans to soak a bit longer. and that's that..

Then our two old fishermen friends, who've been caulking their boat down the beach using a mix of wood-ash, Ethiopian cotton and shark guts (mercifully downwind), come up to announce they're on their way.

As we help steady their sambuk in the surf, we notice a thin stream of smoke unravelling along the horizon. It stretches out into long tenuous skeins, possibly Ethiopian cranes, winging their way north, then crumples up, darkening and ballooning into a massive cloud of sea birds, heading directly towards us.

"*Allah Kareem!*"(God is merciful), shout the fishermen as we hand them the mooring ropes. Then on an impulse, Barnes grabs his fishing gear and yells, "Come on!" And I clamber in too. The stink is terrific but it's the real thing – just what that old bastard Monfried claimed to love! The lanteen sail squeaks up, and before we know it, we're moving fast through the pass.

The swells lengthen. Rock-hard land is soon gone and we're in hilly ocean. The big cloud is now above us, full of all manner of sea fowl: Caspian terns, black-headed gulls, frigate birds and pelicans, like old ladies at a sale, once more wielding umbrellas in feisty combat before crashing into the sea, obviously forgetting, they're meant to be scoopers, not divers. The gulls gather portside, squawking and paddling in the foam of the wake, while the terns hover and dive on schools of smaller fish driven to the surface by skipjack and bonito.

Zing! Zing! Goes Barnes' line as the fishermen haul in theirs. The decks are soon full of dancing yellow and deep-blue enamelled fish (skin, tight as balloons and hard as pumpkins) leaping and skittering all over the place.

A bigger dark shape is snared, comes snaking in under the water, turning this way-and-that, until it too, is heaved on board: blazing silver, with a deep grape matt-bloom to its back, and on the silver of its sides, vertical dabs of pure lilac. The bottle-green flared-sail, in texture like rubbery kelp and as exuberant and ostentatious as the finery at Ascot, now folds down, neat as a Venetian blind. It is a creature of extravagant beauty, but not for long. In a matter of minutes it's turning the colour of coffee stains, then – dark as mahogany.

But it's payday for our friends. Once back on shore, Rix dumps the remains of our ice over the sailfish and runs them into

Shekeik, where they sell it. He brings back a massive ice block, and while the old fishermen pray, we infidels hack-off a corner, bury our milk cartons in it, and wait.

They scoff down my mushy chilli-con-carné, with no complaints. And when they make the pass, we cheer them on through a brisk sparkling sea, towards the Farasans.

58 Late on reef 2

It's dark and spooky and we're spread out like lonely soldiers on the reef-top overlooking a gloomy seabed. There's been no time for getting rations today, so we simply sloshed down a few sids as soon as we hit the beach, and here we are. If we hadn't had the sids, I doubt we would be. We've moved up here with excruciating slowness, if not exactly silence, the idea being, if we can't get something at dusk here, we'll not get it anywhere.

We sense that arrayed in front of us is a wall of small fish. But in the dark, one tends to exaggerate. There are shudders, swoops, fly-bys and massive jerks – seen but not heard – and felt – more than seen. But what's causing it? Eventually, looking up into the undersides of small waves, we make out the slim forms of needlefish lurking in their very apexes. Every so often, one arches its back, doesn't dart forward as you might expect, but hurtles straight down – twists round and is up again – almost faster than one can follow. The bait school doesn't scatter or plummet downwards, either, which would have given us a clue, but rushes outwards like an expanding doughnut.

A pod of Crevalle comes in, sweeps back-and-forth like a brief aurora-borealis, and leaves the punch-drunk school, reeling.

Then things settle down. It must be the famous *quiet period*, we've read about, more than experienced. Begins ten minutes after sunset and lasts about twenty. Basically it's the day-to-night shift-change, and is carried out both by prey and predators, with a small overlap between them.

First the day fish, previously masked from predators below by the sun's dazzle, descend the water column. Then, as the light darkens from the seabed up, grunts and other night-fish gather at reef-side assembly points before making their way out to the feeding grounds, where night-hunters have taken up ambush positions, hunkered down in the turtle grass.

Something nips my finger. Then the little bugger does it again – clicking like one of those Xmas-cracker crickets – and retreats down its hole. I move my hand to a new position.

We are but four gunmen, among battalions of Lilliputian sharp-shooters, manning reef-top trenches and equipped with all manner of gimcrack weaponry. There are jawed polychaete worms (with bristles or living in tubes), pistol shrimps and sea anemones, the latter armed with miniature harpoons, or lassoes, all ready to be hurled at passing prey. Some weapons are fired on orders from the organism, some triggered by prey. Some operators are freelance, mercenaries, available to the highest bidder. The variety of relationships defies my capacity to elucidate them, but I proceed to, anyway.

The marine hydra, a gun-toting version of the little gymnast, we studied at school, supplies a blind flatworm with weaponry. Unlike Warner, the flatworm doesn't even ask to borrow them, but simply swallows the hydra, lock-stock-and-barrel. The consumed weaponry disappears into the belly of the beast, a bit like Jack's spear guns, but reappears, no worse for wear, to take up front-line positions in its new host, no questions asked.

Other hydras are not so easy to gobble up. There's one with its own oxygen-making algae, which inflates an air bubble on cue (somewhat like a car's air bag), and parachutes away.

I move up the reef a bit and find myself confronting a vast expanse of staghorn coral. Even though, or perhaps because it's in three dimensions, it's hard to see anything hiding in it. And soon its endless pattern becomes as irritating as that flock wallpaper which, they say prompted Oscar's exasperated last epigram. 'One of us has to go.'

Then outcrops of different variety edge in, grow denser, interlock. Each an intricate mosaic, expanding in its own area. One moment the original motif holds sway, the next, it's surrounded, as in a game of Japanese Go.

Suddenly, something is breathing in-and-out, right in front of me. Makes me cease my meanderings and freeze. What I'd thought was a hole in the reef, is in fact, a ruddy great grouper. It doesn't react to me, but shifts about to get a better look at things below.

Then it's off, bolting down the reef-face like an animal through dense scrub. Small clumps of blackfish panic as it makes a vicious sortie across a glade, and disappears – swallowed up in the dark.

A small starfish, next to my hand, curls its fingers round a pebble and glides on. Small shells nearby take evasive action and roll away. I look for one with spikes, to place in the starfish's path, to see if they are sufficient to prevent it gaining its deadly purchase. If it gets a grip on a clam, it usually wins the arm-wrestling contest, because many clams lack the more enduring suction power of a starfish. But with a scallop (using hydraulic jet-propulsion) it's usually hop, skip and away!

Around me, I vaguely sense, there's an army of small shells on the move. Maybe I'll see a dog whelk in action. It stops its prey with one narcotic, holds it down with a foot, tenderizes it with a second potion then beats it into submission with its own shell. Another species prowls the mussel beds and, if it gets a leg up, takes its time drilling into them one by one, sucking out the juices as it goes. If it fails to climb up, the mussels surround it and tie it down with glue-like threads, produced by their tongues.

There's also a carnivorous moon snail, the shark-eye, which travels stealthily under the sand, touch like a gloved finger, grip like a closed fist. Then drills in. And there's the prettily patterned cone shell, one venom stuns the prey, the other dissolves the tissues, hot pursuit not being its bag.

There's a fungus, which hurls itself like a net at passing traffic (often a paddle steamer-like rotifer), boards and crawls, cabin to cabin, like animated spaghetti.

I'm beginning to doze-off. The foreground changes. Suddenly, I realize the grouper is back on its original ledge. *No time to lose!* I launch myself forward like a drunk determined to fly. Everything happens at once. A big snapper looms up, dull as unburnished copper. Turns to rose, to styrofoam pink, explodes in a shower of scales as both my spear and the day's last light, strike it.

Leo comes over. A black shark comes right in below us, and almost smacks him in the face as it rolls away.

"It's gone. Thought you hit it fair and square," he says. "Must be around here somewhere." He's talking about the snapper; hasn't even noticed the shark. *He's in another world!*

"Leo, there's a *shark* around too. Keep your eyes open."

Then we hear a second shot. Lambourksi has fired and got his spear stuck. *What a balls up!* Warner and Leo cover us as we try to work it loose. Dust and detritus everywhere, and things going on all around us, I don't like at all. I feel like a member of a road-gang in night fog, stuck in the centre of a Los Angeles freeway. I'm trying to convince myself it's all happening in my head, when the shark returns – white entrails streaming from its mouth.

We finally get the spear out and ease back from the reef front. And have only gone twenty yards when, apart from the silent silver underbellies of small waves gliding overhead, it becomes quiet as a mill pond.

We pause to gather our wits. Some way along the reef, two barracudas, in shining silver, ratchet up ever so slowly, like twin missiles from a mid-reef silo. When they see us, they fire offshore, one after the other: the fastest creatures in the sea from a standing start, save perhaps a lemon shark, which that earlier bugger looked suspiciously like, now I come to think of it. (At night all sharks are dark, unless you have a torch, and that attracts them).

We drift slowly back to shore and almost into another horror, Rix's bare feet. *Aaargh!* He's walked out, ever the optimist, fish-scaler in hand. "What have you got?" he asks.

"Fuck all. Sorry. Total bollocks!"

"Corned beef then." He says, definitely pissed off.

"Great!" Not a murmur from the troops.

"So what happened?"

"Got caught behind enemy lines with our pants down. Drunk on patrol. You name it – we're guilty."

"What about the famous *quiet period*, you were gabbling on about?"

"It's only quiet if you keep quiet. We weren't." And I recall, when last time out late, I'd seen that moray in a school of black fish and quoted from Macbeth:

> Light thickens and the crows,
> Make wing to the rooky woods.

Should have let the bard finish:

Good things of the day begin to droop and drowse,
  While night's dark agents to their prey do rouse.

*You'd almost think Old Will had done some snorkelling,
wouldn't you?* But one who had no need to, was that famous lady
Rachel Carson, who once wrote:
  When I have lingered on the reef flat until dusk fell, a
strange new world, full of tensions and alarms, has replaced the
peaceful languor of the day. For the hunter and hunted are abroad.

59 Samantha

"Come and look at this little critter. It's a nudibranch, sometimes called a sea hare or sea slug," says Barnes to Cowboy's girlfriend, Sam. (Cowboy himself being way down the beach, recording a tape to his wife: "My dearest Rose. I'm walking along this lonely beach thinking of you". Maybe, even sings a song.)

"Men are such mutts," says Sam. "Thinks I don't know. One of these days I'll play it on the ghetto-blaster."

"Stop complaining," says Barnes. "Quick, or it will be gone."

"I don't think I want to see it, not after that cucumber-thing you showed me the other day, which squirted out all that gooey stuff. Anyway, how can something be called a hare and a sea-slug at the same time – unless you mean that creep down the beach, ha, ha! *Wowee!* Isn't that the cutest little thing you ever saw? Makes me feel a bright wee girl again, watching my brother's best marble spinning in the sand lot."

"Exactly!" says Barnes (he's something else when the ladies are around). "It's been called a caterpillar doing the twist on LSD. Lovely names: *Sappho amicorum*, the Spanish Dancer and *Doto coronata.*"

"Sounds more like a bunch of stuck-up hookers on coke." Says Sam.

"Spot on" says he, delightedly. "You should see *Doto coronata,* draped over some hapless hydroid or sea anemone, while trying to remove its side-arms. No truly. She acquires their *nematocysts* and *cnidoblasts,* Colt 45's and lariats, I should say, for her own self-defence. If her dancing partner cottons on to her intentions, or squeezes her too tight, she exudes a purple poison from her lips."

"*Yikes!* My kind of gal" says Sam.

Not so long ago, she and Cowboy had been stopped by the *Metawa* (the Religious Police) and not being married (to each other) thought it was Kingdom come. He for the chop, she for the tip-up truck, with rocks. She was wearing men's jeans, unlaced Doc Martens and sported a page-boy haircut. Scared that her voice might come out soprano, handed over her pass (made out to Sam Johnson, Veterinary Surgeon and signed by the Asir Governor) without a word. The *Metawa* did a double-take, tried to work out something in his head, gave up, and waved them on.

One time I made the mistake of asking her, how we might improve the camp for when Pitsos' wife came out. I knew she wasn't going to suggest frilly shower curtains or anything, but she took it very coolly, "How about starting with table manners?"

I was going to add "But we don't even have a table yet," then decided it was simply too juvenile.

60 "Boy oh boy! Have I news for you!"

Marsden's back from leave. Comes in, huffing and puffing, loaded down with pub and football regalia. Dumps most of it behind the bar and dispenses the rest. "Good job you weren't sleeping under Charing Cross Bridge this time, Stevie". He says. "Thames' embankment's flooded and the Country's in another recession. Taxi drivers, cruising Oxford Street – elbows on the steering wheels – no customers.

"Everyone wearing gym shoes and lugging round plastic bags. And a gent in Harris Tweeds, off Trafalgar Square, asked me for a handout."

"Did you get any spear gun parts?"

"Boy oh boy! Have I news for you! You're the pits. Menace to yourselves, fish, other people, and the reefs. When I asked the guy in the store, selling some Swedish lovelies wetsuits in mauve-and-apple green Lycra, he looked at me like I was some kind of pond scum. When the ladies left, told me he had some flood-damaged inventory in the back."

Marsden now hoists a heavy brown bag onto the bar. "Managed to pick up a few odds and ends." He says.

Among the beer mats and ashtrays, we find rubber catapults, spear tips, piano-wire, even some trigger mechanisms.

"Perfect! Buy this man a drink!"

61 Colour Consciousness

Sir Peter Medawar, a worthy Nobel Prize winner (of slightly swarthy complexion), on proposing to a lily-white English girl, was discreetly (if that's the word) rumoured to have syphilis. And he had a precocious young nephew, who got himself in a real muddle, pondering: If Nature looked like Van Gogh's paintings to Van Gogh, what did Van Gogh's paintings look like to him?

The reflective angles of ribbed scales on some butterflies' open wings can cause them to flash when passing; paint in a closed tin has no colour, and the thickness of black-and-white stripes confuse many of Nature's creatures. The conundrums are legion. Some Africans even hold that tsetse flies (the dreaded 'dudus') prefer dining on dun cattle to zebras, because the latter's stripes cause them to lose focus 'like a drunk on a zebra-crossing.'

Men are also slightly more prone to colour blindness than women, perhaps because, for over thousands of years, they were watching for predators in savannah grasslands, while their women picked berries etc.

It is also said, when a distant zebra herd first clicks into focus in a hungry lioness' eyes, her sudden tiny change of stance can alert a focused stallion, who often continues head-high, dribbling grass -- a picture of equine obtuseness. And only when the pride enters dead ground, does he gently nudge his mares to better terrain.

If the lioness eventually charges, the herd may swing this way-and-that in apparent confusion too, thus allowing any panicky breakaway foal to be momentarily swallowed into a background river of swirling stripes -- and so live another day.

How to interpret fishes' colours is even more of a problem, because the colours they see are often not the ones we do. For example, they see ultra-violet and we can't. They've also evolved ways of making lights, whereas we now consciously design ours. Seeing and being seen by fish makes for some interesting meetings. My own with the fantail grouper (also known as the moontail wrasse), being a case in point.

Sometime ago, I saw one meandering about the bottom of the reef and waited for it to pass behind a rock in the hope of intercepting it the other side. When I dived down and peered round the rock, there was only a surprised brown fish with two stripes, and the grouper had gone.

And not long ago, Warner dived down on another one but never fired. Thinking he might be getting into the big-fish syndrome and need snapping out of it, I swam over to him, and adopting a somewhat severe tone, asked "What about that one? Seemed big enough to me."

"That one? Didn't look good-eating to me." He said. Then it clicked. Perhaps the fantail grouper and the drab non-descript fish, were one and the same. And I remembered reading somewhere of an experiment, where cats were put in empty boxes, and observers watched as the cats checked out their new homes. They only discovered later, the rituals had next-to-nothing to do with the boxes, but were greetings to the observers. Perhaps the fantail grouper has many such greetings.

Today for the first time ever, I saw one really close up. I'd been doddering about with my head just underwater, trying to undo a knot in the string of my spear. In the middle of this meddlesome procedure, I turned round. And there watching me, suspended at eye-level, was this brilliant fish, showing-off completely unafraid, and literally burning with colours.

Talking about this at sundowners, I felt I might be exaggerating, and had difficulty in believing it myself. It seemed to belong to that magical childhood era, when, as a bright-eyed seven year old, I'd watched a weasel performing perfect cartwheels before a bunch of enraptured sparrows, or received a haunting memorial card depicting my father lying beside a burning Spitfire, which he never flew. Or a pod of golden trevally suddenly announcing itself by bursting through the oyster-grey of an undersea dawn like an opening fan. Or the Dorado, the writer Eric Hansen caught just before the yacht he was on floundered down this very coast, 'Its colours, so outrageously opalescent and liquid,' he thought they might all come away in his fingers.

I didn't realise, I'd fallen silent till Warner said, "Why have you stopped talking? It's only a fish. Not like you've seen a vision of the Virgin Mary, or anything."

Somewhat reassured by this assertion, I pressed on. "I think the moontail wrasse, far from scorning to create an effect by piling colour on colour, actually relishes it. Mauve rings encircling emerald; rose, cobalt. Moss-green nestled in a sky-blue oval, hoops entwined in hoops, and all as intricately woven as in a Persian miniature. But also in motion, ravelling and unravelling before my very eyes.

"I think the moontail wrasse has many greetings, and on occasions, likes to mesmerize the company it meets, especially some pop-eyed crustacean or dumb two-toned fish. Then pounce! And in turn, likes to play the dumb fish of but two colours, to avoid becoming unworthy prey, to the likes of us."

Tactful, uncommitted Pitsos, says the moo-moos may be a trifle strong today, but I seem to be handling mine very well.

62 Old Ben's donkey

We're watching the pelicans return, wing-tips not inches from the waves, good family members all, bringing home the bacon.

"Problem is," murmurs Steve to Warner and myself, "we've been looking at women dressed-up as Guinness bottles, and eating Polish beef dressed up as bacon, for so long, we're forgetting what women look like and bacon tastes like.

"In their place we've produced a menagerie. Barnes has his birds. Dundas his fish — sometimes more worried about coming back with no dinner than not coming back at all. Leo his jeep — now a bit too much a homebody, if you ask me — and Marsden, his pub."

A discussion ensues whether Marsden started his pub to supplement his income, to remember what pubs were like, or forget what they were like. "It was a recession, remember?" says Steve, "Public bar full of cigarette smoke, damp carpet in Saloon." Barnes doesn't remember -- had exams to pass.

"Anyway what I'm thinking is, with its fancy bar top and studded leather bar-stools, it's more like a New York cocktail lounge."

"You've never been in a New York cocktail lounge", says Barnes.

"I have that." says Stevie. "On a return student charter flight via Reykjavik, we were dumped in a Newark Hotel. Some of us sneaked into the cocktail lounge. It was so cold, I asked the spectral figure sitting next to me in the blue light, if they were practising us for Iceland. She said, if I was expecting any service, to lay a tenner on the bar. I didn't know if she was a socialite or a hooker. But that's another story. Most early travellers to New York, New Jersey, New England, New Hampshire etc., weren't planning to scatter money about, or leave by the next boat, were they? They were in for the long haul. A new start. Same with Marsden's bar".

"You've certainly got a long way of saying it." Says Leo. "What about Colonel Cufflink's cats? Are they in for the long haul?"

While they sort this out, is a good time to give Colonel Cufflinks a proper introduction. He was a Southern gentleman, of courtly charm when he chose to exercise it, and a drinker when he didn't. He'd originally shared a villa with the Major, who believed officers, when inebriated, should pretend to be sober. Though considerable leeway was given here, the colonel kept forgetting. He moved to skid-row and took to wandering the compound at 2 am in pyjamas, complaining about the frogs and a ghost (a five foot high cauliflower, which showed the richness of the desert's watered soil, and did duty as a scarecrow).

As these twin apparitions (pyjama clad colonel and Rix's scarecrow) passed before me, I recalled the tail-end of one of Van's parties, when the Colonel was holding forth to a bunch of nodding heads on the expense of his daughter's riding lessons, in Switzerland.

As it was the time of night when flubby-faced Americans confided 'between you, me and the doorpost' (one time it was to the doorpost) they worked for the CIA', beefier members of the homosexual brigade request to arm-wrestle (Humphrey Littleton used to suggest 'brain-wrestle') and fierce-eyed Scots demand to know your position on Home Rule ('It's now or never Jimmie, no more sitting on the fence!') my own eyes were most certainly focused on the level in the Colonel's Jim Beam bottle. Yet despite all these concerns, I'll never forget the communal gasp which greeted his mention of the cost of food-and-lodging in Lausanne -- and that was only for the horse.

When I learned later, he was scared of going on leave for fear of spending too much lolly, I merely thought, here was another poor sod, half-killing himself supporting a family in a manner to which they'd become too-well accustomed. And once, when Barnes and I asked him why he fed so many cats, he drew himself up, saying. "Think what would happen if I stopped." At the time we considered it more a threat than a genuine show of concern, and took to feeding them doubtful pieces of barracuda. None have died yet.

Now, listening to Pitsos, it seems he's suggesting that Colonel Cufflinks fed them to show he could still take care of a family. As this smacked a little too much of Freud, I was not impressed, and it took the later case of old Ben to convince me, he might have a point.

Old Ben had found a donkey with a broken leg outside the Compound and, worried that the Koreans were going to eat it, decided to keep it in his villa.

Dr. Metwalli and the medic tried to convince him, as it hadn't signed a Company contract, it wasn't entitled to such accommodation. Old Ben declined to see it that way, and was sent to Riyadh for a check-up. The medic assured us, it was more a ploy to get the donkey out of an institution, than Ben into one.

Whatever they did seemed to work. Old Ben returned to watering the garden, and the green frogs reappeared. The donkey took up residence outside the wall, becoming the football club's most vocal supporter, and eventual mascot.

63 The sense of unease returns

We're back in the glades again, T shirts faded, cryptic as old coral, and expectations high. A couple of mullet pods arrive, circle obligingly, forage awhile, give no sign they know we are here, and move on.

The sense of unease returns. *What could have alerted them?* Pissing in the water? The glint of a mask, sweat on the water's surface, suntan oil, vibrations from our breathing? Or the lot?

A big-butted parrotfish in pasty-pink and pale-blue spandex, upends at the cleaning station to get a facial, and creates a queue. I even begin to feel some sympathy for the underage-suburban kid in the movie the other night, who enlisted in the Marines because his mum spent too long in the Beauty Parlour.

Steve leaves, and I recall that this has happened before. He soon returns and this time, says excitedly. "They're back in my place." We follow him in. Sure enough, not only is the barrier back, but last month's storms have gouged out a considerable pond, with mullet inside. We position ourselves outside it and wait.

Mullet cross the barrier in twos and threes, in sparkling silver, alert and fresh from the sea. Then in fours and fives, both sides of us. *Thwack! Thwack!* One is pinned into the gravel and another spins on a spear, shedding scales like a one-armed bandit loose change. Soon we have four gleaming fish,

Then everything stops.

The water continues going down, and soon no predator the size of medium barracuda will be able to cross the barrier.

"What do you think?" says a delighted Steve, "A good place, yes?"

"Perfect," we say.

"Let's keep it as a safe-haven," I add enthusiastically. "And only pick them off as they cross the barrier." Everyone agrees. "Till next week then", we promise ourselves.

≈

A week later, we arrive in good time. The water is high enough for mullet to cross into the pond. We wait outside, hidden by our usual rock. After a longish wait, many mullet arrive but none enter.

We leave and return in three-quarters of an hour. The water is now gliding over the barrier   in great silken sheets, but only just deep enough for mullet to cross. When we peer into the pond, it's empty! When we leave, the water's below the barrier.

For two and a half months, the water stayed just below the barrier, almost as if the mullet had known it would. A bit of a mystery here.

64 The arrest of Donald Duck

The other day, during a Safeway sales promotion, a Filipino employee was arrested by the Department for the Promulgation of Virtue and the Prevention of Vice. It was a dark day for the Americans and her close allies. Word spread fast, and Marsden was right up there with them. "Haven't you heard?" Were his first words at the bar.

"Heard what?"

"They've arrested Donald Duck."

Some people felt, locking up that obnoxious five-foot duck was the best thing the Saudis ever did. Others, that it required an immediate diplomatic riposte, if not a military one. Others that it was but the first jolt of the gravy train, testing the brakes. The Major sensed it when he reached for the Schweppes tonic on its usual supermarket shelf, and found his hand clasping a can in day-glo colours, named Faygo, with a pesky self-confident effervescence and dubious flavours.

We noticed the change on the way to work, in the first jarring yammer of gridlock. And in the ferocious looks of men in turbans and beards, scurrying to-and-fro, not with Kalashnikovs, but buckets and spades from something looking like Watt's steam-engine, parked by the roadside.

Gone overnight it seemed, were those halcyon days when Mercedes swung like toys from helicopters over Jeddah harbour, and asphalt flowed in a black velvet river from machines like combine-harvesters moving four-abreast towards the horizon. And at dusk, young men raced each other up and down pristine highways, horns braying like demented donkeys.

Soon, some of these abandoned conveyances began to re-emerge from the desert like creatures from the lost ark, sand-blasted and red with fresh rust. Some were pushed in asthmatic bursts by chanting Bangladeshis, and steered by stout Sudanese gentlemen in bed sheets. And others further afield, full of muzzled goats, only glimpsed on moonless nights, guided by Somali trackers crossing the Tihama's remoter saltpans.

65 Zilch!

We're on the broad-backed reef on our way back from Sand Island, and still need three good fish for the medic's farewell party.

You'd think getting a large grouper would be easy enough, but it isn't. You have to spy out and approach one without disturbing it. And because we've long foresworn the use of more powerful guns and (as said before, not for want of trying otherwise), have to get real close.

On these sea-fronting reefs, small dense schools of tiny fish regularly duck down to avoid open water predators. But the first time, we saw a big grouper masquerading as an outcrop of coral under one such cloud, was a right shock.

Only later did it occur to us that such small fish might be earning the groupers' protection by helping lure in passing pelagics. And we began to scrutinise their behaviour more closely, even hoping to use it to our future advantage. It was not to be, till today.

On our return from Sand Island, Warner eases himself onto the reef, "Zilch!" He says disgustedly, and enables a dead still Lambourski, not ten feet away, to shoot a large grouper as it drew back from beneath a rapidly closing umbrella of small fish.

Feeling well pleased, we push on to an area of three submarine gullies we'd earlier seen from the top of Sand Island's highest dune, and now approached from deep water for the first time.

As I slip off my safety catch, everything happens at once. Down one gully pour hundreds of unicorn fish, a cavalry regiment of drab olive-green cut-outs, short lances high on foreheads. Down the next, comes a huddle of Napoleon fish in a ponderous stampede, disgracing their namesake, with a pod of grey trevally riding their backs, and black surgeon fish (an unruly detachment of Cossacks) wheeling beside them.

As they swarm down the slopes, we survey this shambles of a retreat like well-positioned sharp-shooters on the lookout for high-ranking officers and their aide-de-camps. In this case, the vivid flash of golden trevally and the silver plumes of long-finned cavalla, fleeing among the riff-raff.

Thwack! Warner fires into the middle of the mayhem. Sheer madness.

Whoomph! go the parrotfish, and the school opens to reveal, hanging vertical in the water column, a large saddleback kicking on his spear, darkening and flicking on its lights, even as we look.

"There's another." He hisses. I can't see anything, but know what's coming, and hand over my gun. He fires and pins another onto a fretwork of coral.

In the space of twenty few minutes we have all the fish we need: Lambourski getting his, by refusing to be distracted by Warner's "Zilch!" And Warner, his two, by hunkering down and not being swept along in all the excitement. And I recall for what it's worth, how Archimedes, genius that he was, lost his own life for being too focused on his own agenda.

As we slog back over the pass, we meet Barnes by the Egyptian Eagle's nest (which he's now downgraded to a vulture). Here we rest awhile, enjoying the breeze and watching the waves wash over the reefs, far below.

It is turning into one of those days where nature seems an open book. An unusually big fox comes dashing out of the dunes along a sand-spit, crowded with oyster catchers and spoonbills. They take off all at once as it leaps high and snaps twice at the empty air.

After a careful search with the Major's binoculars, we spy the den's location among big rocks, dotted with fish bones and crab shells, but no cubs appear.

Then, cruising slowly along the reef, come two big sharks, one of which, goes to the very spot where Warner pinned the second saddleback.

≈

Back in the compound, everything's laughably behind schedule. The bad news is no alcohol is to be served, third nationals being present. But soon everyone starts arriving, including skid row: Van, Colonel Cufflinks, Cowboy and Old Ben, all of whom we thought might be deterred by the booze ban. Such is the commotion, the jewelled sunbirds retreat to the top of the castor-oil trees, and the green frogs into the depths of the ice plants.

On the long garden table, a lucky dip of goat parts, half-hidden in heaps of saffron rice, full of almonds and raisins (a gift from Colonel Sudais' wife) is placed between a dish of mangrove crabs (hiding modestly in rice noodles), steamed grouper and two saddleback. The latter basking in layers of bay and lime leaves, disguising the severed-halves of a large biscuit tin next to Chowdry's full stop, and surrounded by a flotilla of oranges, small bowls of goat cheese, black olives, dates, bird chillies, squeezed coconut milk, plus an evil-smelling sauce (to accent certain flavours), and pickled Chinese plums (to take them away).

After the carapaces, goat-bones, fish skeletons and orange peel are cleared away. Doctors Metwalli and Sherry praise the cooks and helpers, and present the medic with a two-volume medical encyclopaedia. He jokes about taking a hint as well as the next bloke, then, for the first time, appears lost for words. Dr. Metwalli, a dab-hand at emergencies, calls for three cheers, and to tumultuous applause, the guest of honour, has to be helped to his seat.

The VIP's circulate among the walking wounded, impressed by our football team's most vocal supporter (almost certainly having over-indulged in mash) and pretend to worry, we might all be arrested because the Thais have become inebriated; no one having told them, the Orangeboom beer was non-alcoholic.

66 Last bayad, and a rebuke

Cold early morning. Deep water. We pass over a great gloomy coral head. It looms up and is left behind, but the spookiness of the empty ocean is worse. *Could there be something down there?* Something else nags me, which the coldness is making me push away. *Don't be lazy, go back.* I put off my safety catch and force myself down.

Two great bayads are chasing each other round the base of the sombre edifice. Maybe I shouldn't shoot because there are two. But it's no time for indecision, so I fire.

Warner immediately signals me to come up. "There was a shark behind you," he says. "Came in and turned back, just like that."

"How big?"

"Big enough."

When I get my wind back, Warner covers me while I take another look. The bayad has hooked itself round a spur, way down.

By the time we get the gear untangled and the fish trussed up, it's turned into a glorious day. We lie on our backs and trundle along in a sparkling sea towards the home shore. Every so often we look down. After a while, Warner says. "Do you see what I see?"

I look down and make out two sharks. Then I saw it. A big one, deeper down, moving from side to side.

"What shall we do?" he asks.

"Steady as she goes." I say, or rather it just came out. In fact, I was looking for the ripple markings of a tiger shark. And of course it had them, as at that depth even a bathtub would.

Then I recalled reading somewhere that tiger sharks don't go far up the Red Sea and that one was seen, not long ago, in Jeddah harbour. I mull over these contrary pieces of information, until Warner informs me there's a reef ahead. The distant whitecaps come and go with disturbing irregularity. Twice we bump into each other. "It's a hell of a long way," I say.

We both peer down again. "Could it be a family...?" he says. I think he wanted to add something.

"Excursion, you mean?"

"Whatever you want to call it, excursion's alright by me."

"I don't think sharks are great ones for family excursions, cannibalism's more their thing," but I don't add the last bit, I say. "If it comes to it, we might just have to give them the fish."

At this, he looks horrified. "Just give it to them?"

At that, half my courage comes back. "You're absolutely right. To hell with giving it to them."

We push on.

At last the reef appears. But it's only a hummocky mass of white water. No place to land. One moment it's getting shallower, the next deeper, and the next, inky-black. The good thing is, the sharks are swimming in the same positions as before, neither faster nor slower.

I begin to think about towing the bayad to a safe place. Then remember what our shark psychologist Lambourski, once said. When a child, he'd once opened grandma's oven before the chicken was done, and received a walloping. And adding that to a shark, a wounded fish trundling along in open water, was likewise 'cooking nicely in Grandma's oven, and going no place'. Maybe explains why so many anglers' fish are grabbed by shark just before being hauled into the boat.

Another line of surf comes-and-goes, ahead. It's a long reef. *No getting to the other side of that!* The sharks come closer and we let out more line, not that there's much to let out.

A submerged ledge swirls by.

"Let's dump it!"

"No. Let's get out first."

"Ok, now!" Warner leaps out. Me too, headfirst into a pool, like a palsied frog. There's a tremendous tug and the line snaps. Warner slams down on his butt, back ramrod-straight, spear gun pointing down, looking like a snake-charmer who's momentarily mislaid the snake. I'm too stunned to laugh, then we both have difficulty stopping.

We eventually meet up with Pitsos and Lambourski who have a bayad almost as big as ours -- was. They'd simply waited in a channel and Lambourski had shot it when it came by.

Late at night, basking in the afterglow of Ben's bayad curry and falling asleep in the sand, I dreamed I was swimming alone in a dark sea. There was a violent commotion and a detached arm came floating by. I swam to it, to carry it back to the reef as I used to the saddleback in the old days. And wake up pouring with sweat. I stare at the fire, still pulsing faintly to a fractious wind prowling among the dunes like a restless Djinn.

What is it that causes these brief nightmares? Is it fear of shark, or something in the bayad's flesh, as in some of the goatfish and weke-fish of Hawaii? After eating which, one savant declared 'was like being fired from a rifle barrel lined with Baroque paintings.' Worse than being shot through one of Cezanne's oeuvres!

Or are they caused by Ben's mum's voodoo chutney? The first time we ate this memorable repast, we thought it was going to split us Brits and Americans apart, but in fact, has united us. And ever since, Ben's curry has become to the bayad, as curry is to fire, and nobody wants to separate them, just for the sake of an experiment.

Maybe, the nightmares are caused by all of the above? With sleep the dumbing-down process (the playing possum stage), and the nightmare, Nature's wake-up call.

I drag my eyes from the mesmerizing embers and let them glide along the escarpment's distant silhouette. I imagine I can see the radar perched on the highest point, above which storm clouds, lit by the radiant moon, are stacking high, lightening flickering within, as if in the mouths of giant cannons.

We could be back in the time of the Turks, or when the Captain of Periplus fame, sailing down this very coast, saw the faint fires of the fish-eaters. Or further back still, when early hunters huddled round the first-ever fires: And three fundamental entities: food, fear, and the exultation of the hunt, were bound together by an indivisible and invisible bond. Now we can easily separate these three components, lean forward before the video-thriller, or ease back in an armchair, and pop fish-fingers into our mouths. We have the choice. Upon that reflection, I must have fallen asleep, for I don't recall any more nightmares.

≈

The next evening, a great red sun sinks into the haze above the Sudan. In the lagoon, schools of silversides burst through the reflected mare's tails of strato-cumulous, like flights of high-flying birds.

I'm assembling a new spear. Warner's ripping out the soggy old sack from the inner-tube and threading in a new one. Pitsos is straightening his spear shaft by the simple procedure of pushing it into the sand at various depths, squinting down it and straightening it. Not exactly missile science. And Leo's gone back to applying mercurochrome to his abrasions.

Right at the beginning of our time here, we started with iodine for coral cuts, until Barnes said, "Don't use iodine, coral eats it. Gets it from the kelp." Sure enough, after many months some wounds under rice-paper-thin scar tissue, began to throb. The little critters were still alive!

So we switched to mercurochrome. "Putting on the wode," Leo called it, though we told him it was put on before battle. But it drew too much attention at work. Even the German from the dynamiter's camp, who gave us ice, and was generally a man of few words, remarked. "That's not mercurochrome is it?"

"No, it's strawberry jam," said I.

"It's carcinogenic."

"So is orange juice."

"Suit yourself." So we switched to hydrogen peroxide. When applying it at sundowners, we especially liked the way it fizzed and fussed over the smallest cut or fish-spine prick, yet foamed over acres of fire coral welts and grazes, like a tsunami gobbling up millions of bacteria, before vanishing. But we often forgot what we'd treated and what, not. No big deal, except by mid-week, the odd finger swelled up, turned pink and began to throb.

So we switched to Savlon, 'the germicide hospitals use.' Until Marsden said it was banned in New Zealand for actually spreading germs. So we're waiting.

Every species here spends a lot of time grooming and preening, it's something we all have in common, excepting the really big fish, hence their cleaning stations. And in time, this regular need to get rid of parasites from difficult places, evolved into a bonding ritual within a pecking order. With human warriors, the doctoring of wounds became an adorning process: ash rubbed into cicatrices, tattoos, sergeants' chevrons, and so on.

Getting a good buzz from the sid, I fancy I was feeling something similar to the hunters of old who, unable to make any quantum leap in their technology, simply settled into time-honoured routines. I even thought Pitsos might be charmed by this notion of us as latter day fish-eaters, settling into a *modus-vivendi,* within the *status-quo.*

No doubt these pompous phrases irritated him, for he was neither impressed nor amused. "How can you go burbling on like that?" He groaned. "I agree, we're bringing in bigger fish, but I'm also beginning to think, the more successful we're becoming, the more foolish we're becoming.

"How so?"

"The risks in bringing back bigger fish have started to outweigh the benefits. Or haven't you noticed? The sea gets deeper. The sharks bigger. "

"Maybe. Sometimes."

"And when you and Warner lose a big fish, you concentrate almost entirely on what to do next time, never on what might have happened. Hence your failure to entertain the notion of losing an arm, except in a dream."

A good point, I had to admit. And notice Warner, who's snipping the right-sleeve off a long-sleeved shirt, is staring at his foot, if I'm not mistaken the one the grouper bit, a long time ago.

"A new rule's coming lads, I can sniff it a mile off," says Leo, "Just what we need. Calls for another drink."

When we've topped up, Leo says. "Let's have it then. Keep it simple mind."

Simple it is.

"When you can't see the seabed or reef underwater," says Pitsos. "Put your safety catches on."

"That's all?"

"That's all."

Now, every time we leave the reef behind or the seabed fades from view, somebody's sure to nag. "Safety catch on, Dundas?" I suspect because I told them, I'd once gone spearfishing in Lake Turkana and failed to notice the crocodiles sunbathing on the shore. But it doesn't take me long to realise, the rule doesn't stop us going after big fish, just big fish in open, or deep water, as probably was its original intention.

67 Moonlight and acacias

Tonight by the acacias the heat left hanging in the air and the extraordinarily bright moonlight give the broad wadi the feeling of a summer's day. The sand lies quite still as if under a great weight of water, and the grey earth, laced with crushed mica, glows like the beach of some radiated atoll.

Though the moon itself is hidden behind the massif of the Jebel Adam, I can easily make out, two hundred yards up the wadi, a family of baboons going down to drink in tandem with their shadows, like escapees from the Ark. The bedhu call these nights 'white nights', when no one can approach unseen.

At times the whole earth seems to be holding its breath, then a small wind awakens from nowhere, gently billows the mosquito nets, and passes by as mysteriously as it has come. Something is sitting on the sand beside the biggest tree. Then there are two. "Little owls," whispers Barnes. One settles not two feet from my camp bed and peers at me with wobbly torch-bright eyes. Soon there are four, and the way they fly around with absolute quietness, gives magic to the place.

The mesh of entwined horizontal branches strains above us. The whole canopy stirs and shifts. Those thrusting upwards, unlock, scissor and lock once more.

When the moon rises over the Jebel's rim, light pours through a thousand tiny windows, and all change size together. The kaleidoscope is tapped again. Arabesques dance like fireflies over the sand, and then everything becomes still once more.

Imagine if you can, this multi-levelled intricacy frozen in stone, and you could be in an alcove of the Mosque of Sheikh Latfullah in Isfahan, of which Robert Byron wrote: "The European is astonished because until he sees it, he can have no idea that abstract pattern was capable of so profound a splendour."

Perhaps I had glimpsed something of its origins here, beneath the night sky and a thorn tree's dry branches.

68 Colonel Cufflink's cats

Colonel Cufflinks was officially fired as of yesterday, mainly because of his latest binge, which lasted all of five days.

This morning, he came shuffling into our garden wearing pyjamas and a week-old beard, the whites of his eyes flickering in grey sockets. He showed his termination of contract to anyone who wanted to have a peek – which we all did.

Its terse language hit me like hard rain: 'In spite of three official warnings, you have been absent from your duty station without due cause or notification thereof.... *You have repeatedly exhibited behaviour unbefitting a person in your position and with your responsibilities, etc., and so on.*'

He asked about the green frogs, chuckled over the marijuana plant and otherwise acted like a man at peace with the world. I hadn't the heart to ask him what was going to happen to the cats, but Rix did. "Who's going to take care of the cats?"

"The Koreans. Said they looked in good shape."

"Ah, well. Um... That's good." We said our goodbyes, wished him well, and hoped he'd make it.

The weird and wonderful thing is he did. Dried out, went on the wagon, dragged himself back into harness and became a Manager in one of the Gulf States.

Meanwhile, on the domestic front, the Koreans took their charges to the new airport landfill, where there were plenty of rats.

"What about the dogs?" We asked.

"If the cats survive the rats, the dogs will be the ones to worry."

A few weeks later, a new regulation came out. All accrued leave had to be utilized before year's end. Wives of middle management were however, allowed to visit two weeks in a calendar year, and incremental leave (five days or less) could be taken in Country. This last concession was considered a bit of a joke, like first prize: One night in the old Jeddah hotel; second prize, three nights.

As Pitsos' wife didn't want to be cooped-up in the Compound all the time, we set about planning a five-day trip up the coast, returning by the new highway along the escarp top.

69 The Last waltz

The permit fish remain elusive as ever. A few weeks ago I was hanging off the reef by Black Mountain, when a big wave came in. In the fog of fine haze, I thought I saw the hairline profile of a permit as if etched on frosted glass. But as the foam dispersed, nothing. Coming back in, I asked Warner if he'd seen anything unusual.

"Like what?"

"You tell me."

"Something came straight at me then dived."

"A permit you think"

"Could have been."

Today we are in the lagoon near the kelp beds, and the school of young permit (or not-so-young pompano) are back. This time Pitsos wants to know how they disperse when disturbed, and asks me to hide in the kelp, stay put, and watch what happens.

At first, the school is only a darkish blur, with individual fish no more than vague putty-shapes, and Pitsos himself, a log-like blob in the middle. As the school comes closer, I see the pompano (or juvenile permit) are actually circling him, albeit very slowly, almost sleepily. When almost opposite me, there's a silver-bright flicker, as one of the outermost fish switches direction.

I wondered if this was its way of announcing my presence to its companions. And might be what happens, when a mature fish in the outermost circle sees an angler's boat (or the angler himself) and the information is telegraphed back, circle-by-circle, to the fish nearest the bait. Could it also be what Malcolm McClane (the doyen of American Sport Fishing editors) was referring to, when he wondered if permit sometimes took a vote before the bait was swallowed?

I eased gently back into my hideout. As Pitsos came directly opposite me and began to move in an agitated manner, I witnessed something strange. When one fish disappeared behind him on the left, another reappeared a moment later, on his right, giving him the impression they were circling him, when in fact they were peeling away one by one, so:

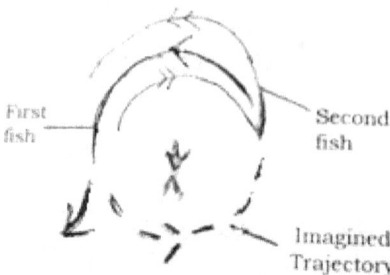

We called it The Last Waltz.

70 Resources and Strangers

Gaspar, out of the kindness of his heart, is going to help us with one of life's impossible problems, how to share a resource with strangers over the long term.

It sounds a mite ambitious to me, but with special sid as the come-on, we set to with a will.

He calls it his version of a problem known as The Prisoner's Dilemma, and begins with an apple (as the resource) and generous portions of special sid as the come-on.

"Two strangers spy an apple lying in their path." He says. "One picks it up and eats it. If he's the smaller, maybe he picks it up and makes off with it. This is *carpe diem* (grab the day), don't look a gift horse in the mouth, tactic. And, complain as much as you like, its good for the one-off meeting.

"But what if these strangers meet regularly and often find an apple lying in the path? They work out a way to share it."

Warner's not happy with Gaspar's mode of questioning. "How do you know if it's going to be long term? What if the stranger pulls out a gun and shoots you?"

"End of story. Not all stories have happy endings, ha, ha! Anyway, after a time, one party usually ends up complaining that he always gets the smaller half. So one bisects the apple while the other chooses, and they alternate roles. Contentment reigns.

"But life, as you suggested, can be a bitch. One day they're both arrested for stealing apples, and get thrown into separate prison cells. The prison warden is not interested in their story, and each is told, if he confesses and implicates the other first, he'll get out quickly, but the other will have to stay. After a time, one can't help thinking: 'If my erstwhile buddy tells on me first, I'll be in the shit and he'll get out. But he won't. But just suppose he does? In the end, he decides to ditch him first. So what's happened here at the resource level?

"I'm confused," says Leo. "You started out with apples as the resource, now you're on about two persons in prison."

"Good point." says Gaspar magnanimously. "Prison is the opposite of a resource, it's being deprived of one, in this case, physical freedom. Looked at this way, a material resource (apples) has gone missing, and to find the perpetrators of this dastardly deed, the local constabulary's been applying a little arm-twisting, in the hope one of the prisoners will betray a higher resource, trust. There's been a ratcheting up and lowering of resource levels. But where does it end? With a regime change, or longer?"

"Maynard Keynes once said, if you'll forgive me mentioning him, 'In the end we're all dead', whereas Mother Theresa thought it went on for ever, in heaven or hell. There are big questions lurking here, as well as one about trusting unknown policemen before your erstwhile mates.

"The average Joe's not entirely thick on this score, either: Where did this set-up all start? Who was the nice guy who put the apple tree on the ground in the first place? Was there ever a Mr. Nice Guy? Perhaps the apple got there by itself, or came from Kazakhstan? Perhaps it's a test?

"Remember in *The African Queen* (we saw the other night), when Kathryn Hepburn said to Bogart (Mr. Allnut!), 'Nature is what we were put into this world to rise above', and Bogie seemed more worried about falling below it than rising above it. The higher you climb, the further you fall. My guess is, with this problem, we all need all the help we can get. This brings us back to the problem of trust, betrayal, and its lesser brethren, cheats.

"It appears some of us, I'll mention no names, are simply unable to keep their part of the deal, and make silly mistakes. But some smart operators, when caught cheating, say the same thing. This drives many do-gooders bananas, and probably explains why cooperatives rarely last.

"However, some small cheats, corner-cutters and their ilk, may become pathfinders! Their short-cuts become freeways, and eventually – you've got grid-lock, ha, ha! And how about in your neck of the woods, Dundas, where they share according to time-honoured traditions, and usually manage to put something away for a rainy day?

"Works okay." I mumble.

"Excellent." He beams, "So you remember our main topic?"

"Um… it's slipped my mind for the moment, but you seem to have pretty much covered everything."

"Ha, ha! I'll be honest, too. It's about sharing a resource long term with strangers. And I've been a bit of a cheat myself. There's been no game-changing strangers. In your case, no Viking's daughter winking at one of your ancestors, long ago -- disrupting more than cash-flow. No intrusion of sheep, as in the Clearances. No killer viruses entering the salmon estuary. No old codger, named Adam Smith dropping by from Kirkcaldy." (Today more likely to be Donald Trump, but of course, we don't know that yet).

As Adam Smith gets no response, Gaspar adds, 'or some lads from St Andrews University, playing hooky in the nearby sand dunes (to avoid King James' compulsory longbow practice) inventing a new game, called golf."

"So what's the answer?" says Warner, whose finding all this name dropping a tad tedious.

"There isn't one; strangers being strange by definition, if you'll forgive me for saying so."

"So why are you bringing up all this stuff, if there's no answer?"

"Because there have been some interesting international competitions set up dealing with this very topic, involving inputs and strategies, from bacteria to bureaucrats, economists, social scientists, foreign policy gurus, military Think Tanks -- you name it, including one devilishly cunning anonymous one, which often came last. (Some of us guessed the CIA, but Gaspar says. 'No prize for guessing, guessing's too easy.')

But the one which stayed the course, best, stunned almost everyone by its baffling banality. Had only two rules: "Cooperate on the first move, and copy your opponent's thereafter."

"Sounds like an eye-for-an eye and tooth-for-a tooth," says Warner.

"It is, except some strangers have four eyes and others rows of replaceable teeth. And others offer small presents which just happen to prove poisonous, and cautious recipients learn to treat as vaccinations.

But it was the only game in town, where the thickest players could understand the rules, pronto, before being sucked into irredeemable follies. Yet didn't stop brain heavy ones from concocting sophisticated psychological ploys, which did little in the long run other than leave them mooning about during the coffee breaks with furrowed brows, like some international chess Masters.

"Coffee breaks? Chess games?" says an astonished Warner. "Sounds more like a Monopoly game played in a Five Star Hotel. If their own money, people play with different rules, and if other people's, other rules again."

"But that's life," says Gaspar indignantly. "I'm only trying to simplify. In fact, some ivory tower types actually set up sessions in the street, with cubicles and individual keyboards, and small groups of passers-by were invited to participate. They were told if no player touched his keyboard for X minutes, everyone would receive Y bucks. After double the time, double the pay-off. But if anyone touched their keyboard in the time set, nobody got anything.
"In one lot, a lad immediately typed in his name. Hadn't understood a word. Another spilled ketchup all over the keyboard. In another, after less than X minutes, a distraught mum remembered, she'd forgotten to pick up her daughter at the bus station, and needed taxi money pronto.

"There were several thefts and on two occasions, when people needed cash badly and lost out, some claimed it was a set-up, a rip-off. In one location, someone asked to see the man in charge, then biffed him one. A big man standing next to him, biffed him one in return. There was a punch-up.

"The main problem here appears to be, our propensity for emotional retaliation linked to improved technology. Sticks and stones, become knives and spears, knives and spears, missiles and bombs, and so on, to World War III."

"Bit of an exaggeration, surely." Says Leo.

"Not if you read history backwards." Says Rix.
"Of course, the cake can get bigger," Gaspar goes on, "the fridge more capacious, but so can the people, ha, ha! With perseverance you may suss out a stranger's motives and work to mutual benefit, but you still have to be wary of Greeks bearing gifts and gifts bearing Greeks, or being greeked, eh' Rixie?" (Some time ago, after driving all night, he'd been invited to take a shower by a friendly coastguard. Not a bad idea to be honest, but he'd been reading too much Laurence of Arabia, and left in inhospitable haste).

To lighten things up, Gaspar now finishes with a cautionary tale about a certain Capt. Kid, from a fishing fleet set far in the future.

"During one of the many declines of fish resources and commons," Gaspar goes on, "this worthy man did his best to help the local community. Held many meetings, pounded the table with the best of them and organised patrols which scoured the sea night and day, to keep out poachers.

When his wife set up the Fisherman's Provident Fund, he bought-up several abandoned wharf-side warehouses for chicken hatcheries, and all the time was secretly catching everything he could, and selling it to an offshore fleet.

When the local commons collapsed, he'd already sold-off most of the old factory ships and entered into a sustainable fishing venture with Namibia and Greenland.

When, many generations later, the global resources collapsed, his descendants had already left by rocket to a planet called Persephone.

"Several centuries later his look-alike, a clone, returned to make good. Said his venerated progenitor was the only one who'd really believed in the tragedy of the commons, others only thought they did. His entourage didn't do too badly, but his descendants proved a poor lot. Went the sexual route, became playboys, and ended up nicknamed the 'Clowns of the Billennium.'"

After that, Gaspar himself runs out of steam, and we all need a drink.

"Sid's finished." Says Warner.

"Can't be."

"Is." Says Gaspar.

≈

It's siesta time, only a few weeks later.

Peace reigns and the sea is so far out, the only sound is the gentle tapping of the tent awning. Far off, just beyond the reef, something catches my eye: A head, then several, bobbing about in the sea and a bit further on, parked in the middle of the sand flats, a yellow Bluebird bus.

"Fucking hell! Filipinos." I cry, "How did they manage that?" And have visions of small figures all over the lagoon, hunting for octopuses with wire hooks.

It's the Prisoner's Dilemma, and we're in it! Cooperate? No way! But wait a mo, that's for the long term, and this is short term. Very short term.

We stealthily angle the tent poles down and wait, not sure what to do. They could be stuck here and if not here, on the way back, when they try to cross the channel by the old Greek camp.

Already a dark stain is beginning to spread over the sand, and we see a man waving out to sea, looking a bit like Fernandes from Toyota.

Figures wave back and a horn blares.

When we look again, nobody is about. But they could be sitting in the shade of the bus, getting a pep talk.

Soon the bus lurches forward, followed by rhythmic chanting. Bodies swarm aboard. And as it slowly moves off, we hear an engine rumble into life.

71 Yemen days

8 a.m. "I've brought someone who knows you," says Rix. A man walks over, pale as marble.

"Lance Corporal Thompson of the Yemen days! Am I glad to see you!"

"Christ alive! Whatever happened to you?" he says, "Skinny as a rake!"

"And you remind me of the day, the Emir of Dhala brought out those four pale bloated humpty-dumpties, chained together in the bottom of that dark well." (Hostages, mere kids, sons of neighbouring Sheiks and had us watch them blinking in the unaccustomed sun)."

There was a kind of sigh. Then he said, half-turning to the others. "You won't believe this, but it was snowing when I left Inverness."

This is too much for Steve, who has a fit of hiccups and inane giggles, giving the impression we're a long shipwrecked band of poor whites, gone simple.

"You'll have to excuse him. Hasn't been on leave for a while."

"Maybe he and I can swap places? Let me check with Mr. Rix, I'm sure he can arrange it," and looks around for him. "Where's he off to now? Amazing fellow! 'Ask the Ancient Mariner' they said, when I first mentioned your name, and this bearded chap comes up, fixes me with a dodgy eye, 'Did I hear you say you were a friend of Dundas? That's your problem. But I can take you to him.' Asked him where you were and he said, 'Down the road.' Never told me how far! And you know what it reminds me of?"

"Of course. The Kureiba Pass, to Dhala."

"Six thousand feet would it be?"

"Almost exactly. But you can't possibly go back tonight."

"Must, Sorry. Already got my ticket to a place called Sharorah."

"The back of beyond! Then we are lucky to meet."

"Mr. Rix also mentioned you might have some old snorkelling gear to spare?"

"No problem." And soon have him toffed up in several T-shirts and plenty suntan oil. "Keep it off the mask dinkhead!"

"Ha, ha! Just like Khormaksar beach!"

Swimming out, we pass the resident barracuda. "What a beaut!" He remarks and asks about sharks.

"Not dangerous, plenty fish to go round, I hope." But as the barracuda seems unusually interested in the contrast of his white skin against black flippers, add that he shouldn't move too fast.

He told me, the patches of cold water we swam through were probably from fresh springs under the sand, and I told him not to try and stand up without looking down first, as there could be stingrays, and so on. It wasn't too different from the times down the coast. He told me about his family and water resourcing job. Then we talked about old times.

5 p.m. He leaves in a whirlwind of dust, and I can still hear the muffled cough of the mortars and another Major's voice.

"Well, what was that all about?" asks Pitsos, when we settle down for sundowners. "Heard you chortling away on the reef."

"I'd better start at the beginning."

"Fire away, sid's in the bucket."

"Pretty small beer. But here goes. "Army days. Late 1950's. There were two Yemens then. The South was known (at least to us) as the Aden Protectorate. And Little Aden was a coaling station, much as San Juan, Puerto Rico and Pearl Harbour, Hawaii, were oil depots to the U.S. in the early days of oil." Then recalled how the Head of Sandhurst had lectured us at Eaton Hall's Passing out Parade on how the Indian Ocean was now a power vacuum, with Diego Garcia in the Chagos Islands, the bull's eye. And things were going to be arranged accordingly.

"Our job was to keep the peace locally. Bit like here, give or take a few hundred years: tiger sharks in the sea, jocks posted with Lee Enfield rifles to scare them off, and up-country, little men guarding the quat fields with all manner of ancient artillery. But as-per-usual, the natives were restless."

Pitsos places an inner tube flat on the icebox, prior to cutting out catapults, and sips his drink.

"Outside Little Aden, we practised crowd control. In the event of a local riot, blanks were to be issued and live ammunition to the marksmen. In those days there were no rubber bullets or tear gas.

In the Company Sergeant Major's (CSM's) scenario, The Front for the Liberation of Occupied South Yemen (FLOSY) was the devil incarnate, and we would be making up the disciplined rectangle, opposing them.

Two warnings to disperse would be given over the loud-hailer in Arabic. If the crowd continued to advance, an ultimatum would be issued. If the crowd persisted, they would be fired upon. In this event, one section would fire at a single target, in practice usually referred to as the man in the red shirt, or waving a red flag.

The CSM had always been a past-master at keeping our attention on the parade ground and outdid himself here. He arranged for one rifle platoon at a time to control the other two (plus some odds-and-sods from HQ, who needed the exercise) and all sections acted in turn as the riot.

Needless to say, the lads took full advantage of this. All manner of insults, plus chanted taunts from the home terraces, including rocks and stones, rained down on us. Though we practised for weeks, and several lads made it to the infirmary, the first practice is the one I remember best, especially the CSM's post-mortem."

Pitsos starts cutting the inner tube into narrow strips.

"The CSM took us aside individually," I go on.

'Lieutenant Cameron, Sir', He started real quiet, 'Resorted to the loud-hailer did we? Couldn't make ourselves heard? Forgotten what the parade ground's for, have we? Well, let me tell you sir; standing like you did with the loud-hailer,' his voice rising like a wave smacking into the seawall at Fort George, 'you're a dead man.' Then he went all quiet. 'I'd be delinquent in my duties if I let that happen, wouldn't I?' He appeared overcome with remorse, almost penitential. 'How would I make it up to you? We'll have to devote more time to it, won't we?' And then, cock-of-the roost again, bawled out, 'Report to the Adjutant's Office, Guard House, 5.45 a.m., for defaulters' drill, 6 a.m., Mondays and Fridays!'

"Lieutenant McLeod was next. 'Your caution was a right marvel,' he began with uncompromising earnestness, the volume rising slowly. 'You stopped south-side of the Murray Firth to do your business in the Black Isle. But because of your utter failure to locate the man waving the red flag, the entire assembly was unaware if it was arsehole or breakfast time, or they'd been invited to the Queen's Garden Party.

'I'm going to give you a piece of advice, for your own sake, Sir.

Next time, get your teeth into it! Or you'll find yourself facing a Board of Enquiry for opening fire without due provocation. We don't want that, do we?' And again, bawled out. 'Report to the Adjutant's Office, Guard House, 5.45 a.m., for defaulters' drill, 6 a.m., Wednesdays and Thursdays!'

"Then it was my turn. 'Lieutenant Dundas. You got in close enough. Highly commendable'. *But spoke so quietly, not another soul heard it.* 'Then ordered your men to fire before giving them the order to load,' and his voice rose, without rhyme or reason. 'Never in my born days have I seen such a right-regimental cock-up at platoon level! You'll not only get yourself killed, but your men too. Men with wives and children, from Moffat, Nairn, Grantown, Inverness, Banff and Dufftown. All by your own foolishness. I'll not have it. We're not playing soldiers anymore. *We are soldiers.* Understand me, Sir.'

'Yes Sergeant Major.'

'Report to the Adjutant's Office, Guard House 5.45 a.m. for defaulters' drill, 6 a.m. Tuesdays and Saturdays.' *Fucking hell*, I thought. *Saturdays! I'll miss the Khormaksar swimming race.*

Pitsos has stopped what he was doing and is staring at the sand. "Slow down a moment," he says. "Let me get something clear. Did you actually have to do any of this?"

"No. But I would have."

"And you're worried about how you could order someone to be shot so easily?"

"All I worried about was doing it right, not whether it was the right thing to do."

He scoops the rubber strips off the icebox into the sack, and continues without preamble. "When I was a trainee pilot, we did a spell aboard ship to see what Search-and-Rescue was like from their end. With us were a small group of officers about to take up their first commands. The last day, towards the end of the Captain's summing up, he asked myself and another, where we were.

"We did our calculations, carefully double-checked them, went up and put a cross on the wall chart behind him. He then asked the Navigation Officer, who happened to come by, the same thing. The Navigation Officer put a large hand over our own mark.

"I thought it was the hoary old dictum, experience knows best," Pitsos went on. "It was, but there was a little sting in the tail. The Captain then added that he'd manipulated us into concentrating on giving a too-correct answer and, almost in the same breath, congratulated the new officers on taking up their first commands."

It was too much for me to absorb in one go, and I only remember asking Pitsos where the CSM fit into this.

"That's easier", he'd said. "He expects to be put in a situation where somebody's going to get hurt. His job is to make sure it's the other guy." I took a good swig of sid and forgot to ask about other ranks.

"So what happened after all the practice?" Steve pipes up.

"I'm just coming to that. We were lucky. Got moved up-country. There our job was to offer assistance to the South Yemenis in case the North Yemenis crossed the border in any force. The border was the problem. To put it frankly, border-skirmishes were as common to them as football fixtures were to us Brits. Many went back generations.

At Mukerias, the locals went into battle at the run, bugles blowing, and ended them religiously at sunset, whereas the Emir of Dhala, lead his men from the rear, and the battles generally ended in confusion.

Tribal loyalties were loaned and exchanged, and every bit as secretive as inter-football club transfers. Diehard supporters were just that. Didn't simply jeer and boo when a former player turned up on the opposite side, but fired bullets, and tried to kidnap his family. One time, a village shot at one of our convoys delivering supplies to a fort. The locals were forbidden to harvest in the area for one season, and then a Hawker Hunter firing a burst over the interdicted zone, hit a woman by mistake. More trouble.

"So where did the border fit into this?" asks Warner.

"Hold on a mo. I'm just getting to that. Originally, it was more or less a joke, more theirs than ours. But it soon began to make these immensely sociable, but moody quat-munchers nervous – like a rumour about a Super League. One now bringing in foreign players, big guns and its own rules."

While Pitsos refills the ice bucket, I place two mugs on the groundsheet, the first, standing for Fort Qutaba, manned by North Yemeni regulars and rumoured to have several T34 tanks. And the other for Fort Sana, opposite it, a Beau Geste-like edifice perched on a small hill, our side of a wide plain.

"Our camp was a few miles back, with sufficient space for an infantry company and support weapons, all tucked rather too comfortably beneath the massif of the Jebel Gehaf. It was protected by four-and-half-foot high walls round the other ranks' area, and six foot high, round the officers', giving each an appropriately graded sense of security.

Sometimes, Fort Quataba would fire its big gun. If the shell didn't explode, an ambush would be set up in case someone was sent to retrieve it.

One day a skirmish developed between our ambush party and a sheep-raiding one, and things began to get out of hand. We were called-out to take up a defensive position by Fort Sana. Live ammunition was issued. Private Wylie from Glasgow, who'd helped our platoon win the Company Patrol Competition (by going behind 'enemy lines' towing a goat) wanted to know if it was for real. A cosy chat with the CSM, who hardly raised his voice, convinced him, it was.

"In next to no time, we were gliding along in our three tonners over the soft sand on the way to Fort Sana. An open-top Landrover sped past us with the long-barrelled 106 mm recoilless anti-tank rifle, already mounted. Cheers went up. Not much later, we passed a donkey with a tremendous stiffie. 'One-o-six fully loaded', shouted Lance-Corporal Thompson, and was greeted by more cheers.

Fifteen minutes later, we were spread out on the stony ground by Fort Sana, where we'd practised so many times. From nearly every position, men were soon squinting down their sights and picking out familiar objects at different ranges.

Over the chirping of the cicadas, I heard the Company Commander, Major Logan, calling on the Levies for mortar support. But nothing happened.

238

Local tribesmen appeared from the direction of Quataba and began to fall back through our lines, waving, laughing and muttering to themselves. Then a group of red-turbaned National Guardsmen came past, carrying a wounded man. Behind them, about a quarter of a mile away, a well-formed line of white-turbaned riflemen appeared, dropped down and began firing in our direction.

I was feeling something of Churchill's 'nothing in life is so exhilarating as to be shot at, without result', when the Company-runner slipped down beside me and whispered, 'From the Major, sir. We're to give one clip from every man to the Bren section, immediately.' This meant that we were beginning to run out of ammunition, which was impossible, or were going to attack, which was unbelievable. The Bren-gunners scrambled away to the flank, using the dead ground well, their backs practically parallel to the ground, excellent lads!

When in position, the Major, bold as brass, walked out in front of us and, in the same voice that I'd heard him say 'Game to Miss Brown' at the Khormaksar Tennis Club, gave us a string of commands, ending with 'B Company. Fix bayonets.'"

I glanced at Pitsos. "I don't know if you remember when the Medic had us fiddling with those new medicine bottle-caps, but that's what our Company looked like, trying to fix bayonets. Another order was given and the Company found itself in an extended line, last adopted when facing a row of swinging sandbags at Fort George.

'The Black Bear, laddie,' said the Major to Piper Thompson, Lance Corporal Thompson's brother. But all that came from him was a pneumatic sigh, like that of a dying cow.

The Major waited no longer but turned about, and facing the distant plain, boomed out, 'B Company advance!'

We walked forward in a numbing silence, but all that came from Piper Thompson, was a blubbering whimper, followed by a squeak.

The sheep's stomach, which he kept hefting-up over his own like a fractious but sleepy child, seemed to be struggling with him. His face grew redder and redder. All of a sudden, a piercing skirl burst forth in full flood and went rolling over the plain.

The white-turbaned figures stopped a moment, before throwing themselves to the ground as the pipes were joined by the muffled cough of the mortars and the clatter of the Brens. It was like the steps of an ancient dance: Yemen mountain troops and a Company of Highland Scots come to give a last hurrah before passing from the stage.

Then two shots rang out, much closer than the rest, and a treacherous clarity gave my story a life of its own. The lenses of the Major's binoculars shattered. Piper Thompson stopped playing and rolled over. I saw the slug pop out from the back of his skull, like a parrot's tongue, followed by gobs of brain.

We laid his body out under an Ilb tree and placed a blanket over him. As we waited, his pet chameleon crawled out slowly as a crab, crossed the path and turned bright green when it reached the other side."

≈

There was one problem with the end of this story. Only a few distant shots were fired, and Piper Thompson was never shot. I made it up for dramatic effect. In fact, Lance Cpl. Thompson later got demoted for allowing his section to leave behind a Brengun magazine, mercifully empty, on the small hill next to our camp.

I eventually told Pitsos, and guess he told the others. For one evening at sundowners, Rix tells us Lance Cpl Thomson is back from Sharorah.

"What?" My face must have fallen, because everyone laughed.

"Only kidding," he said. "But we're all happy to hear that his brother, Piper Thompson is back from the dead. Cheers!"

72 Marsden's last leave

Marsden's handing out the mail. "Donahue! Dundas! Some lovely Norwegian stamps there. If you don't need 'em I'd appreciate them." And throws me a letter. "Jack?"

"I'll take it", shouts a voice. "Owes me thirty bucks."

"Please take note," Marsden continues and drops his bombshell. "Contract ends in ninety days." Everyone receives an envelope, giving the final details of all payments and benefits, plus two forms to fill in. Then nods to our lot, "If you hadn't been gallivanting round the Red Sea so much, you'd already have a nice job lined up, like young Ben here, ha, ha!"

"Breaks my heart," I say. "Pour me a drink."

Some old timers, strangely sober when it comes to finances, stuff the envelopes into their breast pockets and carry on drinking. That's what I do (after a quick peek at my total) and watch Lambourski.

One part of him seems to want to leap up-and-down with the Yanks. For this is the moment he's been waiting – for someone, anyone – to have the decency to kick him home where he belongs. Yet another part of him knows it's not exactly the best moment for an American (same job, more pay) to break ranks with the seasoned journeymen, he's travelled with so long.

For most of us Brits, certainly for me, it's the best pay packet I've ever had; yet some are already expressing dire opinions about the severance pay package and end-of-term bonus. "How come the strange reaction?" I put this to Van beside me.

"Scared of becoming light-headed," he says. "Splurging it on tonight's poker game, I know. I'm one of them."
"For Chrissake Van. Don't even think of it." Then I realize it's meant as a joke. But that's how it usually began, with a joke – a dare. His minders, two beefy men from the Military Mission, come forward and stand beside him. He changes the subject. "How come Marsden's flogging bits of rock and bottles of sand, when he's got a whole pub to sell off?"

"Getting rid of the rubbish first, I guess."

Down the bar Marsden advances a piece of Desert Rose like a small tank through a mine-field of beer mats, towards Cowboy, whose squinting down a long letter. Then he takes a dimpled Haig from behind the bar, filled with compacted layers of coloured sand (ostensibly from the Empty Quarter) and places it before Lambourski. "Shan't be trucking there again," he says, almost wistfully.

"You were never out there." says Cowboy.

"I was, Sir." That ridiculous 'Sir,' should have warned me, but Cowboy is mellow and impressed – or pretends to be. "A piece of Desert Rose?" He muses, rocking back and forth in his boots, hands stuck in his famous belt, and settles down to consider things.

On my other side, just out of view, two old-timers start up, and by their conversation I guess they've still got the Sharorah sand in their ears.

"Your storeman back yet? Sorry. Material Expediter to you."

"Store man you mean?"

"Yes."

"Nope."

"Thought his brother was a Radio Comms on a tanker. Set him up in a VIP cabin for the duration?"

"Well, not this time, he didn't. Locked himself in a five-star hotel. Put his usual call in, though. Hear he had palpitations when the plane touched down."

"Not bad timing, huh? And a little bird tells me you're thinking of flying Concorde?"

"Just an idea."

"Go for it, I say."

"I thought so too. Last time out. Why not?"

Marsden gives them the old eyebrow and gestures towards the piece of Desert Rose. "A memento of the desert?"

A liver-spotted hand comes forward, fingers it tentatively like a camel spider sensing an opportunity, and slowly turns it over. There's an intake of breath. "A mite pricey." He says.

"And you're flying Concorde?"

I can almost see the old boy shaking the sand out of his ears and grinning.

Indeed, there's a lot going on round here, you'd never pick up on if you were new. For example, Rix watching Cowboy.

In the early days of the Club, Rix was Brewmaster, Marsden Treasurer and Cowboy, who sang and played guitar, Entertainments Officer. When he spoke, women didn't pay much attention, but when he sang, it was a different matter (though to my mind what came out was pretty much the same stuff).

One evening he had shown Rix once too often, a photo of himself and the wife on a grassy slope, in front of a log cabin. "How nice," Rix had said "Two acres and a cow." There had been a fight, a terminal offence. Marsden had fined them both for arm-wrestling on the bar. And had a bar-length, leather-cushioned elbow-rest, installed on the proceeds. Disparagingly called the gay bar at first, it was soon thoroughly appreciated.

Then, there'd been my first meeting with Marsden. He'd come over real friendly-like, with a piece of rock in his hand, which he proceeded to crumble into pieces. "As a Scotsman," he'd said, "What do you think this is?"

"A rock."

"It's granite."

"If there's one thing it's not, is granite." I replied, and remember being more worried about the grammar than the rock, having already been accused of spelling cassette with one 's'.

"Want to bet?"

"Sure."

"Ten bucks." And he called over a young geologist, I hadn't noticed (who later got lost in the desert and claimed the young bedhu lasses had given him freebies, while the men were out looking for the camels). He proclaimed it granite on the spot. Said the feldspar crystals, quartz and other minerals, expanded at different rates in the heat, causing it to crack.

"Let you off this time," Marsden had said. "But your round." And rang the bell. A whole table of geophysicists behind me, who'd been unusually quiet up to then, chorused. "Thanks Dave, cheers mate!" *Cost me double.*

Marsden moves down to Lambourski and raises the Haig bottle, with its pretty layers of sand. "How about this from the Empty Quarter, for your kid?"

"Let's put it this way," says Lambourski, "I *love* my kid, but were I to start giving him bottles of sand – no offence – he'd think I was coming up a few cents short on the dollar. While we've been mucking about in the desert, he's gotten himself into computers, science fiction and a ring in his nose."

"What about *Dune* then?" says an already pissed Steve. "Some of these layers could be pulverized dinosaur droppings."

"Now you're talking! Get me a lump of fossilized dinosaur dung and we're in business, but this bottle is too sissy."

"You're missing the point," says Marsden. "Making it too easy for him, because you're on a high roll. Believe me. You did your stint in Sharorah before you'd saved a cent, didn't you? And when you turned up here, were a zombie, remember?"

"Remember."

"Well then, let him see with his own eyes what you had to stare at, day-in-day-out, so you could get him his fancy computer. Package it with this simple bottle of sand, which he can put up on the shelf along with his computer games."

"But I never really went into the Empty Quarter, I sat inside most of the time."

"That's what I mean. You were *in it*. Staring at it like you've been staring at this bottle behind the bar, and never saw it. Oldest form of camouflage in the book."

"Never thought I'd say it, but you may have a point. A lot of the time, I pretended I was working on NASA's Mars Landing Program."

"That's what I mean. Totally spaced! We could all see it."

"Better give it me, before I change my mind."

Cowboy's beginning to sway back and forth before the piece of Desert Rose, like a mesmerized cobra. After a time, he asks, 'How much?'

"For you, no charge."

"Hang on a mo, don't rush the brush." Then without warning, reaches up, clangs the bell and bellows at the top of his voice, "Here's to the best fucking Rose in all the world!"

"Proudly spoken!" says Marsden. "Let me wrap it for you," humming quietly "as they say in the West, the old saddle fits best."

Marsden never came back from his last leave. Died of a heart-attack in London. And we only heard about it later. At his wake, the bar was dismantled, and that's putting it mildly. Behind it, among the beer mats and football memorabilia, we found: Warner's old flipper (the one the grouper bit) all gunged-up and covered in dust, a whiskey bottle half full of sand, the remains of Leo's T-shirt which the shark bit, all tangled up with an Umm Kaltoum tape, and a sepia-tinted photo of Victorian era sportsmen in buttoned-down shirts, holding up an over-exposed trophy fish.

At night in the wee hours, in strangely time-warped dreams, I'd often hear voices whispering, 'Marsden's dead', and all too familiar ones protesting. 'No, not Marsden. Not here, he isn't'.

73 Comeuppance

Warner and Gaspar have been looking at the old tide charts for Karachi and Jeddah, and somehow calculated that within a month the water will fall below the mullet pond barrier. Then, in the next storm, the barrier will probably be washed away.

So here we are two weeks later, at the barrier, and by some fluke, seem to have the timing just right. The water level is a good six inches above it and going down. Mullet are travelling this way-and-that but not entering the pond, though the water is high enough for them to do so.

We move forward and peer in. Half a dozen big mullet, faintest tinge of blue-violet on the fins and tails, are cruising about like carp in a monastic pond; fade away then return again.

When Steve and Warner float off to see if some are crossing further down, I while away the time removing pebbles so one of us can slide in, if need's be.

A frumpish emerald-and-mauve blenny comes out of a nearby hole to observe things, fluffs up its pectorals, back-heels the blind shrimp before it's finished emptying the ashtrays, and ogles me like I'm a photographer from *National Geographic*.

On the past occasions when we've tried to catch these shrimp, they've always escaped with the blenny into a warren of hard, dead coral. Now it dawns on me, if that's the norm, the barrier was probably once a living reef, and the mullets' ancestors been coming here for donkey's years. So perhaps we've been wasting our time waiting for them to enter the pond, as they already know the rhythm and level of the tides, and we don't.

But that said, the shoe's now on the other foot. Ours. As Gaspar has so patiently lectured us, once the habitual behaviour of an opponent and one's own departure date, are both known (like our end-of-contract), nature's winning practitioner is the one who grabs first and successfully absconds.

When Steve and Warner return and report that no mullet are going in, I put my suggestion to them. "Someone should go in and get one."

"Good try," says Warner. "But I thought the pond was meant to be a safe-haven. Or have you forgotten?"

I explain that knowing the contract-end date, probably makes this our last visit, and so changes the situation.

"But with this safe-haven business," says Warner. "It's us you're dealing with, the mullet don't know what you're talking about."

I'm surprised he's being so stroppy about this, and there's an unhappy silence.

Steve tries to help. "On this caper, you started out a fish-hunter, became Mr. Nice Guy – offering the mullet a safe-haven – but have ended up, a fishy-human being."

We move on, but gracious I'm not. And Lambourski's savoury steamed-mullet -- with its nip of chilli, buzz of ginger and tart of astringency of lemon grass still destined to be a memory of thing's past.

74 The Night Porter

"What was that about?" asks Barnes, tapping a piece of wood back into the evening fire. "You were yipping away like Gasper's puppy asleep on the beach."

"A weird dream. I was leaning over the railings of the *Oranje Fontaine* (our ship back from Australia) as it smashed through the waves, and pointing at the flying fish skimming over the sea. A horrified Dutch woman, dressed in a flouncy mauve-and-green dress, not unlike the blenny on the mullet barrier, is bawling at me. I shout back, *'Hou je bek!'* (Shut your gob), scamper away, but don't escape a walloping."

"You're still steamed-up about missing out on Lambourski's steamed-mullet," says Barnes, "but the dream's telling you, no need to go overboard, ha, ha!" Then suggests Gaspar's puppy's dreams aren't just Match of the Day replays, but severely edited versions. "The puppy remembers that ghost crabs have deep holes then forgets the claws down the hole. Hence the 'Yip!'"

Barnes now tells us about Konrad Lorenz's dog, which once barked at him because he was wearing a friend's raincoat, then ran on and barked up a tree.

"Some dreams express feelings covered up by other feelings," he continues, "and as the dream has to grab whatever images are available (the rapid-eye movement), it's often a mix between a mad-hatter's tea party and a post office nightshift (trying to pigeonhole items) but whose work's never done. Maybe explains why, on waking, we sometimes catch members of the dream-staff scurrying offstage with the weirdest props (the night circuits fading as the day ones cut in).

"Some dreams," he chunters on, "are like over-protective mums or feather-bedding union reps, saying, 'No way is our boy going to bring home the bacon today (our bacon too) without a couple of hours more shuteye.' And arrange things accordingly.

"Sometimes they simply get it wrong. Have you never had an important early morning interview, and everything goes swimmingly, till you wake up, and find you've overslept?"

"No."

"Maybe explains a few things. Anyway, whenever we wake up bright-eyed and bushy-tailed, our morning prayers should be, 'Thank you Neurons. Great Hollywood movies last night, slept through the lot.'"

"And if Konrad's old mutt had been playfully scolded for eyeing-up the neighbour's new chickens, it would probably have wagged its tail at being thought spry enough to have a go. Then dreamed of chasing chickens dressed-up as rabbits, and on waking, only remembered chasing rabbits".

"Now you really are talking utter bollocks!" We all chime in. But he says, it's much the same as being served Polish beef dressed-up as bacon at breakfast here, so as not to offend our Muslim hosts and help us forget what real bacon tastes like.
Then he suddenly hisses at Steve, "Hey Stevie! Don't go to sleep on me. You remember Pritchett's dream? The one you used to recite," adding *sotto voce,* "when pissed?"

"About the night porter, you mean?"

"That's the one."

And Steve's off, stopping only to remove a speck of ash from his eye:

"One night, just before the start of the Spanish Civil War, my train stopped at Medina del Campo and I woke up to hear the porter calling the name of the station in an extraordinary measured and resonant manner which I have never forgotten.

Over the next few years, I was liable to nightmares of physical violence in which I was attacked and defeated by terrifying enemies.

When I was in France, I dreamed that the night porter at Medina del Campo had annoyed me, telling me that the train had gone when I knew it had not. I fought and grappled with him and flung him victoriously to the ground on the line before the oncoming train. After this I had no more dreams of violence.

In subsequent years I heard many interpretations of this dream, especially from amateurs of Freud but only much later did the likely fancy occur to me that it had connection with a childish battle with my grandfather, a very alarming man. I once shouted at him that I hoped he would be killed by a train at the level crossing near Sedbergh in Yorkshire.

I got a spanking and I can still feel the sting of his hand to this day."

Hardly has he finished, when the rig begins shaking. A ghostly apparition appears, a camel's head suspended six feet in the air, its owner scratching its back on the corner of the roof-rack. Then a hairy creature, like a mouse, runs down the guy rope and jumps on to Rix's neck before disappearing into the dark. A camel spider! When things settle down, Steve goes on. "I've been thinking, Dundas. This morning, when you tried to pull a fast one on us about the mullet by changing safe-haven to fish-pond, you were strictly right according to that prisoner's dilemma stuff, because our approaching departure date is now known. But maybe, we were wrong to go along with the safe-haven idea in the first place. Too easy to offer, too hard to deliver."

"So?"

"What I mean is, you've kept most of the other rules, haven't you?"

"Like what?"

"Not shooting saddleback in the grouper's playground."

"But I did once or twice."

"In that case you deserve a midnight dunk." He says enthusiastically.

"Let's hear the sordid details first," says Barnes.

"Not much to tell really."

"Let's hear them anyway."

So I told them, spinning it out like Scheherazade. "Swimming back late at night over the lagoon, I came across a saddleback and changed the word 'fish' to 'dinner', much as those noble sons of the desert, the Anazi do, when they change the word 'guest' to 'visitor', and so never steal from guests.

I felt grateful too; left the spear in, so as not to let any blood out. And, as I pushed the saddleback before me, through the last reed bed, its sky-blue dots began to glow. As its jaw opened and closed, a line of tiny midnight-blue jewelled lights came-and-went above its upper lip like some new-fangled fashion statement. And, behind needle-sharp teeth, as closely packed as the bristles on a toothbrush, a filigree of taut silk fluttered palest blue. The whole assemblage became beautiful but alien, like a hot-house orchid or coral bloom, opening to the night currents.

I think the others were asleep by the time I'd finished.

Bye and bye, when we next got a large grouper (a *kushar*, the best tasting), it was served to all but me. No warning, no sauce, just rice. And I thought, how vindictive and petty, but almost effective.

75 Mullet rage

Early morning. Soap and bucket of water. Two freshly washed shirts (no suntan oil) and am out of camp in the pre-dawn quiet.

Give the inshore mullet pond a wide berth and head out to the mullet glades. If I could get a mullet there or in open water, no safe-haven would be involved, and Lambourski's steamed mullet, not necessarily be a dish of yesteryear. Upon such a nicety I built new hope.

I am no sooner ensconced in my usual coffin, like an old club member in his favourite armchair, when a fair-sized barracuda moves in, turns awkwardly round, and is gone. It's as if a senior waiter had plunked a double whiskey before me, only to withdraw it in consternation. And clear to me that these Diagalevs of our reefs, who like others to dance to their tune, can't always dance so well themselves.

After a time I notice a school of plankton-eating mackerel circling in a cloud of sand, near the reef. The fact that plankton-eating mackerel don't usually circle, but patrol in long sweeps outside the reef, doesn't bother me. I decide to exit the glade and observe them closer.

I've hardly gone twenty yards, before I'm in the middle of the largest school of mullet I've yet seen. Had I my wits about me, I'd have done nothing, but as if my action was immune to any long-term consequences, I swing my spear gun uselessly this way-and-that. The mullet bolt all over the place and I end up letting fly at one well out of range. Swear words aren't enough, but I let fly a string of them anyway, to bid them on their way.

I kept this incident under wraps until the morning Warner and Lambourski report seeing a large school of mullet completely by-pass the glades.

When I offer two carefully written pages in my diary by way of explanation, Warner refuses to read them. "Why don't you just say, 'Sorry. Lost my temper.'"

"Sorry. Lost my temper."

Pitsos then suggests my apology is the easy part and the explanation, the hard part. And adds his twenty cents. "When we and mullet meet in open water, I think a tiny change in our body-stance or tensing of the spear arm, tells them the only thing they really need to know: We are not plankton-eaters or turtle grass-munchers, but fish-eaters merely masquerading as the former.

And the thrill to us of any successful subsequent swing-shot (often as exciting to relate, as boring to listen to) is not an incidental technique, but an age old adaption, going back to the first projectile our ancestors ever hurled at a moving target.

But it's maladaptive with regard to the mullet here, because, though a few swing shots may prove lucky, our efforts will eventually drive them away."

And he concludes cryptically. "Some people can stop smoking, when they accept that they're only doing it in order to smoke the next one. That is, it's become an addiction."

Gaspar however, is sufficiently impressed with my explanation, to photocopy it as the first example of mullet rage recorded on our coast. He also adds that with local trawlers now working the Red Sea's deeper water, hand-net artisans the shallow lagoons and us poking our noses into the Tihama's remoter nooks-and-crannies, the mullet are probably being harassed all over the globe! He's even heard they're migrating through the Suez Canal and causing the tastier varieties in the Med, to forage nearer the surface.

≈

A month later, the pitiful episode of mullet rage well behind me, we find ourselves watching a new lad lining up a parrotfish for the chop (despite just being told we don't shoot them).

"Point you gun somewhere else," hisses Leo, "can't you see it's relying on you not to shoot it?" The upset lad explains he was only lining it up for practice. But of course, the unfortunate fish didn't know that, rolling its eyes and banking like the Red Baron, avoiding a Sopwith Camel.

I mention this incident here not to denigrate the worthy lad, but because the phrase 'relying on', being used to express a parrotfish's attitude to us, shows just how far we've come with this fish thing. Not shooting them has become part of our highway code, like stopping at a red light. And anyone shooting one and not feeling

253

our unease, would probably not feel any on deserting us, should a shark come by.

On summing up our present attitude to mullet and parrotfish, I now realize we've ended up (as with the acacias) pretty much opposite to how we began. And the mullets' cleverness, if I may call it that, (at least with regard to myself) lay in the aggravating nature of their boringness. That is, not in whether they knew where we were or not, but in not letting on, either way.

With the big-butted parrotfish on the other hand, not only do they prune the coral gardens, scour and scrub the reef's pavements and help make the best beaches, but also they've built up a massive fan base. They've garnered the votes! On our daytime reefs, happy parrotfish mean happy reefs, nervous ones; nervous reefs.

At night, it's trickier. The big ones wrap themselves in cling-wrap, keep their metabolism to a minimum, and never mind the colour our torches show, hope for the best.

76 The forgotten Tihama road

Behind the bar, Marsden, who has got approaching leave fever (but knowing nothing of his future demise), is telling us we can keep our Red Sea. "Been up it too many times in the Merchant Marine," he says. "Aden, Port Said, Assab, Massawa. You name it, I've been there."

"Massawa's in Israel, you pillock," says cowboy.

"You're thinking Masada," says he, and turns to the Major's *Daily Telegraph* world map behind him. "Want to bet?"

"Then you're a queer." Says Cowboy, and doesn't want to bet.

"How come?"

"You said before, 'Aden's the asshole of the world, Hodeida and Massawa, six inches up it. Ha, ha!"

"Silence!" hisses Rix. "The medic's coming." And he comes in, bringing everyone a pile of envelopes dealing with the reimbursement of our Social Security package and other matters.

While everyone attends to this, Rix whispers to us. "I've got the Red Sea passes, but we have to leave quickly. If there's a Red alert, we'll never get out."

This proved to be the first of our many mistakes; too much haste, too many loose ends.

When Pitsos' wife arrived, he'd had to move to Married Quarters and in the process, half the Red Sea gear had gone off with a family to Atif.

Then, on leaving our compound, we were delayed by searching fruitlessly for it, and were late for our first rendezvous. We pushed on hopefully down the escarp just before the road closed, and have ended up on a coastal strip, which seems to be turning into an island.

At dawn, we search for molluscs and crabs and try using the mosquito net to catch fish. It's too rough and murky, but after long swim we find a large underwater grotto, well protected from the surf and with no photosynthesizing algae in it. I'm delegated to keep watch, while the others explore the reef.

Inside the spacious cavern, the water heaves like a sleeping giant occasionally smacking its lips. One moment the grotto is empty, the next, two big groupers are facing each other just above the seabed. Only ripples of light dancing over the walls from gently fanning pectoral fins, gives them away. Then before my eyes, their cryptic colouring changes into black-and-white bands, as distinctive as two road barriers. A single tentacle comes out of one's gill case and caterpillars towards an eye. The great fish takes an almighty huff and blows out an entire squid. A tug-of-war ensues. Then, one or both, must have seen me, for they explode like dynamited sandbags. Squiggles of ink and bits of squid descend all over the place.

When quiet again, I spy the tip of a crayfish's antenna waving out of a crevice, the other tip possibly keeping tab on the resident moray, which some say chaperones then eats them, when they moult.

Eventually the owner emerges and trips delicately over the sand to investigate pickings.

As the creature passes me, its antennae probe forward, and I grab it. My grip is firm and the sharp points on its carapace don't bother me. But when my own skin, between forefinger and thumb, is nipped by the segmented flanges of its tail, my hand releases it and I'm distraught as a birthday boy watching his helium balloon sail away.

To quieten down, I go on a tour of my surroundings: large domes of brain coral, protecting sunny glades. And when I pause, it takes me several moments to realize, I'm staring at a large snapper right in front of me.

If I had my spear gun I'd have no time to ponder the situation, but now have plenty. Its gill cases hardly move, and though the patina and rough-hewn texture of its scales imitate no specific coral, they reflect and absorb the sunlight exactly as the present surroundings do. It could be just another sculpture in the garden.

When I return to the grotto, I try to get a grip on things and plan a careful manoeuvre. I close my eyes awhile, then open them, sink down and inch forward. Then, taking care not to scuff up any sand with flippers or snorkel, turn slowly on my back, and look up. A crayfish is three-quarters out of a crevice right above me. Even as I grab, remember like an old hand, to shake not pull. But in the last instant, like a fussy art expert, decide the salmon-and-maroon pattern of the carapace doesn't quite tally with the bluey-green of the living creature. Its stippled-striped legs become the flared fins of a lion fish, and I'm spared further serious folly.

The others have also got nothing. Their only excitement, a bloated body covered in sea urchins in another cave -- a baby camel bobbing against the roof.

In the evening Lambourski manages to grab a monster crayfish in the grotto as it chased another along a ledge. It had an over-sized thorax and normal abdomen. He said it was a cannibal, but tasted very good, for all that.

Rix spent his day digging out four mangrove crabs. Tied them up and put them in a box with a rock on the lid. We checked on them every so often, but eyes modestly withdrawn, they remained still as death masks, cast in bronze.

In the morning, they're gone. Our clumping approaches must have forewarned them. And we even saw where one escapee had pirouetted in the sand, waving goodbye.

If we hadn't got off that spooky island the next day, I'm not sure how we ourselves would have made out.

As an afterword, not two weeks later, Gaspar watched three of Rix's bound mangrove crabs starting proceedings by flexing hidden muscles. The narcissistic minimalist performance eventually sent him to sleep until he was woken by scratching noises and saw them clambering onto each other's backs; the last and smallest, getting its lift-up out by refusing to let go. Gaspar then claimed he fell asleep, and Rix, not amused demanded a bottle of sid as forfeit.

≈

Eventually we meet up with Pitsos at our final rendezvous. He has with him his wife, Tee, a friend called Gus, young Ben, the iceman from the German dynamiter's camp, and the rest of the gear, but no food.

Only Tee seems to be enjoying herself, making all the right noises when shown the cannibal crayfish carapace (like we'd slain the local dragon) and had a way, at least with me, of extracting information I usually kept to myself. How a Norwegian girl, who'd put a bunch of us up in her apartment one time, sent me out to buy items for breakfast, the others having opted to go to the airport.

When I returned, I couldn't remember the building, never mind the apartment number.

We trundle on through incredibly tedious windblown sands till we come across deep tracks. The high centre kept lifting our wheels off terra-firma. If we strayed, sand came up to our axles.

There was nothing to be done but start dumping surplus gear. And due to a handling error, the crayfish carapace gets crushed to smithereens. We've off-and-on loaded about four times, when some shifty-eyed characters appear, gutras round their faces, and watch us through narrow slits. Rix and Barnes don't think they're locals.

I almost bump into one round the corner of a dune, adjusting his rifle, and tried him with my best Arabic. Barnes not far behind, says, "That didn't help."

"Why not?"

"You know what you said?"

"Basically, yes: 'Hello, and may God's peace be with you.'"

"You said 'Hello and God willing, goodbye.' " Obviously the strain is beginning to tell.

"Ask them the way to Al Birk," suggests Pitsos.

Barnes asks them, super politely, adding *Ain-al-biblia* (Which way to pray)? They point to Mecca but decide Al Birk is inland, which it isn't.

"Keep calm lads," says Pitsos. We offload the box of wood, some tent poles and the collapsible table for improving table manners. Our watchers are unimpressed.

'The faces of men, but they have nothing for you,' wrote the colonial traveller Kinglake, scarce out of Istanbul: 'No welcome, no wonder, no wrath, no scorn. They look upon you as we do upon December's fall of snow, as a seasonable, uncomfortable work of God that may be sent for some good purpose, to be revealed hereafter.'

However, the old German in charge of the freezer in the German dynamiter's camp, who'd simply wanted to escape his Swiss-style chalet (tea cosy on the toilet, loo-paper coming out of a cuckoo-clock, and baking black tarmac outside), isn't letting on if it's more than he's bargained for. And is heaving the boxes round as if exactly what the doctor ordered.

The sky is now an ominous wall 200 yards off. Our watchers fade away. Pitsos brings over his friend Gus, who's been asleep, and claims is an expert on wind-sheer, having been one of the first pilots to land a Mustang on an aircraft carrier. But not to embarrass him further, adds that as a crop-duster in New Zealand, he'd ended up spraying the wrong farm, killed the sheep, and had to return to driving a taxi in Hawaii. "He's now in the burglar alarm business," he says, "and has never looked back, until this moment, eh Gus?" Gus makes no comment, but suggests we park halfway up the dune, which we do, while black kites wheel about, chasing scores of insects fleeing the storm.

Pitsos, who's been nipping back and forth between us and his wife, like a Jack-in-the-box, produces a pre-mixed cocktail in a thermos and finally relaxes.

"In Auckland," he says, seemingly apropos of nothing, "We were always trying to sneak into our guesthouse with beer in a brown paper bag. Every time, the landlady's cubby-hole would open and she'd tell us to watch our step, as she and her husband had 'never stood for disruptions.' Remember?" Gus nods.

"On Xmas day," he goes on. "She put on a fine spread, and when everyone was quaffing mineral water and masticating over-cooked turkey, came in beaming, to wish us all a happy Christmas. She went over and stood next to the Christmas tree. At first Gus and I thought she was rearranging a festive balloon or two. When she began to shimmy out of her petticoat, we realized we were about to witness a major indiscretion.

"Her husband, a beefy gent of Russian extraction, stood behind her with his massive arms folded and surveyed the room with an implacable stare as if implying, she was as entitled to an annual indiscretion as much as the next person. Then, before she was almost reduced to her state at birth – somewhat magnified by time – he came forward and put his arm round what had been her waist. She stood on one leg, leant forward, raised the other above her head, gave a cheery little wave and departed on dainty steps.

"In the hush that followed, only our table applauded, so Gus cleared his throat. 'No disrespect intended,' he said. 'May not have been *Swan Lake*. But was a love story, nevertheless.'"

Then Pitsos himself is gone, and the wind hits. The vehicle rises as if some practical joker is over-inflating the tires. "Same G's as in wind sheer," says Gus. "But no phosphate fumes blowing into the cabin."

A spadesful of sand hits the window. Then another and another. And I think, if it continues like this we'll all be buried.

Eventually I doze off, half-listening to Gus talking about the ploys used long ago by Polynesian navigators crossing the Pacific in the search of new lands.

"Forget open skies and plentiful islands," he's saying. "Think open water and overcast nights, when navigators had to lie down in the bottom of the hulls and let the ocean currents course through their bones. And sometimes, feigning sickness, lay in nets slung between the hulls, hoping to track, deep down, phosphorescent plankton streams rising from valleys of land masses, yet unseen.

"But under starlit skies, on the remotest landfalls and loneliest atolls, they were even more discreet. A group went a small distance off, to pray in seclusion to the Gods. Half a coconut was placed firmly in the sand and filled with sea water. Then a small secret star map (an heirloom), made of woven bamboo strips and shaped a bit like the Star of David, was laid on top. By peering in and aligning the reflections of known stars with ones never seen before, one specific bamboo strip showed the way they should go.

And before a single mangrove pod came bobbing by, or land bird flew overhead, the navigator was sometimes wont to announce a possible landfall, by surreptitiously sipping sea water. A trick to addle the brains of any spies planted in the boat.

If they brought along enough young women (many escaping infanticide on over-crowded atolls), coconuts, seeds, fermented taro, turtles and even pigs, they stood a chance.

Many adapted in remarkable ways, through plagues and plenty. But sometimes, even on good islands, a few forgot simple sense; cut down their timber, and begged rival ancestors, hewn from mute stone, to carry them home again.

≈

I swear the wind hardly let up all night and a fine sand to pour at irregular intervals through tiny holes in the roof. Once a light came down and danced on the dunes.

I woke repeatedly from tangled dreams. Once to hear the Icemen, usually as tight-lipped as the proverbial clam, talking about the time he'd spent in a Yugoslav prison, with Serbs, Croats,

Royalists, Stalinists, Albanians… all sorts. "I could accept it was my due," he said, "because I'd been caught trying to drive some Croats out of the country. But what you're asking me about, Rix – the worst thing, was that they thought I might be an informer, because I'd driven the last lot out for money.

"There was a gypsy, completely apolitical, who'd pissed on a wall poster of Tito, and did odd jobs – replacing burst sandbags and cleaning up generally. One day my friend Lucas, who spoke his mind too much, was given a cardboard shoebox with a clean shirt, trousers, and a bar of soap. He thought his appeal had been approved, and was going to be released. But the next day, he was shot. The gypsy gave me a small piece of his skull with the hair still on it, and told me it would protect me. Every so often, he asked me if I still had it. It began to haunt me. When I was finally released, I buried it by the first tree I could.'"

Hour after hour, the wind thumped away. The lowest point was, when woken by a vile stench and Rix complaining "how could it be scrambled eggs, when I haven't eaten eggs for a week?"

"Christ! Grow up you guys," growled Leo. "We're trying to get some sleep."

"It's dawn," said Rix. And dawn it was, chinks of light coming through the canvas instead of sand. Stepping out of that awful fug was like stepping into a blast furnace.

In the distance we could see scudding waves and a lime-coloured lagoon. Pitsos and Lambourski come over, carrying a sack and bunch of spearguns. "I'm fucking starving," says Pitsos. His wife slithers out of the vehicle like a hibernating snake and scowls at the horizon. "The missus would like some breakfast too.'"

"Coffee and kippers, right?" Says Steve. "There's a cosy little café, lee of the point."

We slog towards the shore. In the sea, the first creatures we meet are two jellyfish, one a monster like an elephant's tumescent penis, and the other, a small grey hand, severed at the wrist, clasping and unclasping under a bell jar, "like a Roger Bacon painting," says Steve, and I take his word for it.

In the shelter of the point, the reef below us looks as moribund as an unvisited tomb. A fidgety remora comes by. Then we saw it, an enormous grouper covered in reef detritus, as if in a fur coat. There could be no delay. We struck it down with three shots, like murderers in a back alley, and it fought back.

We almost get the lines round it, but it thumps us away. Only one spear, bent like a horseshoe, prevents it disappearing down a hole. The second spear snaps.

"Fire the goddam gun, Steve!"

"Where?"

"In the head!"

"Where in the head?"

"Through the gill opening. Friggin' hell man, shoot!"

"Look out!" He says. *Thwack!* The fish goes into spasm. The great mottled jaw, spotted all over inside like a giant cowrie, packed with quill-like teeth, snaps shut like a steel trap. Steve's spear bends slowly upwards but doesn't break. As we tighten the noose around the fish, several hands slip into the claws of its gill-rakers. We push it through the surf, and takes four of us to carry it ashore.

When we dump it down, Pitsos' wife leaps about like a cheer-leader, then takes off. The grouper's maw opens one last time, gills wide like a wire-cage, disgorges a skinless fish, and one end of a spear drops out. Warner waves both hands about as if they'd just been dipped in a can of tomato puree. We're exhilarated and drained, like streetwise shits who've just done in an old lady, who fought back.

"Wood," says Lambourski. And off we go, Ben and I to the right, others to the left. Two things, you can be sure that remote beaches have here, are plenty reef shark offshore and plenty driftwood. After tying some logs together to make a sledge, we sit down.

"I'm knackered. How about you?" I say.

"The same." Says Ben, though he's done little enough. In fact, why he's here at all is a bit of a mystery considering he's local squash champion, secretary of the Squash Club and, if not arranging competitions, studying for his accountancy exam and sending every penny home.

"How did you get on with Pitsos' wife, stuck in that vehicle?"

"Had some great conversations."

"About what?"

"Family. When you've got kids, it's natural. And you guys?"

"Same, only opposite. Jail and scrambled-egg farts."

Then it all comes out. Apparently, Lt. Mufti had hauled him into his office only last Thursday, and asked if he'd been making alcohol. He said no. Lt. Mufti then produced an open-dated ticket to Heathrow made out to him, and asked again. Ben said yes.

"Get rid of it," said Mufti. "In the meantime, I'll hold on to this."

Now that I understood better what Lt. Mufti and Ben actually did in their spare time; both rocket-up in my estimation. "Where was the still? On the villa roof?"

"Behind the squash court. I only sold to upper echelon."

"Of course, goes without saying. What's-his-name of B.A.C. wouldn't have gotten the O.B.E. for anything less. Bit of bad luck. And just one other thing, Ben. I don't know about in the Seychelles – but you see those smooth patches of sand over there – with whorls on them like hundreds and thousands, made by tiny crabs?"

"Yes".

"It's always firm there, don't ask me why. That's where we're headed. No more through the soft stuff.

"Why didn't you tell me earlier? No problem. If you can pull the sledge over the last stretch and anyone notices, just say I hurt my arm in the Squash court. Ok?" And off he goes, straight as a die through the soft stuff.

Back at the fish, things are looking up. A fire crackles away. Gus has a bag of mesquite chips and the Iceman brings over a vacuum-packed loaf of black bread. "Reserve rations," he grins sheepishly, "Thought we might need it."

Tee's set up a dispensary with Warner acting as medical assistant. To my horror, the bowl of hot water in front of him is already a bilious pink. "Not your blood I hope?"

"Mercurochrome. Any stronger, it would stain. Not help our case – if you get my drift."

This is the first time anyone has hinted about being late. The problem was, we'd already been warned, being late back from the Red Sea would result in termination.

"What do you mean?" scoffs Rix, "After this lot, we'll be home and dry before first prayer-call, Inshallah." It's the *Inshallah,* which worries me.

As Tee swabs our worst cuts, you can sense that the cool touch of a feminine hand is something we've all been missing. Only Ben says "Ow!"

"Hurt his arm in a fall on the Squash court", I pipe up, a mite tardily. Tee peers at it cautiously and applies a heat-inducing balm to his elbow, which he then flexes with a cheerful smile.

After we've applied hydrogen peroxide to lesser abrasions, we're soon queuing up again for a new plastic spray, which she applies with gusto, sealing up any remaining wounds with icy blasts.

Rix, having cleaned the fish and, already hacked-off the head, passes a big chunk to Lambourski, who proceeds to cut it into paper-thin slices, with surgical precision.

The great head, left up-ended on the beach like an emerging sea-serpent, jelly eyeballs turning to sandpaper, transforms an already bleak scene into a macabre one. As the rosy blood runs into the sea, whip-lashes of sand skitter along the beach. Sweat pours off us. Eyes streaming, we're soon all chomping away on smoked grouper-on-toast, like a bunch of cannibals on long-pig.

"Beats the old fish-and-chips shop, eh Ben?" Grins Steve. "With the missus plunking herself down to rest her ankles and you ending up, having to pay VAT."

When we've finished we lick hands, humming with lime juice. Steve drags the remains of the skeleton into the surf and gives thanks to the fish itself.

We eventually clamber aboard our vehicles, drive off, and punch-drunk on protein, promptly get stuck. We dig out of a mulch of hot brine, kelp and blood-worms and, peering through windscreens sand-blasted like frosted-glass, press on.

3 pm. Hard sand, and my turn in the donkey spotter's seat, requiring oodles of tact, particularly with Leo driving.

In the Tihama, camels move silently and hit windshield high, but donkeys don't budge. Barnes claims they like to stand on the warm tarmac of road-cuttings out of the wind. And treat trucks bearing down on them, all lights blazing, as expanding silhouettes, staying in one spot. Whereas, something with moving parts like a charging lion, would have had them kicking up their heels and away, so he says.

"You were saying Leo?"

"Wasn't saying anything? But don't you dry up on me."

All I can come up with is the incident with the bedhu woman, who panicked crossing the freeway, went sailing into the air like a rag-doll and nobody stopped, including us.

"When?"

"Last year."

"Can't you tell us a funny story or something?"

All I can come up with is the tale of two Saudi lasses, who got sucked into a street-cleaning machine. "If you were to go a wee bit slower I might be able to do better. But my eyes are getting confused. How about you?"

"Yes." And sure enough, a herd of camels, silently and without breaking stride, glide across the track as if it were nothing more than a line in the carpet – their carpet.

"How come, in the *Saudi Gazette,* it's always us who run into the camel, and the camel which runs into the Prince's Mercedes?"

In the end, we bring Gus over to entertain us with some of the weird places he's been to: Stumbling into a Communist camp above Kyoto, martial music blaring, banners waving. Not a film set, but a cadre of North Korean POW's about to be repatriated into the bosom of The Great Leader.

Then camping with a naked German, eager to have a swim in a beautiful reed-fringed lake near Gifu, but totally ignored by the crowd of gawping villagers, fascinated by Gus making scrambled eggs.

In the rainforest of the Mazuruni in Guyana, they searched for the Chinnipaw falls under a sky with but a single cloud. When they found the falls, it was the cloud, and they leapt about and gibbered like Chimpanzees, but didn't know that either!

On a stopover off the Rio Branco, he'd seen from his US Army hammock (zippered mozzie-net, cords impregnated with ant-repellent) a herd of wild pigs pass, followed by a bunch of Indians with blow-pipes, then their women with *wairichis* (tall backpacks), children and their silent dogs.

He saw them and they hadn't seen him.

And later, when they docked by a once flourishing plantation, looking as if mechanized earth-movers had dug it up, couldn't believe it, when told it was the work of wild boar.

≈

8 pm. Long ago, this corner of the globe had more than its fair share of mythical cities: Ad, Om and Hud, but I don't recall Dogwag and Mutlag being among them. Nevertheless, the highway signposts first one, then the other, and widens respectfully for each, as if we were about to enter fabled ruins.

"I believe, there was to be a secret airstrip here," says Barnes, "before Nasser banned the Muslim Brotherhood and bumped off Sayyid Qutb, 'a man with courage beyond most men, and a dream beyond simple sense.' Devrill-Smith had said.

Mutlag has the same desolate esplanade as Dogwag, but includes a donkey in the middle of the road, with a hard on.

10 pm. The first tarmac appears, and though dead straight, drifts this way-and-that, as if we were in the diorama of some infernal driving-test. Then it happens. We're sailing off into space. *Bounce, bounce, bounce!* Leo continues driving. *Clunkity, clunk*, and we stop. No sound but the ticking of an overheated engine block about to crack. Leo turns on the emergency lights.

Pitsos lands somewhere near us and comes over. "Everything ok?" A few muffled grunts. "Handled perfectly", he says. "No panic."

11 pm. Braying of car horns and high curtains of swirling dust caught in the sweep of headlights. Pick-ups and trucks mill around like cattle in an abattoir. A convoy is waiting to go north, but for some reason the road is closed.

Rix comes out of the night with two wizened old fuckers muttering *"Hamour, hamour."* He wrenches out the ice box, opens it and hands them a fair sized-chunk of grouper, and we receive enough dates for a pilgrim's feast.

1 am. Total silence. A horizontal strip of pure white beach. A vertical line of moonlight. A scene of utter simplicity, and beneath the water, full of conflict and duplicity.

We all go and cool-off in the shallows, lying in a cosy semi-circle with two lizard fish in the middle, still as chinaware bookends. Pitsos clicks his fingers and phosphorescence winks on-and-off as its telegraphed, left and right along the line of reeds. Tee is delighted.

And I think *what an excellent early warning system for night fish and squid, when the hammerhead come prowling!*

One lizard fish bares its teeth (it has lots, sports a moustache of them and even has some on its tongue). Leaps at a passing guppy and returns to ceramic immobility. I detect no subsequent motion – as if its digestion was entirely a matter of acids.

Among the reeds, it's a world of bubbles and beetles. A small crab tucks himself up for the night in a puff of sand. A flute-fish, looking like a model of the alimentary canal in a Perspex tube, noses towards us then shunts about awkwardly, tiny fins fanning energetically. Yet this fish, according to the folklore of Palau, is said to go into the most dangerous place of the reef, the mouth of the moray. They say it darts forward and, in an instant, siphons out food while the moray goes into a temporary spasm.

I don't believe it, but later, scribble in my diary: *With regard to the most innocuous looking creatures, one is well-advised to adopt the least complacency.*

They also say, the moray eel sometimes threads itself through a loop in its body, lets an octopus envelope it. Bites it near the beak, draws itself back through loop, turning the octopus inside-out in the process. *Hard to believe, too.*

2 am. Tongues of sand cross the road, and hit with the unforgiving thump of sandbags.

3 am. My last spell in the donkey seat. Barnes takes the wheel. We drop the Iceman off the back way.

"Where am I?" he says.

"Home sweet home." Rix gives him a chunk of grouper.

He peers at his watch. "I sink you will make it." Gives us the Churchill V sign (wrong way round) and is gone.

We climb up the escarp in the usual endless zig-zags, slipping every which way, getting out to shove rocks behind the wheels and taking turns to suck the grit out of the fuel filter. At the top, I am completely exhausted and collapse.

Through a gap in the dawn sky, come griffin vultures, lammergeyers and Egyptian vultures winging their way over the Plain of Scorpions, all using the confusion of air currents like sophisticated gliders.

They come to ride the thermals above the cairns (we once mistook for a troop of baboons) and rise like bubbles in a kettle to

267

their work stations in the sky. The pecking order: kites first, then Egyptian vultures and griffins last. And to those with any energy left to listen to a still ebullient Barnes: "In India its the small King vultures which go highest, the turkey vultures, strictly mezzanine, quartering the forest at speed and sniffing out kills under the canopy. The King vultures and kites, then follow them down, and help rip open the spoils."

A mighty lammergeyer swooshes above us, legs feathered like an eagle. Old ossifrage, the breaker of bones, he's called, for his liking of bone marrow, prepared by dropping prey from great heights.

When the Griffins reach the top of the cumulus, they peel from the gyre. And on unmoving wings, scour the four corners of the Asir: for goats, donkeys and camels, once left behind by slowly moving caravans and now laid low, by flash-floods of steel.

The muffled bark of a baboon comes from under the mist (lying like milk in the wadi), and a rumble of thunder from high above Suda (which Leo thinks is aircraft).

We dally no longer. Something is also going on our side of the escarp. Points of light move slowly below us through the mist. It's a backed-up column of traffic. *Bad news.* We could be delayed for God knows how long. And going the long way round, we'll be late for sure.

But Barnes and Rix race on like they're in the Dhakar rally, past ancient Juraish, past the Toyota on the rock and enter the compound on the tail of the radar shift. We just have time to shower and clamber on the bus.

The noise level seems to be very high. No one takes the slightest notice of us and many are half-blitzed. I do up the last of my shirt buttons with tingling fingers, and keep mum.

Though none of us knows anything about Marsden's death yet, and thinks he's still on leave, it appears Bradley has already stepped into his shoes, and is winding up a Country cousin. "We may have lost the contract, buddy," he says. "But half Northrop's Compound is to be turned over to the R.S.A.F and all female secretaries out by the end of the month."

"You aren't screwing any, so what's your worry?"

"I'm not worried. Just telling you. It doesn't always pay to think you're the elite round here."

"Sod's army!" roars Van. And I glimpse the driver's face in the rear-view mirror as he hunkers down. *One of Mufti's men, no doubt.* And recall how the medic, first day of the week, sometimes used to patrol the bus, peering into the faces of the comatose, like a prim but conscientious undertaker. Specially the time, the driver drove all of us to the police station, and the medic said, we were suffering the effects of Fansidar (the new anti-malarial medication) after a couple of deaths from cerebral malaria in Gizan, and didn't think too much should be made of it.

The bus groans up the final incline, the cairns springing briefly into view, and shudders to a halt before the Radar Station. Old timers brush away their dreams: a retirement villa in the Algarve, a bar in Baguio or Costa Rica -- sights the desert traveller oft-times glimpses before he's reached the shade.

Everyone shuffles forwards, adjusting their attire in the windows. Then we see them, parked well beyond the end of the runway, big white planes with long drooping wings and small leaner fighters, canvas already pulled over their insignias.

A babble of voices breaks out, all asking the same question. "Where the fuck did they come from?"

"Air Traffic Controllers guided them down in the early hours," says Bradley. "Iran and Iraq are at war."

"Whose side are we on then?" A thrilled new lad pipes up.

"Iraq's obviously, unless you think all these planes have been hijacked."

"Hope we win soon."

"Not the idea, either." says our new Mr. Know-All.

77 Things move fast again

Things move fast again.

When we're told we're the first base to be handed over to the Saudis, even we cringe at the tactless phrase, specially as the event seems to have been engineered so nobody knew it happened (if it did happen) save perhaps for one occasion when the duty officer, possibly inebriated, climbed the Control Tower to scramble the F5's.

One bright morning, our new Project Officer departed for Taif in his own transport. Then resurfaced in Jeddah, with a Ph.D. after his name. Rumour said, he'd picked it up on the Christian by-pass (used by us infidels to avoid Mecca), accompanied by a blinding light, like Paul's experience on the road to Damascus, or Lawrence's at the prospect thereof.

Next, all villas are to be wired for cable TV, and no more movies held in the Recce Hall, a better idea, but not as good as the old days, when Ali's kitchen staff cheered on the opposition at the Battle of Omdurman and Rorke's Drift.

International phone calls become cheaper. Barnes even gets a call from his niece, desperate for the gen on Hamilton's Rule, 'a dead cert for mid-term orals and no time to swot it up,' she said.

Hamilton's famous rule of altruism! Which we'd so often witnessed in action every time ants and termites carried their eggs through the flames of our fires, now become to her what Joule's famous equation had once been to me: a pain in the ass.

Lambourski also turns briefly weird again; thinks of signing on with the AWAC's Early Warning Radar Program, until Louisa tells him. 'You've a son now, who hardly knows you.'

And Ali, as mentioned before, has gone into a fast food venture, Ali's Pizza Parlour. Business is booming.

The tennis court also has a new perimeter fence and a superior green rubberized surface, much easier on the ankles. And far less tennis balls get whacked over the wall for the bedhu girls to make off with like the wind.

A big snake appears in the garden, and we're ordered to fill in the pond. Devrill-Smith says, in the ancient times, when a great drought moved from Oman across Arabia, many oases probably had such visitations. 'So now's a good time to leave, ha, ha!' But he told no one where he was going. Some said it was to Oman, and some, to one of the Gulf States as a translator at a new TV station opposite Col Cufflink's base.

Over the past several years, the Major has also managed to squirrel away a small budget from late library returns, for some Natural History videos. We were eagerly looking forward to these when the wiring for cable TV was suddenly put on hold.

An enterprising bunch of Filipinos had been caught copying porno in the test villa, possibly infiltrated by a Mufti man. It was the first time I sensed our lot were falling behind the information-technology learning curve.

In the meantime the Major suggested we put our over-ambitious hunters' role models, such as barracudas and sea otters on the back burner. This seemed a pretty good idea as they were becoming too serendipitous and disconnected. As if a boxer could learn a good move from a chicken; or a Greenland shark pluck seals from Californian kelp and peel them like oranges.

But more to our immediate concern, the Major offered us two bottles of his finest vintage for the best quotes on Natural History and hunting. More on which later.

When the Red Alert moved from the Red Sea to the Persian Gulf, we began to plan a proper going-away party for Tee on our beach.

≈

At Abha's new Toyota garage for our annual servicing, I am surprised to see Fernandes has been made Manager.

When the conversation somehow drifted to the subject of beaches, he mentioned he'd once organized an outing to the coast and been surprised how differently people behaved, when they thought they were on holiday.

"The same with our lot," Pitsos nodded sympathetically. "Long before there was any road south, our Company provided 4-wheel-drive vehicles for recreation. But when the Company got bigger, people simply drove them all over the place. And when they got stuck, blamed the vehicles. Now they have no more 4-wheel-vehicles to complain about, ha, ha!"

Fernandes then asked how we'd managed to end up getting our brake-pads so caked with salt, and brake-drums so rusty.

"Same thing again," said Pitsos without missing a beat. "Only takes one dunderhead, who shall be nameless, to go charging over the sand flats, and the next moment, we're up to our axles in green slime."

I was impressed by the nameless driver and the green slime, but surprised when Fernandes seemed genuinely disappointed – as if our odometer readings and the sand-blasted windscreens, demanded a more dramatic series of mishaps.

Pitsos gave him no satisfaction on this score, just sighed, thanked him for a job well done, and paid the bill.

78 Tee's party

"There's three more coming" says Lambourski. "Be a sport and get us another fish, even a parrotfish. It's an emergency."

I'm totally knackered and to be honest, can't believe I've been at this caper all day and only got two small fish. "Who's coming?"

"Fernandes and his wife. And Cowboy, maybe later."

"Are you crazy? No way! They'll never forgive us." He thinks I'm referring to the guests but I'm referring to the parrotfish.

Dusk is approaching, and with it, the dreaded quiet period. Warner's hands are still healing (despite having used up all the plastic spray) so he's out of action. Leo is willing – but possibly dangerous.

"Stay close," I say, "but not too close." If he's offended, doesn't show it and comes anyway.

Off the reef, it's the usual wall of lead. Invisible hands gouge out slivers of bright metal. At longer intervals, there's a rushing like grain flowing down a large chute, possibly instigated by no more than a single snapper, moving in that hypnotic way they employ to lull a school into complacency, before pouncing.

Eventually Leo admits, he can't see bugger all, and eases back. I hang on a bit longer, hoping to catch a glimpse of the phantom snapper turning at the end of its pendulum swing.

One moment there's nothing, the next, a large fish with big silver scales, has stopped right in front of me. I can't miss and I fire.

I stare down at the seabed, put out my hand, and touch something soft. *Sand.* Close my eyes in disbelief. We've drifted inshore and the fish, all seven inches of it, must have stopped about the same distance in front of my spear tip. Leo thinks, I've fired to unload. I do not disabuse him and wait for him to do likewise.

Back on the shore, after a shower and putting on a clean shirt, Leo's his usual cheery self – giving Tee a rundown on the Natural History of our beach and, apart from calling a tern, a seagull, doing very well. He even imitates the long mating-call of the deep sea halibut (related to the Sausalito drum fish, according to Barnes) which so impresses Tee, she wants to tape it for her sister's fourth grade.

When Fernandes and party arrive, Fernandes immediately makes a beeline for the beach and is downright shocked to see how far the water's in. Wants me to show him where he was the infamous day of the bus. I point over to the left and move us way over to the right, not wanting it to look like we were a bunch of schmucks.

"Learned a good lesson that day," he says. "A bunch of Greeks helped us." But I can't help feeling he may be in for another shock, like *not being offered enough to eat*. And leave him examining the rig, while I pop round to get him a drink and check on Lambourski. "Had no idea that Tee knew Fernandes's wife," I say.

"Thick as thieves". He replies, but I can't help noticing, the fish seem to have become even smaller. "How are you going to cook them?" I ask.

"Surprise."
"They're not very big."

"That's the surprise. Now buzz off. I've work to do." He's in his *Mussolini-Toscanini* mode, and there's also been another balls-up. Apparently, half the cutlery got dumped by mistake last trip, and Rix is making chopsticks out of bamboo.

Eventually the fish are brought over, one with a mustardy sauce, lying on crispy-brown potatoes, the other with gooseberries from the garden on top of it.

"Wowee!" Goes Tee, "*Nouvelle cuisine!* Or is it *nouveau*?"

This culinary assessment is entirely wasted on Leo, who's setting to in the old style, like a basset hound on the heels of an escaped convict. Then Warner, despite being *hors-de-combat*, nips playfully in with his chopsticks to bear away the food, Leo's carefully mustered one side of his plate.

At this Leo downs tools and begins baying at the moon with little regard for the assembled company, other than to demand the immediate restitution of his rightful portion. "You've the manners of an Ik," he growls. "Worse than a guitar fish." *Harsh words.*

Warner is taken aback. Sits bolt upright, face red, like one of those fastidious crabs which raise claw to mouth parts, but never take their eyes off you. Our female guests carry on, dignified and calm as a couple of anthropologists invited to dine with a tribe thought to be extinct, and possibly cannibalistic.

"My, that was yummy!" says Tee with a palpable exhalation, and puts down her chopsticks, "I could have eaten half a dozen."

What a faux pas! An icy chill settles on my skin.

In the long pause which follows, I hear a single wave slap down on the beach. *Where's the sid?* And rise to get it.

Careening round the back of the vehicles, I almost bump headfirst into Pitsos, bearing a platter of sizzling pork chops, and Fernandes with a bowl of steaming Abogado.

A bottle of bourbon is produced. "We owe you an apology." says Pitsos. "To make a hunter go out and get dinner at such short notice is not the way things should be done."

"Jesus, I thought you were taking the mickey."

"We were, we were," says Tee, "But not the way you thought". And hands me a bourbon on ice. "So here's to you. We thought you might never come back. Cheers! And plants a kiss on my cheek.

I take another toke on a joint for my back's sake, and the jagged corners of the evening begin to smooth away. Everything becomes mellow. I fall asleep and wake to two female voices, calling like seabirds flying above the churning surf of cowboy's base:

'Don't leave me my soldier boy.
Don't leave me for the war.
I'll cut off my hair and march by your side.'

"Depends," says one, followed by laughter.

We all end up skinny-dipping in the Mullet Pond. If anyone kept guard, I wasn't aware of it, though Barnes says I took my turn on the dune top, like everyone else.

"Did I fall asleep?"

"Not as far as I know. In fact, you said you'd protect us with your life." But all I remember is the silvery waves crashing on the beach, which I thought strange, as there was no longer any moon, only the ghostly jewelled *noctiluca*, surfing in the waves.

I woke one more time, to ask Barnes if everyone had left.

275

"Yup. Pitsos and Tee, only a moment ago, after a last swim. Left you a present though."

"What about shark?"

"Don't know about shark, but they certainly freaked-out the mullet..

79 Role Models or What happens to the hunter?

We are sitting on the beach in a depressed state and partaking of the remnants of the hair of the dog. "Tee was right," I mutter, "A hunter's not meant to be a short-order flunkey. From now on, guests popping up at short notice should bring their own rations or take potluck."

"What if they bring Ali's Pizzas, and we're stuck with Rix's leftover ring-stinging curry?"

"Share!" Goes the chorus.

Only Barnes stands firm. "We'll become lazy. All those endless swims and long hikes will become memories of yesterday. And if I've learned anything here, it's that the best part of hunting is being able to enjoy the labour, many labour-saving devices deprive us of."

Though I can't remember Barnsey being particularly enthused by the long-distance swims, and myself by the long slogs, he has a point.

We decide to leave the problem till Pitsos returns, in the hope he'll come up with a simple rule which actually works.

Then the Major and Rix arrive, delayed by a long night spent avoiding a coastguard patrol (which turned out to be a road-surveying party).

Their arrival puts an entirely new complexion on things, because the Major has brought down two prize vintages, to dispense to the winners of his competition (for the best quotes on Natural History and hunting). And Rix also informs us, Fernandes has agreed to buy both vehicles and the rig!

To be honest, I can't remember who won the Major's competition, other than that Warner was particularly clueless. But I did learn that the early enthusiasm of the nature lovers Wordsworth and Thoreau, waned a bit in old age. Perhaps a need for creature comforts had something to do with it; the former ending his days an apologist for the landed gentry, the latter as a surveyor of city lots.

The author Gerald Durrell, on the other hand, stayed the course, starting life by putting creepy-crawlies into matchboxes (only to be exhibited at the best locations: a maiden aunt's soup or his kid sister's pillow) and ended up, trying to return rescued creatures to viable habitats.

The winning quote was from the first President Roosevelt (who started badly but got better) to the man who camouflaged the U.S. Navy, then told him that flamingos were coloured pink, to look like sunsets. To which Teddy, if I may call him Teddy, retorted. "Then so would a baboon standing on its head on a beach at sunset, with its ass in the air." The funny thing was, our flamingos over at Shaban did look like sunsets, and sufficiently so for us to start sundowners at 3 pm on a couple of memorable occasions.

Four of the longest quotes in the competition, starting with the youngest, I copied into my diary. (If you'd like to guess the authors, the answers are given at the end of this chapter.). A couple of hints, here: The mother of the first was said to have suffocated a serf with a pillow, and the last was a turkey-hunter).

1. "My father often took me hunting with him. And I enjoyed it immensely! I shoved my trousers into my boot-tops, put a flask over my shoulder and imagined myself a sportsman! I was dripping with sweat, small pebbles got into my boots, but I didn't feel any fatigue and didn't lag behind my father. And when I saw a bird fall, I skipped about and even yelled – I was so happy! The wounded bird struggled and flapped her wings in the grass or between Trezor's teeth, blood poured from her, but I felt happy all the same and had no feeling of pity at all. 'Wouldn't it be wonderful', I thought to myself, 'if I could kill such a huge bird – why I should be the happiest man in the world, if I could do that!"

2. "I waited all afternoon, growing colder with each passing crow, and with each rheumatic groan of the labouring windmill. At sunset, a lone duck came out of the west, and without even a

preliminary circling of the air hole, set its wings and pitched downward. I cannot remember the shot; I remember only my unspeakable delight when my first duck hit the snowy ice with a thud and lay there, belly up, red legs kicking."

3. "We poisoned out the prairie dogs, and incidentally did in the black-footed ferrets that lived on them – ferrets that are now the rarest North American mammals. We didn't even know they were ferrets; we called them big weasels. But we killed them as we killed everything else. Once I speared one with a pitchfork in the chicken house and was sickened by its ferocious vitality, dismayed by how hard the wild died. I had the same feeling when I caught a badger in a gopher trap. I would gladly enough have let him loose, but he was too fierce, and lunged at me too savagely, and in the end I had to stone him to death.

"Nobody could have been more brainlessly and morally destructive. And yet there was love there too. We took delight in knowing intimately the same wild animals we killed. Our pets were all captives from the wild – burrowing owls, magpies, a coyote pup, a ferret I caught in a gopher trap and kept in a screened beer case and fed with live gophers."

4. "The trick is getting them where you want them, on your terms. Then you have the options. Pull the trigger or don't. It doesn't matter once you've got them where you want them. The important thing is, knowing that it is in your hands, that you can do whatever you determine is in your interests to do"

≈

And that would have been that, had not Steve piped up, "What about your uncle Bob? He was a hunter, wasn't he?" And had to go in, too.

Uncle Bob's wife (she who had flown the Spitfires) was a tough cookie in her own right (often taking the same medicine as her horses). On the occasion Steve's referring to, she'd ordered me over to cheer up her husband, as he just taken a bad fall.

I brought along a book, *Mr. Sponge's Sporting Tour* by Surtees, which I thought might fit the bill. It was about hunting's heyday, when every yokel, horse and hound, went charging across the countryside in pursuit of the fox, a convenient scapegoat for the ills of inertia and alcoholic dementia brought on every sodden or leaden winter. Townies had to make do with footsie, so called because it was played on foot, rather than by foot; a distinction fortified by the landed gentry donning pink coats, top hats, silk cravats and generally upping the expense, till class war was once again restored. I didn't say the last bit, for I noticed my uncle beginning to eye me queerly, so merely said, I hoped he'd like the book.

He then informed me how he and the wife, had spent many a long winter's night pondering what manner of house vermin had made off with this particular item.

Seeing my face crumple like a novice steeple-chaser having negotiated Beecher's and now facing the Canal Turn, a smile pale as a moonbeam momentarily lit up the wintry landscape of his J.P's countenance, accompanied by a chuckle. The death rattle of an Ik, coming to mind.

They then conversed, and after a bit, decided to crack a bottle of best claret to celebrate the occasion.

≈

Our own general conclusion to the Major's competition was modest, to put it mildly: Hunters change through the ages and as they age.

And I think it was this modesty, more than anything, which prompted Gaspar to produce his dreaded history, or rather story of hunting. And risk life and limb bringing down his special sid, from God knows where, to render it more palatable.

*1 Ivan Turgenev, 2. Aldo Leopold, 3 Wallace Stegner, and 4. James Baker.

80 Gaspar's Story of Hunting

     Gaspar's story of hunting starts with an arboreal ape, grabbing a colobus monkey making its way to the high canopy, chomping into its pulpy brain and handing a piece to its buddy. There's a slapping of hands, a lot of hooting and hunting's begun.

     "*Space Odyssey, 2001* did it better," says Warner.

     "That was the start of technology and weaponry," replies Gaspar amiably enough (and am pleased to see, with a bottle of sid in hand). "This was the prelude, hunting in the raw." He goes on. "When our ancestors left the forest probably due to the great drought, we soon realised, modest dentures, picky nails and loping gait were no match for tusk, claw and hoof. And beating hairy chests and yodelling, no longer cut the mustard.

     Females gathered berries, nuts and shellfish. Males helped bash some open, pulled up the occasional obstinate root and made furtive sorties to scavenge. Very occasionally, a few deluded individuals took off on hair-brained hikes to the horizon after some impossible ungulate, never to return. The females crouched down to wait, perchance to dream -- of salad days in green mansions, their infants clutching them like teddy bears, as they sailed together through the trees.

     There were dark dreams too, when the earth shook and red-haired ogres appeared at the forest's rim, while their male progeny patrolled the perimeter of dad's domain, trying to intimidate any immature females they came across.

     Over time, our omnivore diet made up for a much shorter gut than herbivores, and released more blood and cholesterol to nourish and insulate our brain neurons. Many activities were increasingly undertaken by freed-up arms and hands. And the cranium, released from the pressure and tugging of multi-tasking jaw muscles, expanded. But for what?

     Gaspar, knowing we have the attention span of sand shrimps, opens the sid, then quickly draws a picture in the sand

and explains. "When a dome is placed on four arches, four spaces called spandrels spring into existence. In mosques they are often filled with marvellously interwoven calligraphy, praising God: In Byzantium, with golden mosaics, and in the cathedrals of the West, with fountain-like tracery in stone, all, expressing the very impulse that called them into being.

But when our apish ancestors first stared at herons spearing fish among the reeds and weaver birds making their nests – was anything special going on upstairs? Not just a finger-twitching motor urge to imitate, but an ability to comprehend what they were witnessing, and adapt it to their needs?

I doubt there was a Eureka moment, any immediate explosion -- as when Rixie's bougainvillea reached the greenhouse roof – ha, ha! No quantum procreative leap, employing legions of tiny couriers. Or was there a buzzing inside the hive? Millions of nanoscale fireworks in the night sky above the cerebral cortex?

Whatever. Our brains were indeed different, but I doubt as different as some later imagined them to be. For example, our early apish ancestors were not as well-prepared as the oryx or the crocodile for the coming of the drought; the former well able to sniff the dewless winds far-off and head south, the latter, to seek refuge on the mud banks of underground streams.

Likewise, those of us who'd migrated north, were less well-prepared than the woolly rhinoceros, mammoth and cave bear for the coming of the ice.

In the meantime, many primates died.

Over generations, large numbers of infants born of big-brained mums, though up-and-about in the next-to-no time, perished of cold, or starved. Others, conceived by smaller mums, had big brains, but died in childbirth. A few babies, with pliant skulls, allowing the cranium to contract down narrow birth canals (the downside to upright posture) survived.

These slowly maturing brains put the world together a bit differently. But their precocious young owners demanded almost constant attention.

Through the ice ages many such infants survived, in no small part due to the copious milk supply and massive hushing bear-hugs of den-mothers clad in the odoriferous skins of wild beasts, killed by their men.

Yet in time, marathon runners evolved on the savannahs, not with matted hippy hairdo's but fuzzy-wuzzy air-conditioning ones, almost hairless bodies, and well able to pursue the self-same ungulates, which had eluded their forbears.

81 The Diaspora

Ice ages came and went. No one realised this had happened before, again and again, in expanses of time beyond man's knowledge, but not natural selection's.

Some of our early ancestors' remnants were preserved in desert, ice, peat and cave. But many of those making their way along coastlines and foreshores, left us without trace; buried in the deep sea.

To hold our interest, Gaspar now presents us with a brief cameo between ice ages.

Three exhausted primates, well apart, come loping along this very beach, only further out in The Red Sea. The first enters the unruffled water and spears a sea creature. Hoists it belly up onto the beach, turns it over, and stares at the indentation left behind. As it fills with water, he carefully marks the sand above the waterline, then hoists his load and moves quickly on.

The second primate sniffs excitedly at these marks, sees nothing and hurries on too.

The third, more badly wounded, collapses in the shallows. And sensing something moving there, drags himself up the beach. Half-awake, half-asleep, his mind floats free. Then, not a yard from his head, notices a creature watching him: the image of a large stingray. One moment, he's at death's door, the next, he's up and on his way.

Most of this little band soon die, poisoned by fish left behind on the outgoing tides. But not before the third primate shows them something, he's painted in a cave $\vartheta^{\sigma\sim}$, before which they prostrate themselves and beg for their return. Only one, with a few females, manages to leave for the high wadi, where they hope to find pools above the flash-flood line. The spirits there, could not be seen, but only danced and sung. And soon, parts of the cave walls became crowded with prosaic marks, showing where water and game might be found.

Over more time, paintings from hundreds of schools of thought, including kids' stuff and graffiti, appeared in the Red Sea Hills, faded, and were buried under sand and sea.

Gaspar now draws in the sand what appears to be a woolly rhinoceros, which turns into a bison or musk ox, dunging heavily (but no reindeer for some reason). This is followed by the sleek full-bodied bulk of an eland, hoof-prints slightly askew (Picasso-like) as if the artist was putting in a plug for his main job, as a tracker.

Then hundreds of eland appear on the cave roof, fetlocks bearing no weight, as if passing in a dream. An intruder next appears. A creature with mad staring eyes, topped by a fine spread of horn, with a deer's body and one testicle swinging like a bell-clanger. At first it seems to us a bit of a joke, but no doubt, lit by a flickering torch, after half a mile in chilling darkness, not so.

To Gaspar, he's the linkman, the messenger between two worlds, and we who are the intruders. Beyond that, it's Gaspar's imagination working, not theirs, or ours.

Sometimes, he implies, the painter was more like a desperate coach, trying to get an exhausted bunch of savages up for one last effort. At others, the cave is full of leaping bodies, heels stomping, bull-roarers twirling, palms splayed against resonating stone, drinking in the echo from the chthonic god (the god of the underworld).

Many hunters followed the returning game as their life-line, and settled into the loops of local migrations. Some protected smaller herds, over-wintered in favoured places where they'd eaten fruits, cracked nuts, and old women had noticed new shoots springing up on past middens.

Some camped by estuaries and favourite coves, where shells and carapaces were heaped. (Nothing like an old oyster shell to gouge goodies from the new, or the hooked tip of a crab's smaller claw to extract the flesh from the bigger).

In time, larger middens appeared, some now over 1.8 million years old, containing thousands of flattish teardrop-shaped stones ⬠ , many strangely awkward to hold. Hence, many weird theories have arisen as to their use. The one Gaspar favoured was that they were mainly blade-dispensers, but only producing the goodies if knowledgeably bashed, as with some old vending machines.

Thus what remains for the souvenir hunter today, are mostly poor samples, bashing stones, and discards. But this doesn't deter Gaspar from maintaining that in the elite of these establishments, high fashion also flourished, where only the finest razor-sharp flakes and needle-pointed shards were struck, and not merely ochre and ashes put to the grinding stones, but secret herbs and healing balms.

Here were first produced the stunning raised cicatrices on a chief's plumpest daughter's tender parts, denoting her betrothal to a lion-blinded warrior, possessor of the first herd of ungulates.

Some small bands, passing through these crossroad middens, ended up in the rich alluvial soil of estuaries, but found themselves tormented by swarms of seasonal insects. Others got lost in hallucinatory deserts, where new categories of thought arose: worlds of mirages, magic and miracles -- where powerful djinns protected their own, bent light, and sometimes made the carefully poised spear miss the fish.

Others, left behind, were trapped by the rise and fall of great river systems. Still others ended up in miasmal swamps, and suffered the phantasmagorical fevers of malaria and dengue. Others escaped on rafts of reed, were lost at sea, or swept along sinister shorelines to end up on quiet beaches of shark-filled lagoons.

On the plains, as game grew bigger and more cagy, extraordinary kudos began to accrue to successful hunters, some of whom distributed largesse to whom they fancied.

At the close of one such hunt late in the season, discontent bubbled up among the young Turks, and mums with babies on the way. One young primate, just beyond the arc of firelight, began to thrash the undergrowth, not too unusual, then suddenly attacked. The alpha's cohorts were upon him in a flash, but he jumped back, and to much glee, they fell into a pit packed with bracken.

There were some excited barks, but when the crowd saw he was more interested in leaping about and bashing rocks from a safe distance, than in bashing the chief, lost interest.

After a time, from pretending to savour his pointless thrashing, he forced himself to pay attention to its unusual, if not finer points: his swing and the direction, distance and astonishing trajectory of some of his projectiles. The knot of angst within him began to loosen, and after the sort of perfectly executed chip shot which comes to us but once or twice a lifetime, he felt a novel contentment sweep over him. But it didn't last, other interests intruded.

That evening, watching the bimbos round the fire, he noticed one young female discreetly rolling a pebble to and fro. That night, searching for his best projectile, he found a small pile of berries, then another and eventually herself, munching on some more, of which she offered him one. Then, giggling, one by one.

To show his appreciation, he gave her his favourite cowrie, which she hung between firm breasts and Gasper tells us, was the first time such a spandrel was ever so adorned.

Her canny younger sister also had to have a peek, and to her first reasonably clued-up admirer, daintily touched her earlobes. Cost him two gut-busting dives. She wore them but once, implying she had more important things going on -- between her ears.

In due course, this admirer found himself dispatched into the hinterland with more pretty shells, stingray barbs and salted fish. He returned with skins, strong gut and bone needles, and not being a total numbskull, something which he dangled in the firelight. 'Show me, I want,' her eyes said, and she made a playful grab. The alpha woke, beat the shit out of him and threw the earrings on the fire.

After the last hunt of the season, this same younger sister, pregnant by the alpha and wearing earrings of gleaming copper, stood beside her young man, some grim looking elders, a motley collection of young Turks, a bunch of mums with babes-in-arms, and the largesse was distributed somewhat differently.

Over generations, children began to play games, where capricious sounds were bestowed on playthings. Sometimes they swopped this-for-that, and if not at hand in the required number, denoted by splayed fingers.

Several chiefs didn't get it either. And one (my own ancestor for sure) on wandering into the mist one morning to avoid the senseless chatter, came across the first ecologically naive mastodons of the new world.

And for some of us, the rest is history.

"To reassert his status," Gaspar goes on, "this hunter went down the slippery slope into show-off and over-kill. Others, wary of this flaunting of ancient taboos, fled to the mountains.

Some years later, two old chiefs, still fearful of pursuit and that the young had so little notion of what could befall them, met (as if by chance) while gathering fallen fruit in the woods.

The elder tried to convey to the younger, the previously unthinkable notion that young females of his reed people might now marry young men of the other's mud people (after a bath, of course) and vice-versa. The younger, sensing something perilous in this intention, made an emphatically dismissive gesture (diplomatically put 'and bid adieu to le droit de seigneur, for what?')

"Be gone soon enough." Sighed the other.

'Speak for yourself'. Huffed the younger. At which the elder did just that. "Ripeness maybe all," he declaimed in quavering voice, 'but a little bird has told me, a touch of over-ripeness properly matured, may also hit the spot.' But as neither spoke the other's tongue, came across as gibberish, till he simply grabbed the younger by the shoulder and led him to where the hooch lay long buried.

Here they became so happily inebriated, they forgot the purpose of the enterprise, which was a pity, as at its core lay a touch of genius: Forgoing a natural right in exchange for a cultural reward.

Not so an old crone, who witnessed the whole pantomime from the shadows. She kept it in her memory then persuaded some beefier members of the sisterhood (who'd conveniently lost theirs) to help her bury the rest in a new place.

82 Maven and Shaman

Gaspar now says he must introduce two new characters, the Shaman and the Maven. Shamans we know a bit about, so he doesn't need to go on about them, but about Mavens we are so clueless, he's allowed to proceed as long as the sid flows.

Apparently this old crone wasn't simply a long-lived matriarch, due to the benefits of menopause, but also sagacious, and held as such by many, as are some senior sperm whales and orcas by several naturalists, today.

In Gaspar's story she was the first of our species to see that concealment of overt-sexual receptivity, not only decreased sexual harassment (and not to put too fine a point on it, rape and infanticide) but allowed secondary sexual characteristics: bosoms, derrieres and blushes (now bestowed on upper cheeks rather than lower) to be more subtly deployed by the fairer sex.

How the maven conveyed this to both headstrong and shy bimbos, Gaspar doesn't let on, but mentions other skills. For example, that grannies in the frozen north, despite moistening sealskins with toothless gums, stitching many pliable waterproof garments (never worn when in danger of perspiring), endlessly trimming oil lamps and happily intoning long bedtime lullabies, also expected and accepted (when the first ice cracked beneath a fully laden sledge), to being given the old 'heave-ho!' Before the cooking pot!

And even when shamans chose to pontificate about menstrual blood polluting hunter's spears, held her peace. For though it sometimes helped deflect attention from the alpha's own hunting shortcomings, also kept some young Turks quaking in their moccasins.

But on one important matter, shaman and maven were of one mind. 'And could we guess what it was?'

Luckily, Steve's up for it. 'To find the hidden hooch', he pipes up brightly. For a moment I thought Gaspar was going to cap the sid, but only hissed between gritted teeth, "To find an alpha with both brawn and brains."

The shaman's and maven's choice on this score was of course no little Lord Fauntleroy. By the tender age of five, he'd invented the slingshot (no rubber for catapults, yet) and lent it to his brother, who promptly shot him in the eye by mistake. After which he didn't talk so much as listened.

One day, when the tribe was aroused by something strange in the air, the maven gave him the option to speak out at once, or forever hold his peace. He spoke up a trifle shrilly, but he spoke. "Stop behaving like headless chickens, make babies! And they'll be born bright as a new sun."

Then the whole earth went dark.

After which his reputation was further boosted by his talent for treating the maven's memory as if his own, especially with regard to forgotten water resources.

He was also brave, led all raids from the front, a practice frowned on by both shaman and maven as providing far too brief a career prospect. They warned him of young females being used as decoys and of massive retaliation when things settled down. But the young Turks forgot the lot, and he had to spend a lot of time on defence. In the end, 'make love-and-war, but not on my patch,' became the order of the day, and pretty much still is.

When trouble came, as is often the case, it came from an unexpected quarter. Not from the mountains, but the sea, announced by smoke signals and the sound of drums.

Reaction was neither paralysis nor panic, but in between. The mud people agreed to join the reed people, and the latter even donned some greenery for propriety's sake. But due to a too hastily fermented brew to boost their spirits, it ended up in a colossal gang-bang, headaches all round, and troths earnestly pledged the evening before, forgotten by morning.

Yet the strangers made no move.

Better counsel soon prevailed, and new strategies were set in motion on the home-front; fanciful items left on sandbanks, and cheerful maidens glimpsed. Secret emissaries despatched, and much dressing-up and dancing practised deep in the forest. Careful fermentations were carried out in caves, watched over by stooped crones, said to copulate upside down, like bats, and sink their talons into the tender flesh of all inquisitive youngsters.

When the great day arrived, the young alpha went to meet his bride, who impressed all, by her strange disingenuous smile.

The mud people, covered from head-to-toe in white clay and adorned with feathers of the blue heron, danced alongside the reed people, in vivid greenery. Opposite them, leapt the strangers, striped in vermillion, men representing fire and blood; the women, the playful enticement of flowers, lips and tender fruit, shadowed by the forms of giant locusts, rushing, whirling ,leaping and dancing, the wind of stones. The massed lines of bodies almost touched, but drew back time and again, while piercing ululations split the air.

When the dancers finally collapsed, all were served a light honey brew by blushing maidens, not all of whose blushes were owed to nature.

The alphas, in the meantime, plied each other with the very best liquor, and such felicitous speeches made, no one could remember more than a word or two. And Gaspar tells us, ever since that day, champagne has always been served at the very best weddings.

To end things, the maven bestowed upon the bride, the sacred earrings of beaten copper and of immemorial antiquity ⬦⬦ .

But nothing has ever been found of their delicate artefacts of reed and feathers, only a large midden of obsidian and flint in a bend of the river.

And so the magic diorama of my childhood in the Natural History Museum, South Kensington, depicting dutiful domesticity, still rules. Where, on inserting grandma's penny, a stony-faced caveman wearing govt-issue smock to hide his bollocks, chipped flints and his wife's jaw dropped each time she let fall another pot.

Somewhat sad to relate, Gaspar's alpha never really fulfilled his early promise. Took too much to the bottle and was finally deposed by the same young Turks, he'd tried to teach defence. But not before making, probably his finest career move, the institution of ancestor worship.

83 Hunter to soldier

To keep tabs on the different threads of his story and recap the main events, Gaspar stows the gab awhile and draws his own Bayeux tapestry or frieze, in the sand:

After the Mother of all Rays and her retinue of fishes, comes the woolly rhinoceros, which becomes a bison or musk ox, then the gliding eland, but as we said earlier, no reindeer, then the sorcerer, with an impressive spread of horn and mad-staring eyes. Next comes the fertility goddess, the den-mother, we called the Michelin woman, who hushed the children when the cave bear prowled.

Now he adds a simple circle, with an arrow planted dead-centre

, depicting the hunter's main epoch. It comes from the account of the explorer Frobenius, when his pygmy companions, before hunting a deer for him, fired an arrow into a circle with one drawn in it. And after success, plastered some hair and blood on the drawing, and erased the picture. "

Gaspar thinks most early hunters were actually no great shakes, and it took time for them to follow the gatherers' code: 'Eat my fruit and plant my seeds', which slowly became: 'Ask permission to hunt a certain animal, kill and eat it. What you don't eat or use, water with blood or cover with sand. And in due course, the game will return.'

But as the game grew more cagey, with kudos came danger, and not a few hunters began to wonder, how their own passage to the next world might also be better assured.

Many fanciful and extravagant ideas took hold. The first myth preserved in understandable written form, was about a leader, who'd lost his best friend in a hunting accident, and determines to find where his spirit has been taken. (So as not to distract us, Gaspar left out the best bit, where a beautiful temple houri is sent to test if his brilliant hunter friend is really man or beast).

Anyway, in Gaspar's version, shortly after setting out on his journey, our hero passes a lively lass who sings to him, "Where are you going Gilgamesh? Why not tarry here? For what you are searching for, you will never find." But on he goes.

He comes to the seashore where an old man, who is immortal, tells him, being immortal is no great shakes, either. In fact, it's a bit of a drag, like trying to stay awake. And gives him a test to see if he's up for it.

During one session he falls asleep, but on being nudged awake, insists he'd only just dropped off. He's shown five loaves of bread, one baked for everyday he slept, the first already gone mouldy. Nevertheless the old man, admiring his stubbornness, gives him further instructions.

When he eventually spies the reef-fringed island that the old man described, he swims out to it using an inflated sheep's stomach as a float. After a series of deep dives, he succeeds in bringing up the plant of immortality. But is so tired, he falls asleep. While sleeping, a snake steals it. He then has a dream in which he's told he can succeed, but to do so, may have to die first.

When he wakes, he hears again the song of the girl coming over the reeds, and decides to indulge in no more deep dives. Sits down in her beach hut and has a Mesopotamian beer.

After this somewhat chicken-hearted ending, Gaspar moves

quickly on, and draws his last figure in the frieze, the buffalo dancer of the Blackfoot Indians from the other side of the globe.

"Bit of a jump, isn't it?" says Steve.

On the scale he's talking about, Gaspar says, it's only a blip, and will enable him to finish, before the sid runs out.

Thus reassured, we put up with a few more stories, the first from a gentleman called Bird Grinnel, who'd witnessed one of the last old style buffalo hunts:

It was accompanied by a legend, where a young girl playfully leads some buffalo to the edge of a cliff by promising to marry one. She'd only been joking, but when they stampeded over the edge, was so upset, she married the one who'd successfully jumped the furthest.

Her father, angry that she'd married someone with no more provisioning skills than cropping grass, tried to steal her back. The buffaloes trampled him to death. She managed to restore him to life. And so impressed were they by her devotion, allowed her tribe henceforth to take some of their number every year, provided the dance was always performed as ritual prescribed.

Here an amicable agreement was reached, albeit through the words of man put into the mouths of beasts, and frankly, apart from oracles, Gods, the mother-in-law or the senior wife, what other choices did early man have?

Elsewhere, some tribes had a very different problem. Too much of plenty. They'd taken to giving ostentatious feasts, where priceless blankets and other heirlooms were burnt as if each was trying to outdo the other, but some also said, to stop jealousies erupting about who was to get what, when an old chief died. Fierce battles also took place on river banks about resources, and worse. On some occasions when truces were signed, assassinations occurred even before the signatories had left the table.

Eventually common sense prevailed. Great meetings were established, called Messenger Feasts. All widows and orphans were invited, but the widow-makers (the chiefs' war clubs) had to be left behind. Only small gifts were exchanged and some say, recipes (though Gaspar had his doubts) and the latest designs in fish-traps and spear tips amicably discussed among erstwhile, stony-faced killers.

A paramount chief was elected, and a big blanket filled with eagle feathers, scattered far-and-wide to express everyone's heartfelt contrition.

Peace lasted a goodly while, until another lot of strangers appeared with new deals and fire-power, and the iron-horse cut across the plains.

Then Gaspar hits us with two quotes from General Sherman: 'The buffalo hunters have done more in the last two years to settle the vexed Indian question than the regular army has accomplished in the last fifty.'

And: 'Send them powder and lead, and let them kill until they have exterminated the buffalo.'

That is the hunters, by killing off the buffalo, did more than the soldiers in finishing off the Indians of the Plains. (Though they saw it more as harvesting skins than a process of extermination).

While sipping Gaspar's excellent sid, I began to enjoy this oft-told tale of plenty, death and destruction followed by new prosperity, trappers and fur-traders, whale-oil, whisky and women, and plenty blankets. Even taking the side of the Indians, until Gaspar interjects, "And where does your lot fit into this, Dundas? In the southern hemisphere?"

"Who, me? Southern hemisphere?"

"Yes. You're always going on about your lovely grans in Tasmania. How about Oct 7th 1830, when Major Douglas of the 63rd Regiment, led every white man (about a thousand muskets all told) in the Black Line across Van Diemen's Land, to wipe out the natives and make room for sheep?" But before I can say 'old hat', he's telling us how a young Reverend, tearfully admitted (after vain but sincere efforts to school the locals) that he doubted, they had souls. And if no souls, could be hunted. So hunted they were.

After an animated discussion, I eventually admit, I would have joined in the hunt, but hoped what I'd do now, they would, too.

"And what would that be?" asks Warner.

"Be more circumspect. That includes, checking how your own ancestral lot avoided the trip to Bounty Bay. Probably find they were the paper-pushers who booked others their passage."

"And you may find, your lovely grans were also half-abo, and too ashamed to admit it!" says Warner.

"Easy on lads." says Gaspar. "There's nothing so strange as to find the stranger is oneself. The local aborigines too, thought we were their ancestral ghosts, till one tried a little hands-on science and exclaimed, "By Gum. Dem fellahs, just like us!" And later, showed us some of our own kind, were also cannibals.

"So what's happened to the hunters in the meantime?" Gaspar goes on. "Some ended up on the periphery, became bush-meat eaters, poachers, but many became soldiers. Dependent on the alpha, for pay, promotions, pensions, and other perks. Essential for defence, but much harder now to know what to do when your side's no longer in the right, or vice versa. And here everyone is going to need all the help they can get.

"Remember the early hunters who distributed largesse to who they fancied, and the young ape, who whacked the rocks?"

"Almost got clobbered, didn't he?" says Warner.

"Started the ball rolling though, didn't he? In World War I, it was two other ranks Tommy and Fritz who reinvented golf, trench-war version: Two shots fired high overhead meant 'when can we go for chow, Fritz?' And two returned into no-man's land. 'Now, Tommy. Commandant Kurtz's just gone for his cabbage soup and schnapps.'

"In Nam, it was Tim, but few remember. Having shown he was no coward, and finding the weight of what he carried in his head more than what McNamara had put in his backpack, began to signal safe-coordinates back to HQ as enemy positions."

Then Gaspar goes on too long. "When a neighbouring Country was bombed on the sly, a chaplain, navigator and ordnance man (I forget exactly who) wrote to their Congressmen, giving their facts. One was issued an honourable discharge, just before his court martial."

"Big deal," I interrupt, "should have insisted, it went ahead."

"And have you written that letter to the Queen about Diego Garcia yet?" Says Gaspar. "All I'm saying is, if you're thinking of soldiering on here, don't sign away your future to alpha or shaman."

I begin to doze. Thoughts pass before me like sailboats before the wind, and find myself travelling again, back from such myths to modern times. Gilgamesh had tried to pierce the veil into the afterlife head-on, and cut out the deep dives. Theseus's quest was cleverer and he got his tactics right. Went down into the labyrinth and lifted the pall of paranoia from a bunch of hapless virgins, by somersaulting on the back of the Minotaur, then, after raising a smile, led them to safety with a little help from his girlfriend.

Icarus was ahead of his time. In what is sometimes called the first novel, Don Quihote also opted to tackle his odd interpretations of reality, head-on. Tested a helmet made from a barber's bowl, 'and with one mighty blow, instantly demolished the labours of a week'. Repaired it and decided it was in 'no need of further testing'. In the Joseph Conrad novel we're now reading, Lord Jim badly fails his first test. Goes over the side of the Patna (in real life the SS Jeddah, right off this very coast). And in the process (despite time standing still), betrays a bunch of pilgrims.

Conrad gives him a second chance, but I feel sorry for his wife.

Now young people's Stars come from every walk of life. We also listen to Jim Morrison, who went down into the labyrinth, true enough. Thought he could make it out the other side. Never did. His better angel defeated by his worse.

"Science predicts and tests. But sometimes is so complicated we take its experiments on trust. Other peoples' myths tell us how they put the world together. Ours, how it is put together, ha, ha! Levels of belief remain legion. There are some who believe the world will end tomorrow," concludes Gaspar, "And when it doesn't, simply say it shows their belief was not strong enough." So it goes.

84 The Turkish forts

Over the whole waking sky nothing moves from horizon to horizon. Its sleeping partner, the sea, barely stirs.

We dive like otters, only a ripple and a gurgle. In fact Lambourski's and Warner's vague snufflings are the sole disturbances in our world.

It's a while before we sight the first of the coral bastions, we call the Turkish forts. Nothing disturbs the seabed around them, either. But on my next dive, I notice the faintest of vapour trails, about a foot above the sand. And just glimpse a large, perfectly hydrodynamic shape moving arrow-straight into the distant haze, no fins showing, no tail flapping. This isn't a big grouper giving anyone the royal run-around, this is one going to home base with minimum fuss and maximum haste. And who would have thought, it would prove to be the last bit in an old jigsaw puzzle?

I click off my safety-catch and drift towards the first ramparts. A small grouper, we call the gentleman in the striped suit, feels no need to slide off his perch. I watch him awhile.

Close up he's a dressy little item, toffed up in bottle green, with smart, ginger, yellow and purple stripes. But observed from farther off, he's the drabbest of the drab. And that's his cleverness, for in silhouette he looks like the business-end of a moray, and is probably why so many reef predators let him be.

Nothing stirs. I drift on. The second fort looms up. Vague moving shapes firm up into the plump lead-grey bodies of bream, neurotically circling round and round, in-and-out of the coral and up-and-down its gullies, never repeating the same paths twice. Then, having given every fish a wake-up call, disappear.

As I move cautiously from battlement to battlement, squirrel fish dart about below, and end up in a tight spiky ball even a hagfish would hesitate to chomp.

The only fish of any size about is a yellow-fin grouper at the base of the fort, lying between two levels of a fancy coral table, tiered like a wedding cake. He is cream-coloured, the colour of the coral, with pale orangey-ginger dots and darker ones, mimicking the gaps between the splayed fingers of the lower tiers.

I notice him because he peeks out in time to the gentle rhythm of the sea. Whereas if he'd been in his usual kelp, they'd both have been moving in tandem, and I'd have missed him.

Peering ahead, I can just make out the fuzzy outline of the last fort, and above it, fainter forms which come and go. Maybe I've never seen them before, because I've never looked hard enough. Even now I'm not sure I could call them fish, never mind big snapper, but that is surely what they must be. One by one, they fade away.

After a time I have to change my grip, causing consternation among the local Lilliputians. Tiny puffs of sand and detritus rise out of small holes, no doubt caused by nervous nematodes or those annoying clicking zooids. But this time I hear something more resonant, the unmistakable thump of a large fish shifting some way below me.

For a long time, we used to think that the forts' early-warning-system began with the neurotic circling of the bream, but now I think it often starts with a big grouper travelling home, probably one of the very ones, we thought we'd driven away in the early days. Its retreat is picked up by big snapper watching for prey above the forts, which then drop back, one by one, fort by fort, towards the kelp. And the warning system ends with a final wake-up call from the bream.

All of a sudden, between the last fort and the kelp, shafts of the dawn sun spill onto a school of long-finned cavalla, their glittering silver streamers as astonishing as mariachi trumpets piercing the cool colonnades of a Mexican zocalo. There's a hint of menace too, as if they could cut your hand or electrocute you were you to touch one. Then they turn as one and seem to disappear before they reach the kelp.

We swim in swift pursuit round Eagle Ray Point and are brought to a sudden halt by a wall of fish, with a great barracuda hanging before them. They shudder like 'the unsheathed steel at Balaclava', and we back off.

Yet only a month later we see the great barracuda suspended motionless in a channel between the Point and the shore.

Not unlike a famous dreadnought, accustomed to review the fleet at Spithead, now come to the knacker's yard at Scapa Flow.

And one day, looking for crayfish in a kelp-fringed cave, we came across a barracuda's skull, who in his prime probably ambushed pelagic hunters off this very spot. Then collected his pension so-to-speak, until the day, like some long-suffering servant, the school took a step closer and the balance of power shifted. Now the self-same fry he'd started out on have picked him clean.

Can't be much fairer than that: like a salmon returning the best nutrients to the source of the river which bore it.

≈

Later that evening, because something was moving in the salt bushes nearby, I shifted my bed closer to the fire. Not always a good idea, once hearing myself referred to as 'that nutter Dundas', because long ago I'd gone spear-fishing in Lake Turkana and failed to notice the crocs on the beach.

This time I overhear Pitsos say to Gaspar. "Didn't know you could retire in you line of work."

"Ticker's the problem," he replied. "And now the Ruskies have left the sub-refuelling depot at Socotra and the Listening Post in the Dhalaks, our legit business here is over."

This proved to be Gaspar's last visit. He and his wife continue to send us a lot of stuff, but I still haven't told him I now believe he once stood eye-to-eye with a houbara bustard.

≈

That night I had a naive, but disturbing dream. Gaspar's frieze or Bayeux tapestry, with its prosaic circle and arrow, became two seascapes, one at sunset, one at dawn, but I couldn't tell which came first. One showed a battleground of sunken oil rigs in a blood-red sea, the other, old Soochow's endlessly modified fishponds and kelp beds beyond the Yangtze, where bobbing lines of bamboo poles let smaller fish pass, but larger ones were restrained. Tiny figures also dived; apprentices inside, graduates outside, facing the open sea, ha, ha!

Occasionally they fired DNA samplers into selected fish, while here and there, trained porpoises leapt about, herding schools to automatic feeding stations in the centre of a vast lagoon.

85 Et in Arcadia Ego

6 am. We are gliding along a brand new highway, now crossing the Wadi Adam by the acacias. And we get a shock. Pull into a fancy lay-by and walk back.

The biggest acacia has a rusting grader pressed against it. Most of the other trees have gone. A goat mounts the top of the grader, playing I'm King of the Castle. On its opposite side, the big tree bustles with a colony of weaver birds' nests, bobbing away on the very outriders from which our mosquito nets used to hang.

We take a leak then tear small strips off our old T shirts to lay across the lower branches bedhu style, by way of thanks, and walk back to our transport.

We pass through seas of sorghum of the usual blinding greenness, where once there was nothing. See all sorts of birds and wish Barnes was here to tell us what they are, albeit briefly, but then of course, it wouldn't be Barnes.

I also remember, Pitsos once saw a green pigeon here, but never told Barnes in case he was told, he couldn't have.

9 am. You can only reach Shaban once or twice a year, by slogging through soft dunes for most of the day. But this time we are lucky. The wind has carved out a long valley, with a high dune at the far end. We slog up it and the great bay hits us like a second sky.

My eyes drift over countless shades of aquamarine and turquoise, acres of jade-green turtle grass and shimmering coral. Then without warning, inky blackness.

Long ago, when camel and dhow were king here, new crew hands must have been stunned by such chilling abruptness. And when home again, instead of regaling their erstwhile peers with tales of night ambushes under the acacias, told of shooting the reefs off Sulawesi, the Moluccas and the Maldives.

Now, gazing into that immense inverted vault of sky, I imagined some awestruck stone-mason's apprentice, fresh from the quarry's dust, dreaming of future domes inlaid with lapis-lazuli and Byzantine green.

We descend to the water's edge. Not a yard from shore, large guitar-fish scoot away. While pulling on our flippers, three black-and-white rays come lolloping over the shallows and flap about us, like the winged-headgear of nuns at an alfresco baptism. Skittish terns dive and whip back to repeatedly scold us, as once again, we're the new boys on the block.

A school of big mullet passes in the middle distance, disciplined and compact, like a military fly-past.

We take our time, and it's a good two hours before we reach the reef. There we see the largest bump-headed wrasse I've ever seen. Till then it had been twenty or so off Palawan, moving over the gloomy sands, like elephants in river mist (at least to me, they did) but this one was the most beautiful. With its dragon-green scales and owl-bright eye, it could have been lifted from nursery wallpaper or a child's dream. "Chagall would have loved it", said Steve. Then, as quickly as a stained-glass window loses the sun, turned, and drained of colour dove gently down into the deep.

We swam along a broad reef, bustling with all the usual life, and then it all unexpectedly, stops. The drop-off is sobering. Here is the spot where the entire bay flows in-and-out of the sea. It should have warned us that we were entering another dimension, and were now among the big boys.

Sunlight played over thousands of fish. Schools of snapper and golden trevally came past in an unending procession. Stately bayads cruised by, cautious and dignified. A solitary white permit, sheen of buttercup-and-gold, moved way down through thousands of sweet lips, which stirred slightly, like the leaves in an old avenue of trees.

As they drank in our presence, the entire choreography subtly changed. Those going away continued as before, those approaching seemed to make no progress, while those directly in front, to recede as if drawn away by the very depth and weight of the sea. We could sense, any sudden motion on our part and the entire company would move off, like a dance-hall crowd when the music starts.

"We better get some dinner soon," said Lambourski, "because they're not going to hang about." We waited a little while, then, like children caught up in a fairy tale, forgot the warning: by all means partake, but the moment you do, you go down on the menu.

A pod of queenfish came past. I swam down and shot one. It shuddered, and Leo put another spear through it, but dropped his gun in the process. I dived down, picked up the fish and gun, and armed with this cumbersome ironmongery, rose slowly to the surface. Suddenly, two enormous sharks came swimming up out of the depths. As the first came weaving in, all I can remember is with one blow of its powerful jaws, half the fish disappeared. The second one moved in, directly in front of me. Its jaws opened. I hit down with all my might, with both spear guns. The great jaws clamped down. It turned, shook its head, once, twice, like a dog with a rabbit and the rest of the fish disappeared. The freed spear guns dropped down, and the shark wove away into the depths to join its mate.

They were like two professional kidnappers and I, some inconsequential neighbourhood kid, standing on the pavement with his new bicycle. I turned round, fully expecting to see the loyal band with spear guns at the ready.

That was another shock. Leo was staring in my direction, like a blind man waiting for his stick, and Lambourski and Warner were still in the process of turning round. Pitsos, whom I hadn't noticed on my right, seemed surprised at the spear guns some twenty five feet down, and proceeded to dive for them.

I couldn't believe it. They'd seen nothing!

≈

That night, on Beer Bottle Beach, I woke to mumbled conversation and laughter. Further down the beach, I saw Rix's eyes roll as he helped pull something heavy across the sand then fed more wood to the fire. Half of Pitsos' face is hidden under his floppy hat, only his teeth flash. They're eating the crayfish, caught on the way in. Butter runs down their chins.

"Go on, tell us then." Barnes demands of Steve.

"My dad said it was the most beautiful song in all the islands."

"You've told us that already, dinkhead."

"I mean the most poignant." They help him with the pronunciation of 'poignant'. "It was called *Arua Hape* or *Le Patrou Hellaby*, I can't remember exactly. You know what it was about?"

"Of course not! Tell us you mullet head."

"About a girl who could eat a whole tin of *Hellaby's* corned beef at one sitting, ha, ha!"

They've obviously moved on from sharks, seen or unseen and are in unchartered waters, so I'm tempted to join the drunken sods. Before I do, I'll tell you one thing, when we all saw that pig-eye shark, way back, nobody stopped talking for half an hour. But this time, because they hadn't seen anything, it was an effort for them to even listen.

What are they drinking? They've dug up the beer, a whole crate, buried four months ago, for God's sake!

A fish jumps in the lagoon and falls with a flat splash. Someone throws a stone. I must have fallen asleep then, because I don't remember going over.

When I wake, all is quiet. A marsh harrier moves silently and low above the saltbushes. The stillness, close to me, where nothing appears to be moving, is actually full of tiny sounds, high-pitched squeaks – of crickets, mice? God knows.

Over the moonlit water, garrulous wildfowl chatter. Sometimes they go on all night. Tonight there aren't so many really: some oyster-catchers, stilts, crab-plovers, all huddling nervously together with a few diminutive waders running this way-and-that. When the moon slips behind a cloud, their cries grow more plaintive, less assured, as if, having just crossed from Ethiopia, they're worried the others might leave on the night wind or rising tide, without them.

The stars come out again, 'all quietly flowing in glittering rivalry along the Milky Way, and I sense vaguely the unwavering, unstoppable racing of the earth beneath.' So wrote Turgenev in his *Sportsman's Notebook*, a hundred years ago, and so it is exactly, here and now.

The night becomes increasingly restless and alive – presaging hours of wakeful watchfulness. I put one of Devrill-Smith's tapes into my Walkman.

Agonizing discords assault me like a fever. A tremendous struggle is going on. Themes gain strength but have no trace of arrogance, gain lucidity and become tinged with anxiety. Glimpses of serenity come and go, as if seen through small passing windows.

Another presence enters the dance, and with it comes doubt. The whole music becomes this doubt and must be expressed too. Lightly, fancifully, the new partner begins to lead. *Hurry!* I want him to depart. *Hurry!* But the coup-de-grâce is brutal, sudden, over. And two sharks come weaving in among the dunes.

305

86 Pursuit of the permit

The small fire saws in the dawn wind, guy ropes throb.
"You'll be okay, Rixie?"

"Aye." And off we go.

"Always finds something to do," muses Steve, "whether making a forked stick to automatically prop open the icebox, or clothes pegs strong enough to stop wet gear sliding down the guy ropes."

"Bit like your Alexander Selkirk on his island, eh Dundas?" Says Warner. "Screwed the goats too."

"Ah, hah!" Just the sort of contentious issue we need to get us to Sand Island without being distracted by too familiar places.

By the time we arrive, the hammer blows of the sun make us collapse. Pitsos and Leo build a lean-to, not far from Pompano Point. Then, the wind freshens and sends up whitecaps, Lambourski and I decide to try the point. For it is on mornings like this, with seas running fast, that the big permit seem to favour.

After a while it becomes more like open ocean than our Red Sea, and frankly, is beginning to turn into a bit of a farce.

Sometimes I'd see Lambourski in the trough of a wave below me, peering into its depths, sometimes he'd see me likewise; rarely are we able to communicate.

After half an hour or so of being buffeted about in the swell, we're about to give up, when two lots of permit sweep by. I felt a stomach-churning thrill of excitement as two broke away and veered towards us. God knows if we twitched. I think we did, but it was probably swallowed up in the general commotion.

At some point we sensed they were going to pass in front of us, and we turned away a shade to pique their curiosity. They came in fast, and switched direction right in front of us. I fired and missed. But one tilted, its sheen darker, canted the other way, catching the light, and began to sink. Lambourski had a spear in it, but didn't know he'd hit it.

Then the line broke and it took off. We chased it a good hundred yards. As it bolted along the reef we chased it again, this way-and-that. When it tried to force its way into a gully, I managed to grab the spear shaft, both sides of the body. It kept going down, then up, till my mask filled, first with water, then air.

Minutes later we lay on the lava. Black crabs with obsidian eyes, scuttled about, excited by the big fish and the blood.

We swam back with it towed between us. In the strong currents of the channel, four eagle rays, coal-black with white spots above chalk-white undersides, came swinging by and turned towards us all together. Sideways on, their whip-like tails gave them a dangerous look. But head on, their hooded-eyes, housed in smooth dome-shaped conning towers, gave them a futuristic one, like emissaries from outer space. Seeing the permit in company as formidable as their own, they promptly wheeled about, and with extremely slow and graceful wing beats, faded again into the bright blue racing sea.

We rested on the island to take stock of what had happened. Lambourski had aimed at a permit going left-to-right, and hit it travelling right-to-left. I remembered writing in my diary: *With regard to the most innocuous looking creatures, one is well-advised to adopt the least complacency*, never thinking it might be used by permit with regard to us. But on this occasion one must have over-estimated us, and been hit because Lambourski was way too slow! Not the way we'd planned it at all.

≈

Sunset is a good time to walk back. Breezes nudge us gently along. The entire western sky is back-lit with an intense orange glow. In the east, the moon hangs like a lantern before a purple curtain, night and day meeting in the middle.

Seagulls join us over the sand flats, wheeling and screaming and falling out of the air in their excitement as we slump our burden down before the waiting team of Rix and Leo, sharp knives at the ready.

Driftwood, dragged by Leo and Rix all the way from Sand Island, is fed to the fire. We throw buckets of water over ourselves. Lambourski makes the batter, and Rix cuts up the fish. Old one-leg gets a piece of liver.

Through all this cacophony, Pitsos, whose done nothing all day except put up a sunshade, moves with a calm and preoccupied air, which usually means he's up to something. But as there's been no sid since the trouble in Meccah, we have no idea what to expect.

There's another problem. He and I may do breakfast, the washing up and even collect wood, but we never do anything during sundowners. Once, when we were camped at Suda, Barnes tried to quieten him because there was an unknown bird in a juniper bush nearby. Pitsos threw a stone at it and carried on talking.

But how can we make our stand here, albeit sitting down, if there's no sundowners? "How come, my back never hurts when I'm in the horizontal?" I blurt out to no one in particular.

"How come it didn't, when you were carrying the permit?" Says Leo.

"My! What good eyesight you have, Leo. The permit must be a pain-killer, boosting serotonin, or something."

"Endorphins, specifically encephalin," says Barnes, "for brain and back." *Where would I be without him and Pitsos too?* For lo and behold, our old pain-killer now appears – with a dash of angostura bitters to disguise the taste of the new tonic. In big cold glasses, plus beautifully cut slices of lime (not bludgeoned by a blunt instrument and squirted all over the place as Rix would have done). And as always, served fifteen minutes before sunset, give or take, half-an-hour.

Truly, there are in these latitudes, two special times of day, one at sunrise and one at sunset that should be savoured like fine wine. And this we do now.

We watch the night inch over the sky, and appraise those most punctilious citizens of the reef, the pelicans, as they skim low over the waves, shopping bags full.

"Not so," interjects Barnes. "They're empty." Apparently the fish are already in the gizzard or stomach, or whatever pelicans have, and the empty pouch, with its copious spread of capillaries, now operates as a light-weight air-conditioner. And instead of having to lug groceries up to Pelican Heights, they rise easily. And glide in cool as cucumbers, to offload hot home-cooked meals straight down the chutes of their squawking offspring.

I begin to doze, wondering vaguely how the first permit crossed the ocean, from the old world to the new, or vice versa. As young fry in the mouths of leviathans, or like schools of dorados, under ship-wrecked sailors' drifting rafts? Or before all that, during the time of continental drift? *How ignorant, I am!* And think of strange creatures, like the blue ghost: chooses the quietest corner in a wreck's inner sanctum, never moves out, and like buried treasure awaits its seekers. Or the convict fish, turns out her brood each morning (whose look-outs work in relays) and like Fagin, checks their takings every night. "This sid is excellent, Pitsos." I say. "Cooled a long age in the deep-delved earth, no doubt?" But the old fox is still not letting on where it's hidden.

Instead, a plate of steaming hot fish-and-chips is thrust into my hands. "Get that down ye, me handsome!" says Rix.

Everyone sets to with a will, and nothing is heard but the steady munching of the contestants. Finally plates are put down with a sigh, and Steve stokes up the fire.

It's going to be a great night! But I've forgotten one thing. It's the second one, when the tiredness really hits.

We fall asleep where we are, and wake with the sun.

87 The last day

Early in the morning, an enormous deep water ray followed by two jacks, comes slowly along the reef. Its barbed spine is broken and exposed to the bone. A semi-circle of puncture marks arc across one wing. It seems to glide on forever, as if its wings are fixed. Then just when we think perhaps they are, the tips ever so slowly begin to curl upwards, and it fades into the distant haze.

After breakfast, we walk over to Beer Bottle beach, dig up the wine and leave the beer. Someday, someone will find it. *May God have mercy on them.*

We put the wine on ice to drink later with small heart-shaped shellfish we've scooped out from the water's edge. This was meant to be a restful occupation, but isn't. Sand-shrimps, sharing the same gritty beds, nip us on the ankles and behind the knees.

When we come to eat the shellfish, Barnes tries to be particularly helpful. "If they don't open, it means they're dead."

"I thought that's what cooking did?" says Leo.

"I mean, don't eat them if they don't open."

"That would be difficult too," says Leo.

For some reason we seem to have difficulty expressing ourselves.

Rix then presents Leo with one of his most cherished possessions, his home-cured goatskin, to thank him for all the work he's done on the vehicles. But when confronted by this odoriferous mass of uncombed hair, he refuses to accept it, and I thought we were going to have an international incident on our last day.

In the end, Pitsos and Lambourski suggest we offer it to him 'as an honorary Brit', an offer he can't refuse. "Ancient Brit, more like." He mutters.

"It's a pity we can't give Warner a call," I say, "There must be permit in that vast lagoon at Um Ladj. Maybe he could get one."

"Let the precocious little prick find out for himself," says his good friend, Leo. "Remember, it wasn't just guns which did in the passenger pigeon, it was the telegraph." I have to admit, the idea of a telephone call being an upgrading of our technology, wouldn't have occurred to me.

When we've packed everything up (accompanied by Warner's chain gang music), Pitsos turns the vehicle on a high dune and we look around for the last time: Sand island, Grouper's playground, Eagle Ray point. These work-a-day names, brief visitors too, will go with us.

Then we have to wait as Steve's forgotten his socks, not something we want to leave behind. I watch the kelp disappear on the incoming tide, while dapper little waders run this way-and-that on its soggy mattress, and with it comes a frisson of fear.

When we leave, the tide is almost as high as on our first day. And there's nothing to tell a newcomer what lies beneath the surface. It's just an ordinary beach and the sea, ruffled by the wind.

THE END